Angels, Elect and Evil

C. FRED DICKASON
Angels
ELECT & EVIL

MOODY PRESS

CHICAGO

© 1975 by
THE MOODY BIBLE INSTITUTE
OF CHICAGO

Scripture references from the New American Standard Bible
are used by permission of the Lockman Foundation, La Habra,
California, © 1960, 1962, 1963, 1971, 1973.

ISBN: 0-8024-0222-4

19 20 Printing/LC/Year 92 91 90 89 88

Printed in the United States of America

To
my wife, Jean,
an angel of light and love
in our home

CONTENTS

CHAPTER   PAGE

Introduction   9

Part 1—THE ANGELS OF GOD

1. The Existence of Angels   17

2. The Origin of Angels   24

3. The Nature of Angels   29

4. The Position of Angels   47

5. Names, Classifications, and Abode   58

6. The Angel of Jehovah   78

7. Number, Organization, and Rank   85

8. The Ministry of Angels   90

9. Development and Destiny of Angels   102

10. Our Relationships with Angels   107

Part 2—SATAN AND DEMONS

11. The Realty and Personality of Satan   115

12. Names of Satan   120

13. Original State and Fall of Satan   127

14. Satan's Present Character and Position   138

15. Satan's Present Power and Activity   141

16. The Reality of Demons   150

17.   The Derivation of Demons   155

18.   The Description of Demons   161

19.   Duties of Demons   169

20.   Domination by Demons   182

21.   Distractions by Demons—the Occult   196

22.   Defeat and Destiny of Satan and Demons   210

23.   Defense of Believers Against Satan and Demons 216

      Appendix: Difficulties in Angelology   222

      Notes   228

      Bibliography   232

INTRODUCTION

WE HAVE BEEN INVADED by the occult! Astrology and spiritism are on the upswing; but more astounding, even the once rejected and shunned witchcraft and Satan worship are rapidly gaining devotees. Though parts of Africa, Asia, and Europe have felt the force and bondage of the occult for centuries, now the United States is staggering under its revival.

Interest in the supernatural is kindled not only by those directly involved, but the mass media has promoted it by both responsible and irresponsible reporting on the fads and wickedness of the occult. At least 1200 of the 1750 daily newspapers in the United States cater to those who want astrology columns and advice. Popular Magazines such as *Cosmopolitan, Harper's Bazaar, Ladies Home Journal, Time,* and *Newsweek* have carried cover stories and have devoted large sections to the secret arts, and some repeatedly so. Screen and television films and radio programs feature the satanic, the demonic, the horrific.

Various estimates contend that there are as many as two-hundred thousand witches in the United States. Arthur Lyons states that black magic groups have been long in existence and continue to practice black magic on a large scale.[1] Journalist Knaut claims that at least three million West Germans subscribe to some form of the occult.[2] The popularity of seeress Jeane Dixon, who uses a crystal ball and lays cards and has visions to predict the future bears grim testimony of the growing obsession with the occult.

Spiritist churches continue to gain members. Three denominations of spiritualists in the States now total more than three hundred churches.[3] The defection of the noted Episcopalian bishop James A. Pike from professed Christianity to spiritism through the influence of the Rev. Arthur Ford is famous.[4] Other ministers claim to find in the occult some of the answers that they missed in their churches, such as "contacting the dead" to confirm life after death. Spiritists teach that Jesus was a great medium, the oldest and most evolved spirit. Others hold that He was a witch with a coven of thirteen members; He supposedly held a seance on the mount of transfiguration and communicated with the dead when He raised Lazarus.[5]

ESP (extrasensory perception) and telekinesis (moving objects without physical means) are serious studies on the psychic frontier. Arthur Koestler of England, the Maimonides Medical Center of New York City, J. B. Rhine of the Foundation for the Research on the Nature of Man in North Carolina, and scientists in Russia are seriously investigating these matters. The Philippines have become a center of psychic surgery. Russia has experimented with Kirlian photography that captures energy discharges from the human body.[6]

More blatantly wicked and increasingly open is Satan worship. Anton La Vey's Church of Satan, located in California, stopped giving out membership figures when they exceeded ten thousand.[7] The Process Church of the Final Judgment worships Satan as the god of this age and holds that Christ is the Reconciler of God and Satan. The Charles Manson "family," responsible for the cultic slaying of Sharon Tate, followed a man who had announced that he was simultaneously Jesus Christ and Satan. Manson was declared sane; but he and his followers were under satanic power.[8]

The young Israeli psychic Uri Geller astounds laymen and scientists alike by his power to cause uncanny physical feats. He confessed to the investigators from the Stanford Research Institute that outer-space intelligence directs his work.[9]

"Committed Christians need to hear what the growing numbers in the occult religions are saying. Occult people are excited about a new age, an age that has 'outgrown' Jesus Christ."[10]

Most occultly involved people consider themselves very religious and seeking the good of mankind. Some are overtly or secretly seeking power and knowledge for their own self-advancement, even at the expense of others.

The popularity of the occult is bringing more participants out into the open. It is not only more acceptable; but it works, and it gives meaning and power to a person's life. Major colleges and universities are offering courses and degrees in the occult and witchcraft. Among these are Bowling Green State University, The University of California, San Diego State College, and the University of South Carolina.[11] Occult stars are played up on television interview programs, and occult publishing firms are putting out thousands of books and raking in millions of dollars.

The recent popularity of the book *The Exorcist* and of the film by the same name have attracted many more inquirers to the questions raised by the occult and demon activity. Even Christian book publishers have followed up on the interest in seeking to expose and explain the occult from a Christian point of view.

As Christians, what should our reaction be to the invasion of the occult and increase in the demonic? We must know the truth about the occult and the spirit world to combat erroneous and increasingly popular views. We must recognize the titanic struggle carried on every day between forces of darkness and forces of light.

Christians need perspective, lest we belittle the enemies of righteousness, or lest we give them more than their due. We need to be confident of the truth and life we have in Christ and His Word.

Neither should we, while investigating Satan and demons, forget the great power and activities of God's angels who remain holy and true to Him and who resist Satan and his angels.

Christians must have an answer for ourselves and for a needy and confused world. We find that answer in biblical truth and its authoritative and balanced presentation of the spirit world. This study is designed, in view of these needs, to survey the scriptural teaching about angels, Satan, and demons. Its outline form and discussion are aimed to help the serious Bible student to trace this area of doctrine.

In turning to the Bible, we turn to the only trustworthy source of God's truth about Himself, man, and the spirit world. It is totally inspired by God (2 Ti 3:15-17). It excels man's experience, research, and reason, and discloses what man cannot know about God's truth if left to his own resources (1 Co 2:9-10, 14). The Bible gives evidence and explanation for the spirit world, and gives insight into man's insatiable interest in the occult and the supernatural.

There are benefits from studying biblical doctrine on this subject. First, understanding the nature and activities of the spirit world will increase our appreciation of a sovereign God whose creative ability, control of the universe, and interventions on our behalf assure His glory and our good.

Second, we should gain comfort. Angels minister and evidence God's concern for us. His use of angels does not detract from His personal concern for us, but illustrates and expresses it. Angels do not replace God or His love. We have God plus angels.

Third, this doctrine should help us to appreciate God's holiness and righteousness. He actively opposes corruption and wickedness among angels and men. There are solemn judgments on sin and rebellion.

Fourth, this doctrine magnifies the grace of God. God could judge all at once, but He patiently delays. And out of the midst of wicked men influenced by Satan and demons, He rescues all those who trust in Jesus Christ and delivers us from demonic power right now. One day, in righteousness and grace, He will establish a new heaven and new earth, in which Satan and demons have no more influence and the occult is dead.

Fifth, it should challenge our Christian living. We will become more aware of spiritual realities and release our thoughts from their too-often confinement to the material world and our senses. There is a whole world of spiritual beings and moral issues that affect us directly or indirectly. We need to take our stand against spiritual wickedness by submitting to Christ and resisting evil forces by His power (Eph 6:10-13).

Finally, the truth of God's angelic ministry should encourage us and assure us. Angels deliver us from physical and spiritual danger. We can trust our lives to God who sends them (Heb 1:14). Angels present to us an example of complete devotion to God and readiness to obey Him. This can motivate us to worship and serve Him more fervently.

When we study angels and demons as presented in the Bible, we are not engaging in groundless and fruitless speculation. Most speculators, whether pagan (notably Persian), Jewish, or Christian, have ignored, denied, or distorted scriptural teaching. Popular imagination has run wild throughout centuries, unbridled by the truth of revelation. So multitudes in many lands have lived and died under the domination of fear and superstition. It has not been only the credulous masses, but priests, professional religionists, rabbis, and Talmudists have in many cases promoted speculation, perversion, and bondage.

From our sure footing in the Bible, we note that in the Old Testament angels appear often, even from earliest times, as messengers from God to man. They are cast as working behind the scenes in the drama of world events as agents of God to promote His program. They execute His judgments and convey His blessings.

In the New Testament, parts of the gospels and epistles make little sense without the reality and role of angels. The Revelation depends upon the activities of angels for its existence, narration, and structure. Though angels are not the main characters of the Bible, they are indispensable supporting actors.

In 34 of the 66 books of the Bible there are specific references to angels, in 17 books in the Old Testament and in 17 books in the New. The word for angel is used 108 times in the Old Testament and 165 times in the New. To those who respect the Word of God, the evidence for angels and demons is so widespread and substantial that it is positively overwhelming.*

The Bible classifies angels as either good or evil. The good are termed "elect" (1 Ti 5:21) and "holy" (Mt 25:31). They worship God and serve Him with unswerving allegiance. The evil angels include Satan, their leader (Mt 25:41), and demons (Mt 12:26-28). They oppose God and His servants, human and angelic. These two armies engage in a great warfare that exceeds human thought and affects the course of nations and the world.

This, however, is not dualism, a struggle between two eternal and equal forces. God who made all rules all. It is only by His permission and support that any creature, no matter how small or great, can survive for one moment. After He has used wicked angels, who delight to oppose Him, God will finish them.

On, then, to the study of angels, elect and evil.

---

*Karl Barth claims that angelology is not a proper consideration for the theologian. The Bible recognizes the existence of angels but never refers to their creation. They are part of God's government, but we can have no knowledge of their nature (Karl Barth, *Church Dogmatics*, III.. [Edinburgh: T. & T. Clark, 1960], pp. 13-14).

Part I

THE ANGELS OF GOD

1

THE EXISTENCE OF ANGELS

THE FACT THAT ANGELS EXIST is as certain as the fact that God exists. The Bible reveals the certainty of each. Though angelology is not a cardinal doctrine, its acceptance opens the mind to a better understanding of the Bible, God's plan of the ages, the Christian life and ministry, as well as world conditions and course of affairs.

I. THE WITNESS OF THE OLD TESTAMENT

A. THE BOOKS OF LAW

The word *angel* appears thirty-two times in the writings of Moses. Hagar was comforted by the angel of Jehovah (Gen 16, 21). Abraham conversed and ate with angels, and two angels delivered Lot and his family from Sodom before the fire fell (Gen 18-19). Jacob dreamed of angels ascending and descending upon a ladder to heaven (Gen 28:12), a dream recognized by the Lord Jesus (Jn 1:51). Jacob also wrestled with an angel and was crippled; yet he held on until he received God's blessing and a new name, Israel (Gen 32:24-28; Ho 12:2-4).

In Exodus, Moses was called by the angel of Jehovah to deliver Israel from Egypt (3:2, 10), and an angel led Moses and the Israelites through the wilderness journeys (14:19; 23:20, et. al.). Leviticus seems to refer to demons promoting the sacrificing of animals to idols (17:7). Numbers records that God dealt with both Israel and the false prophet Balaam through angels (20:16; 22:22, et. al.).

Never in Mosaic writings are angels considered mere illu-

17

sions or figures of speech. They are an intregal part of the story of God's dealing with men. Men recognized the reality of the beings they contacted, and in most cases recognized them as messengers from God. Moses, however, regards the Angel of Jehovah as more than an ordinary angel wherever he appears in the narrative; he regards him as deity.*

B. THE BOOKS OF HISTORY

The word *angel* appears about thirty-seven times in the books of Joshua, Judges, 1 and 2 Samuel and 2 Kings, and 1 and 2 Chronicles. Most occurrences are in Judges where the Angel of Jehovah, who is more than an angel, conversed with Gideon and Manoah. In 2 Samuel 14:20 and 19:27, King David is compared in comfort, wisdom, and power to an angel of God. An angel smote David's people in judgment when David in pride took a census of his army (2 Sa 24). From the account here and from the parallel in 1 Chronicles 21, we note that it was Satan who tempted David to sin, and it seems it was the Angel of the Lord who executed the judgment and then directed David to build an altar on the future site of the temple.

C. THE PROPHETS

In the major prophets, Isaiah makes two references to the Angel of Jehovah as defending Israel and defeating her enemies (37:36; 63:9). Again, this is not an ordinary angel. He also refers to seraphim (6:2), but does not use the term *angel* of them. Jeremiah and Ezekiel do not use the word *angel,* but Ezekiel does mention the cherubim (10:1-3, 6-8 et. al.). Angels intervened in the record of Daniel to deliver the Hebrew children from the fiery furnace and Daniel from the mouths of lions (Dan 3, 6). Gabriel, who later appears in Luke 1, appears first to Daniel with a revelation of the future of Israel (Dan 9:20-27). Michael the archangel (Jude 9) is identified as "one of the chief princes" (Dan 10:13), and stands as Israel's principal defender against men and other angelic beings (Dan 10:13; 12:1).

*See chap. 6 on the Angel of Jehovah.

In the minor prophets, Hosea identifies the "man" that wrestled with Jacob (Gen 32) as an angel (Ho 12:2-4). Zechariah contributes substantially to the Old Testament doctrine of angels, with twenty occurrences of the word. He pictures angels as God's reconnaissance agents (chap. 1), as interpreters of His visions for Zechariah (chaps. 1-6), and as agents of God's activity and judgment (chaps. 2, 4). The Angel of Jehovah is identified as the personal representative of Jehovah, even Jehovah himself, who intercedes for God's people (chap. 3).

D. THE BOOKS OF POETRY

Job and Psalms contribute to our knowledge of good and evil angels. Though Psalm 78:49 may be a reference to human messengers instead of evil spirit beings, there is no doubt that Satan is represented as one of the spirits called "the sons of God" in Job 1:6 and 2:1. His evil design against God and Job, the man of God, is obvious. The Psalms picture angels as protecting and delivering God's people from harm (34:7; 35:5-6; 91:11). They are God's energetic and fervent servants (104:4) and His devoted worshipers (103:20; 148:2).

The only reference in Ecclesiastes warns man not to equivocate in the presence of an angel concerning his vow, for the angel is a representative of God (5:6).

Summary. The Old Testament presents angels as genuine personal beings who serve as messengers and ministers of God. Their character, position, power, and activity are revealed in some detail. These creatures of God are either good or evil, depending on whether they serve God or Satan. They are so essentially bound in the narrative that to rip them from the record would do violence to the cause and continuity of many significant historical events and would destroy the concept of a moral battle that involves and yet transcends the human race.

II. THE WITNESS OF THE NEW TESTAMENT WRITERS

Though we will yet consider the witness of Christ, we will here look briefly at the reality and role of angels as seen by the writers of the New Testament.

A. THE GOSPELS

All four gospel writers report the existence and activity of angels. Matthew and Luke tell of the signicant ministry of angels connected with the birth of Christ, its prediction, and its announcement (Mt 1:20-23; 2:13; Lk 1:26-38; 2:8-15). The first three gospels (the synoptics) are full of references to angels and demons. All four record the appearance of angels at the empty tomb of the resurrected Saviour.

B. THE BOOK OF ACTS

This New Testament history by Luke has many references to the ministry of angels. At the ascension of Christ, two angels announced His second coming (1:10-11). When the apostles were cast into prison, an angel opened the doors and freed them (5:19). An angel directed Philip to a new place of ministry (8:26). Appearing to Cornelius, an angel directed him to send for Peter to learn of salvation in Christ (10:1-7). Later, Peter was again delivered from prison by God's angel (12:5-11). Paul, in a turbulent storm at sea, received encouragement and announcement of deliverance from God through an angel (27:23-25).

C. THE EPISTLES

The epistles abound with teaching about angels. In them, angels are classified as either elect (1 Ti 5:21) or fallen (2 Pe 2:4). They are contrasted as living realities with the living Christ (Heb 1:4-5). Paul declares that the cross of Christ defeated evil angels, and he warns against the worship of angels as promoted by false religionists (Col 2:15, 18). Peter speaks of Christ having declared victory over angels and then having ascended above them in authority (1 Pe 3:18-22), as also does Paul (Eph 1:20-21). Paul, James, and Peter regard Satan as the believer's angelic opponent who can be overcome only through Christ (Eph 6:10-12; Ja 4:7; 1 Pe 5:8-9).

D. THE BOOK OF REVELATION

There are sixty-five clear usages of the word *angel* in reference to spirit beings in John's Apocalypse. The remaining eight usages may also refer to such or to human messengers as representing the seven churches of Asia Minor. In this book, which contains more references to angels than any other Bible book they are portrayed as worshiping the Lamb of God (5: 11-12), preserving the servants of God (7:1-3), and administering the wrath of God (chaps 8-9; 15-16). Angels are basic to the structure and significance of this great capstone of God's revelation.

Summary. If there are no such beings as angels, then we must doubt some direct revelations and key attestations of truth presented as coming through angels in the New Testament. We must then also doubt the miraculous deliverances and interventions by angels in Acts and consider that the epistles are pure imagination or accommodation to ignorance when they speak of Christ's superiority and victory over angels. We must ignore any reference to supernatural enemies and spiritual warfare in the Christian life. We must also regard the book of Revelation as either a fictional masterpiece of deception or a figurative mass of incoherent revelation. Furthermore, the more highly developed doctrine of Satan, his angels, their system, and influence found in the New Testament revelation is complete speculation without any real correspondence in experience. And this is probably what Satan would desire to have us believe. But the New Testament gives abundant evidence of the existence of angels.

III. The Witness of the Son of God

Speaking with the authority of the Father who sent Him and with His wisdom and integrity as the Son of God, our Lord Jesus Christ gave in His speech and action more than sufficient testimony to the reality of angels. Some doubters might say that Christ was accommodating His words to the popular belief of that time that angels were real and exerted power in the realms of the natural and supernatural. But to those who highly regard Christ as a teacher of truth, and especially to those who know Him as the truth, who always spoke the truth,

such a thought is next to blasphemous (Jn 8:31-32, 45-46; 14:
6). To say that Christ spoke of angels and demons just because the people believed there were such, while He Himself
knew that there were none, is to make Him guilty of perpetuating error and falsehood. However, He who is God's truth
would not gain in perpetuating a lie. Neither does the extent
and nature of His testimony concerning angels support any
idea of accommodation. He believed in and taught the reality
of angels.

A. IN HIS TESTINGS

When Christ was tempted by Satan in the wilderness and
afterward was helped by angels (Mt 4:11), who was with Him?
He was alone. This is *His* record. Was He bordering on the in-
sane when He spoke to Satan as a real person, or was He the
only fully sane and sinless man, the God-man, battling with the
greatest of all evil angels who personally enticed the first man
into sin and darkness which was his originally by reason of his
own brand of insanity?

B. IN HIS TEACHING

Several instances demonstrate that Christ positively taught
the existence of angels as personal creatures of God. When
the Sadducees who denied the reality of angels and of the resurrection sought to discredit Christ in regard to the teaching
of the resurrection, He not only affirmed the resurrection but
compared our state in the resurrection to that of angels who
do not procreate (Mt 22:29-30). In doing so, He placed the
doctrines of the resurrection and of angels on the same plane
of truth. If we believe in a resurrected Saviour who will raise
us from the dead, we must also believe in the existence of
angels.

When our Lord prophesied concerning His second coming
in power and great glory, He predicted that angels would gather
the elect (Mt 24:31). The holy angels will be associated with

Him in His glory, and the evil angels along with Satan will be cast into the lake of fire (Mt 25:31-32, 41).

Could Christ have been accommodating when He rebuked Peter's use of the sword and said that He could, if desired, have the help of twelve legions of angels (Mt 26:53)? Or did Christ continue a notion of ignorance when, speaking to His disciples privately, He told them that they failed to cast out a demon because of lack of faith and prayer (Mt 17:18-21)?

C. IN HIS MINISTRY

An outstanding feature of Christ's ministry was the casting out of demons. The synoptics make much of this, recognizing that such miraculous actions testified to Christ's authority in the realm of the supernatural (Mk 1:27). If we assume, as the facts forcefully indicate, that demons or evil spirits (sometimes called devils) are wicked, fallen angels, we have strong evidence for their existence in the ministry of Christ. He spoke to them in intelligent conversation, rebuked them, and cast them out of men's bodies which they had entered (Mt 8:28-33; Mk 1:32-34; Lk 4:33-36, 41).

SUMMARY

Evidence abounds from Christ's personal narratives, ministry, and teachings that angels do exist. He spoke of holy and evil angels; He did battle with Satan; and He put the reality of angels on a par with that of the resurrection. For the genuine believer in Christ, when He speaks on an issue, it is settled.

The combined witness of the Scriptures, the Old and New Testaments, and of the Saviour, assure us that there is a world of intelligent, powerful, invisible creatures about us and above us that warrants our prayerful and careful study and challenges us to expand our categories of thought and to change our conduct of life in accord with God's truth. Though much was revealed of angels in the Old Testament, the progressive revelation of God has culminated in the New Testament with a highly developed angelology.

2

THE ORIGIN OF ANGELS

THE BIBLE DOES NOT ANSWER all questions about angels, but it leaves no doubt concerning the main facts about the origin of angels.

I. THEIR ORIGINAL CREATION

A. AGENT OF CREATION

Genesis 1 states that God created all things on earth, even the crown of creation, man. Since man was not present to behold the creative act, the fact of man's creation is a matter of revelation. The creation of angels is also a matter of God's disclosure. Psalm 148:2-5 indicates that the angels with all their hosts (armies) along with the sun, moon, stars, and all heavenly expanses are God's creative product.

John 1:1-3 teaches that the Lord Jesus Christ, the eternal Word, created all things. He acted as God's creative agent, for, "All things came into being through Him; and apart from Him nothing came into being that has come into being" (Jn 1:3, NASB). Logically this would include angels.

However, the apostle Paul specifically declares that Christ, who is Himself God, is the creator of all things, including angels. The eternal Son of God was the cause of every creature: "For in Him all things were created, both in the heavens and on earth, visible and invisible, whether thrones or dominions or rulers or authorities—all things have been created through Him and for Him" (Col 1:16, NASB). The similar terminology applied to angelic creatures in Ephesians 6:12 and Romans 8:38 allows us to interpret Paul as declaring that

24

Christ created all angels. They find their origin in Him and depend upon Him for their continuance and welfare. He is their sovereign.

B. ACT OF CREATION

Scripture implies that the angels were all created at or near the same time. The Greek tense (aorist) of the word translated "created" (Col 1:16) may indicate an act or a culmination of a series of acts completed in time past. Angels are not eternal as is God alone. They certainly did not evolve, nor were they formerly men, for they were created *as angels*. Each angel is a direct creation from God, for they do not procreate as do humans (Mt 22:28-30). Perhaps this is why they are sometimes called "the sons of God" (Job 1:6; 2:1). The word *sons* seems to indicate a direct creation of God, as Adam is the son of God (Lk 3:38), and believers are recreated in Christ individually as "sons of God" (cf. Gal 3:26; Eph 2:8-10; 4: 24). The exact time of their creation is not certain, but we know that "all the sons of God" sang with joy at the creation of the earth" (Job 38:7, cf. vv. 4-7), and that Satan, an angelic creature, appears in the Genesis 3 scene. From this we deduce that God created all angels before He created the earth.

The method of their creation seems to be by direct command or fiat of God. In Psalm 148:2 angels are commanded to praise God, and they are included with other creations when in verse 5: "Let them praise the name of the LORD: for he commanded, and they were created." The language is similar to the direct creations of Genesis 1, marked by, "And God said."

C. AIM OF CREATION

The primary purpose for the creation of angels was that they might glorify God and His Christ, for they were created "for him" (Col 1:16). The creatures of Revelation 4:6-11, probably angels of highest nature and rank, confess that they with all things were created for God's pleasure and ascribe to Him glory and honor and power.

In their intricate natures, angels reflect the creative wisdom

and power of God (cf. Eze 28:12-15).* In their activities
they worship and serve God in the administration of His will
(Heb 1:7). They execute His commands with swift obedience
and delight.

II. Their Original Condition

A. Holy State

All angels were created good and holy, just as God made
and pronounced all His creation good (Gen 1:31; 2:3). It is
inconsistent with God's character that He could directly create
anything wicked. It may be that all the angels ("all the sons
of God," Job 38:7), even those who later rebelled with Satan,
were yet holy and rejoiced in God's creation of the material
world. God's angels are specifically termed "holy" (Mk 8:38).

Not only were they holy in nature, but they were surrounded
by every good thing and influenced by every holy thing. They
were not holy creatures in an evil or even amoral atmosphere,
but holy ones in a positively holy atmosphere. They enjoyed
God's presence (Mt 18:10) and heaven's environment (Mk
13:32). This made the rebellion of some the more sinful.
There are now two moral classes of angels: the elect, who remained loyal to God (1 Ti 5:21), and the evil, who followed
Satan in his rebellion against God (Mt 25:41). But originally,
all were good and holy.

B. Creaturely State

All creatures, including angels and men, were made to serve
God. All are privileged, limited, and responsible in all things
to Him.

1. Angels had great privileges. Originally all angels had the
joy of knowing God in a holy relationship. They were His sons
by direct creation, and He was their Creator-Father. Each
one bore the creative marks of an individual, with probably no
two being alike. Knowing God, they had the pleasure of worshiping Him in the joy of their relationship and in the beauty
of holiness (Ps 148:1-2). At His bidding, they would congre-

---

*Many regard this as referring to Satan, highest of angels. Note pp. 127-29.

gate before Him (Job 1:6; 2:1). They beheld in wonder His creative works (Job 38:7), and were granted the inestimable privilege of serving the God of all creation as quickly as wind and as fervently as fire (Heb 1:7). They undoubtedly were given some insight concerning God's purpose and program of the ages.

2. Angels have certain limitations. One limitation is that of space. Since an angel is a creature, he cannot, as does God alone, possess omnipresence. Angels are primarily spirit in nature, yet they cannot be all places, or even many places, at once. An angel must move spatially from one location to another (Dan 9:21-23), and this involves the lapse of time, and on occasions, delay (Dan 10:10-14). Angels, then, are localized.

Another limitation is that of power. Of course, only God is omnipotent. God can by unlimited power speak and have His will done. But angels, though greater in power than man (2 Pe 2:11) and under God controlling even some elements of nature (Rev 7:1; 16:8-9), are limited in authority (Job 1:12; 2:6). They are sometimes taxed in the accomplishment of their duties, as in the struggle of elect with evil angels (Rev 12:7), and stand in need of assistance (Dan 10:13).

Angels are also limited in intellect. Mighty as they are in wisdom, inherent and acquired, they do not compare with God and are in need of His revelation, as concerns the hour of Christ's return (Mt 24:36). They are amazed and seek to learn through investigation something of the marvels of salvation (1 Pe 1:11-12).

They were limited in holiness. Theirs was not absolute and unshakable as is God's for some fell into sin and bondage through defection from God's will (Isa 14:12; Rev 12:3-4).

3. Angels are responsible to God. As creatures, they must answer to the Creator. God's society of intelligent creatures is governed by moral laws. Failure and rebellion require judgment. If Satan, the highest of all creatures, has been and shall be judged, then all the lesser angels are answerable to God (cf. Eze 28:12-19; Mt 25:41; Jn 16:11).

SUMMARY

Angels were created by God through His Son as agent. The time of creation was before the creation of the material universe, and all were created at or near the same time as direct and individual products of God's fiat. They were created to honor, worship, and serve God and Christ. Originally they existed in a holy state with great powers and privileges but limited in space, power, intellect, and holiness; and as creatures they are morally answerable to God their Creator.

3

THE NATURE OF ANGELS

WHAT SORT OF BEINGS are angels? May we think of them as persons? What are their attributes and abilities? A survey of biblical information allows us to reach some definite conclusions and some tentative. Theological categories and philosophical considerations may help us, but the determining source and limiting judge is the Bible.

I. PERSONALITY

Whether we may properly consider angels as persons depends upon our definition of personality. Here we are not speaking of personality as that which manifests itself to us for description and reaction, but as the essence of being a person. Do angels fit the category commonly conceived as persons?

A. DEFINITION OF PERSONALITY

1. Archetype of personality. The definition of personality does not find its roots in what man is, but in what God is. God is basically a person. Scripture reveals God as having one essence and manifesting His existence in three persons. This is the doctrine of the Trinity in which we recognize God the Father, God the Son, and God the Holy Spirit. As a person, God has the ability to create persons other than the persons of the Godhead. It is conceivable that these persons may be human (generally recognized) or angelic. In each case, then, a genuine person should genuinely correspond to what God is or has in the line of personality, for He is the archtype of all persons.

29

2. Attributes of personality. It can be demonstrated from the Scriptures that God's personality is basically manifest in the possession and manifestation of three faculties: intellect, sensibility (emotion), and will. God alone is self-existent, and no creature can exist apart from God. Yet all persons are, as the result of God's creation, self-conscious, self-determining, moral individuals. These qualities distinguish persons from things or animals. So then if we demonstrate that something has intellect, sensibility, and will, that something we may call a person.

B. DESCRIPTION OF ANGELS' PERSONALITY

1. Elements. The Scriptures witness that angels have all three attributes or elements of personality. They have *intelligence,* as evidenced by their desire to learn of our great salvation in Christ (1 Pe 1:12) and by their ability to communicate intelligently in speech (Mt 28:5). Though there is evidently difference in the capacities of various angels, it is obvious that most of them possess great intelligence, and their knowledge exceeds that of man. The wisdom of God is reflected in their created abilities. Before his fall it was said of Satan, probably the greatest of all angels, "Thou sealest up the sum, full of wisdom" (Eze 28:12). After his fall, God said of him, "Thou hast corrupted thy wisdom" (Eze 28:17). Other angels, informed by God, are aware of such things as men's prayers, and future events among men (Lk 1:13-16). They know by revelation God's plan for the world (Rev 10:5-6; 17:1-18). Even the demons know Jesus to be the Son of God (Mk 1:24, 34) and know of His great power (Mk 5:7). Demons also know the place of their confinement (Lk 8:31) and their inevitable torment (Mt 8:28-29). God's angels are intelligent enough to carry out His wise and great tasks (Mk 13:27; Heb 1:7, 14). They may perceive the purposes of men on occasion (Mt 28: 5).

However great their intelligence, it is limited. They are creatures; they are not as God, omniscient. Furthermore, there are some things they do not understand fully, such as our redemption and the wondrous humbling work of Christ in His incarnation and death (1 Pe 1:11-12). From this fact, we also note that their understanding may be improved through observation and investigation. One fact that angels do not know is the exact time of our Lord's second coming. Though they will participate in the events of that day, they do not know the day or hour (Mt 24:36).

Angels have *emotions*. Highly blessed as they are in intelligence, angels, we might well suppose, have deep and sensitive emotions. Scripture bears this out. Struck with God's power and wisdom, they respond to His wondrous creation with joy (Job 38:7). Angelic seraphim worship God with a deep sense of awe and humble reverence, crying, "Holy, holy, holy" (Is 6:3, cf. vv. 1-4). Angels, recognizing the deity of Christ and His redemptive work, worship the Lamb ascribing to Him, with God the Father, blessing, honor, glory, and dominion forever (Rev 5:13, cf. vv. 11-14). Angels either rejoice themselves or view with understanding the rejoicing that takes place upon the salvation of a repentant sinner (Lk 15:10).

Angels also have a *will*. Angels have self-determination; that is, they can choose from various courses of action and seek to carry one through. They were created to do the will of God intelligently and faithfully. God appeals to their wills by commanding them to worship Christ, His Son (Heb 1:6). Originally they all chose to do those things which were within the will of God for them. But in the case of some, their wills opposed the will of God. The leader of this willful rebellion, Lucifer, also called Satan, declared his rebellion against God with five assertions of "I will" (Is 14:12-15). It is obvious from the Bible that many angels joined him in his defection, and they are now called his angels (Mt 25:41). In following Satan, these angels exercised their own wills against the will of God. It is implied that those angels who remained loyal to God exercised their power of choice (an aspect of will) in resisting the test of Satan and in continuing in subjection to God.

An awesome and terrible exercise of angelic will is seen in

Satan's influence upon the unsaved. Either through the spirit of the age engendered by his world system or through direct intervention by Satan or his angels, Satan works his will in unbelievers (Eph 2:1-2). Demonic spirits seek to seduce men away from faith in Christ and biblical teachings (1 Ti 4:1). Evil spirits (demons) may also indwell and control men, exercising their will over man's. The demons in the possessed man of Gadara exercised their will over his, and appealed to the will of Christ, asking for mercy (Lk 8:28-31). But note the power of the will of Christ over the will of a legion of demons. He commanded them to enter a herd of two thousand swine; they obeyed, and the swine dashed into the sea under the power of the demons and perished.

2. *Essence.* It seems scriptural to say that angels were created in the image and likeness of God just as was man (Gen 1: 27). It is rather doubtful that the image of God in man consists in the so-called three-part nature of man—body, soul, and spirit—as if to correspond with God's essence existing in three persons. Is there a true correspondence, as "image" implies, between the three parts and the three persons? What shall we do with man's heart and mind, which are vital parts of man and are mentioned as much or more often than the famous three above? Is man five parts? Or is he simply two: material and immaterial, or matter and spirit?

The image of God seems to consist rather of personality and holiness. Personality gives the basic capacity to have fellowship with the person of God (for only persons may have fellowship), and holiness is the character required to enjoy that fellowship (for two cannot enjoy fellowship unless they are morally in agreement). As sons of God by creation (Job 1:6; 2:1), angels possess the image of their Creator-Father. It is in this same sense that Adam is termed the son of God (Lk 3:38). The image of God in angels, as in men, was marred in those who participated in the fall; still they are essentially persons though their holiness was lost. Essentially, then, and originally angels were made in the image of God.

II. PROPERTIES

How may we describe angels? What attributes or characteristics properly belong to them?

A. SPIRIT BEINGS

Angels belong to the class of spirit beings, that is, they are generally understood as immaterial and incorporeal beings. They certainly do not have a material, fleshy body such as humans have. This follows from the fact that (1) angels are described by Hebrews 1:14 as "all ministering spirits," and (2) demons, if assumed to be fallen angels, are called "evil spirits" (Lk 8:2) and "unclean spirits" (Lk 11:24, 26).

Angels have spatial limitations. The concept of spirit is not irreconcilable with location. When Jesus said, "God is a spirit" (Jn 4:24), He was emphasizing that God is not limited to a particular location as Mount Gerizim or Jerusalem (vv. 20-24), but is essentially spirit. God is an infinite spirit Being, uncreated; however, angels are finite spirit beings, created. Therefore they are limited with regard to space. This is evident because they must move from one place to another. In Daniel 9:21-23, an angel moved swiftly from someplace probably in heaven to Daniel's side. In Daniel 10:10-14, an angel was delayed on his errand by another spirit being. Here a time limitation corresponds with spatial limitation. If a time lapse is involved in their changing locations, this means they are localized.

We may conclude from these facts that angels are creatures and that they have spatial and temporal limitations; that they are not omnipresent (present all places at once); nor ubiquitous (present many places at once); but defined and with one location at a time and always somewhere.

B. SPIRITUAL BODIES?

1. Type of bodies. The Scriptures do not attribute directly to angels any kind of bodies. But some have supposed that they have bodies of refined matter or material different from humans. This issue has always been disputed.* Those who support the idea that they have bodies† appeal to two grounds: (1) the idea of a purely spiritual and incorporeal nature as metaphysically inconceivable and incompatible with the concept of a creature, and (2) the fact that angels are subject to spatial limitation, move from place to place, and are sometimes seen by men. It may be that angels have some sort of body structure not known to man as of now. A body that operates by principles other than ours is not inconceivable. There are various kinds of bodies, and our resurrection body is called a "spiritual body" (1 Co 15:44). Any such body as angels may have is not usually or necessarily visible. They can be present in great numbers in a very limited space, just as many demons had entered into one man's body (Lk 8:30).

2. *Sex.* Angels are apparently without sex. We say "apparently" because we are limited to human concepts of sex and its powers. It is obvious from Matthew 22:28-30 that angels do not procreate and are not a race. So they are without sex in the normal sense of the word. Perhaps due to the limitation of human language (though neuter expressions were available), angels are generally referred to as masculine. They are sometimes described as men, and the masculine pronoun is used of them (cf. Mk 16:5-6; Lk 24:4). When they appear, they generally take on the form of a man (cf. Gen 18:2, 22; 19:1; Dan 10:18).

3. *Lifespan.* Angels are immortal. Once created, they never cease to exist. They are not subject to death (Lk 20:36), so that any body they may possess is immortal and incorruptible.

C. SPECIAL APPEARANCE

1. *Freedom to appear.* While angels are normally invisible (Col 1:16), they do have the ability to appear on occasion.

---

*The Council of Nice, A.D. 784, decided that angels had bodies of ether or light. The Council of Lateran, A.D. 1215, held that they were incorporeal (see Charles Hodge, *Systematic Theology*), 1:637-38.

†Even after the church of the Middle Ages came to the conclusion that angels are pure spiritual beings, some Roman Catholic, Arminian, and even Lutheran and Reformed theologians ascribed to them a certain corporeity, most subtle and pure (see L. Berkhof, *Systematic Theology*, p. 144).

This freedom to appear is, of course, subject to the will of God but evidently operative at the will of the angel (cf. Lk 1: 11-13, 26-29).

Angels have appeared in dreams, as to Joseph (Mt 1:20). In visions, God has disclosed something of their appearance to man. Isaiah's vision centered upon Jehovah, but it also included an astonishing sight of winged seraphim worshiping and serving Jehovah (Is 6:1-8).

On one occasion, God granted to the young man with Elisha the gift of supernatural vision to see the normally invisible angelic army surrounding and protecting them (2 Ki 6:17).

However, beyond dreams and visions and apart from supernatural vision granted to man, angels have actually appeared to natural sight. Sometimes they were recognized as angels (Dan 8:15-17; Mt 28:1-7), and sometimes their actual identity was temporarily or completely withheld (Num 22:23, 31; Judg 6:11-12, 21-22; Heb 13:2).

2. Forms of appearance. It is surprising that angels appear as often as they do in the history of scriptural record. They appear in the pleasure and purpose of God to man in his need. When they do appear, there are several points of description we may note.

When angels appear on earth to men, they generally appear in the *form of men.* This human appearance may be so realistic that they are mistaken for mere men. Abraham welcomed three "men" in the plains of Mamre (Gen 18:1-8). He witnessed them walk, talk, and sit as men. He invited them to eat as men, and they did; but they were angels (18:22; 19:1). Two of these angels journeyed on to Lot in Sodom, where he invited them to stay for physical refreshment. Their physical realism is underscored by the desire of the wicked population of Sodom to misuse them sexually (Gen 19:1-8).

They generally appear as males. Mark refers to a "young man" in the empty sepulchre of Jesus (Mk 16:5). Luke records the sight of "two men . . . in shining garments" (Lk 24: 4). The only exception may be in Zechariah 5:9, where angels may be represented as women, but the interpretation is not sure. But the rule is so apparent, that if we read of men supernaturally appearing to speak or act for God, as the "two men . . . in white apparel" of Acts 1:10, we may immediately presume that they are angels.

Some angels have a youthful appearance, as witnessed by the two Marys who came to the empty tomb of Christ (Mk 16: 5).

Angels may appear in any number it seems, from one (Lk 1:26-29), two (Jn 20:12; Ac 1:10), three (Gen 18:1-2), to a multitude (Lk 2:13).

Sometimes a vision on earth may picture an angel in the *form of an unusual man*. An angel that appeared to Daniel had the general semblance of a man, but his supernatural splendor obviously differentiated him from a man. This man-like creature had arms and legs resembling polished metal and precious stones; his face was like lightning, and his eyes as lamps of fire (Dan 10:5-6). The manifestation of the vision was selectively limited to Daniel, for the men that were with him did not see the angel (v. 7), although they sensed a supernatural presence.

The sight of the angel that appeared to the two Marys at the empty tomb of Christ caused fright because of his unusual appearance. There was something obviously supernatural about him, just as there was an unusual angelic look on Stephen's face when he was stoned (Ac 6:15, cf. vv. 8-15). Matthew tells of the angel that rolled back the stone from the tomb: "His countenance was like lightning, and his raiment white as snow" (Mt 28:3). His brilliant face and clothing were probably an outshining of the glory created in him. The dazzling garments of two angels impressed the women (Lk 24:4).

When angels appear in visions that center in heaven, they may appear as men; but it is not certain that they do, even though some human features are mentioned. More certain is that they appear in the *form of unusual living creatures*. In Revelation 4:6-8, what are probably angelic creatures are pictured as having many eyes, faces resembling a lion, a calf, a man, and an eagle, and six wings each. The angel of Revelation 10:1-3 is clothed with a cloud and has a rainbow on his head; his face is as the sun, and he has hands and feet and a loud voice as a lion. Sometimes angels are clothed in pure white linen with golden sashes (Rev 15:6). One angel, at least, has such glory that his presence will brighten the earth (Rev 18:1).

3. Force of appearance. When angels do appear, their presence produces various effects upon men. No special effect is noted upon Joseph except the allaying of his human concern about Mary and his obedience to the revealed will of God (Mt 1:18-25).

Mental and emotional agitation came upon Mary when Gabriel announced to her the news of the virgin birth of Christ. Nevertheless she conversed with him and accepted his message as from God (Lk 1:29, 34, 38). Zacharias was troubled and gripped by fear when an angel appeared to him in the temple (Lk 1:12). The shepherds to whom the angelic messenger announced the birth of Christ were very much afraid (Lk 2:9) at first; yet they rationally investigated the news and marvelled at the message (2:15, 18).

Mental and physical weakness, sometimes accompanied by complete lack of composure, result from angels' presence. Consider the Roman guards who saw the angel who rolled back the stone from Christ's tomb. They trembled from fear and became as dead (Mt 28:4). When Daniel saw an unusual manlike creature of brilliant appearance, he was left without strength and comeliness (Dan 10:8). Even those who did not see the vision trembled greatly. Strange sensations caused them to flee from Daniel's presence with fear. Animals may in the will of God see angels and so hesitate or fall, as did Balaam's donkey (Num 22:26-28, 31). It saw the angel with drawn sword in his hand before Balaam did; and when Balaam, granted as much sight and sense as the animal had, saw the angel, he then bowed his head and fell flat on his face.

Man does well to ascribe to angels the majesty and dignity God granted to them, and he should not think of them lightly. We need to take seriously the glory of spiritual realities.

D. SPIRITUAL WINGS?

It seems to be a common conception that angels have wings. Artists picture both good and evil angels as humans or grotesque composites of men and beasts and almost always with wings. Does this agree with Scripture?

On some occasions, the Scriptures picture angels as having wings. Isaiah's vision of Jehovah included a description of the seraphim, angelic beings who stood above the throne of Jehovah. These awesome creatures each had six wings. With two each one covered his face, with two he covered his feet, and with two he flew about his duties. It seems that his hands were separate from his wings (Is 6:2, 6).

Another class of angels described as having wings is the cherubim. Ezekiel's vision portrays them as having four faces and four wings each, with hands under their wings (Eze 1: 5-8). Their wings evidently provided the swift motion ascribed to them (1:13-14), and their movement caused a noise like many waters, as a sound from God, like an army moving; and when they stood, they let down their wings (1:24). Imagine the terrifying sight and sound. Here are two classes of angels, seraphim and cherubim, that definitely are pictured with wings.

Do other angels have wings as well? There are some occasions when angels are said to fly. The angel Gabriel was "caused to fly swiftly" to Daniel's side (Dan 9:21; cf. Lk 1:19). The reference to flying may imply that Gabriel has wings, though the means of movement is not specified. Revelation 14: 6-7 records the vision of the apostle John of an event in the coming great tribulation. He says, "And I saw another angel fly in the midst of heaven" (v. 6), announcing terrible judgment on unbelievers. What sort of angel this is, we are not told. We may surmise that he is a lesser angel than Gabriel or Michael (Rev 12:7), just as the other angels of judgment in the same book. This angel also seems to have wings, and so may those who seem his equals.

Do all angels have wings? We cannot say. Are the wings literal? They may be. Are they material? Not in the usual sense. (See the discussion of angelic bodies, above.) Angels certainly could move without physical wings. The wings pictured in angelic visions (note they do not always appear with wings) may be symbols of their swiftness to execute God's wishes, just as wind and fire symbolize their fast and fervent service (Heb 1:7). It may be that the wings of the seraphim in Isaiah 6:2, which cover their feet and faces, symbolize their reverence of God's presence. Surely this is not the commonly conceived use of wings. Wings, then, may be pictures of angels' genuine complete swift obedience and service.

E. SPIRITUAL CONDITION

1. Classification. Angels fall into two spiritual or moral categories. They are according to their nature termed "holy" (Mk 8:38) or "elect" (1 Ti 5:21), and "evil" or "unclean spirits" (Lk 8:2; 11:24, 26). According to their allegiance they are called "the angels of God" (Jn 1:51), or we read of "the devil and his angels' (Mt 25:41) and the "dragon and his angels" (Rev 12:7). It may be that a third of the angels belong to Satan's camp (Rev 12:4).

2. Cause. What caused the separation, and when did this occur? We are not told exactly how or when this came about, nor do we have all the details we might like; but we do have adequate revelation to know some basic answers that are satisfying to reverent faith.

We must first consider the *creation* of angels in a holy state. All angels were created by God through His Son, the Lord Jesus (Col 1:16-17). There is no creature that was not created by Him (Jn 1:1-3). God cannot be directly involved in the creation of evil, even though He allows it to exist temporarily; for He is holy (Hab 1:13a). So it is obvious that all angels were originally created with holy natures.

Next we must consider the moral *choice* of angels to do evil or to remain holy. Despite their holy character and their holy surroundings, some used their God-given power of choice in rebellion against God. The Scripture pictures Satan as the leader in the defection. With unexplained origin, evil thoughts of pride influenced Satan to exercise his will to seek to overthrow God and His program (Is 14:12-17; cf. 1 Ti 3:6). Of course, he failed, as any creature must fail in rebelling against the Almighty. But in the process, he drew with him a great number of angels who became loyal to him as their new chief (Mt 25:41).

3. Continuation. Once the angels were put to the test to remain loyal to God or to rebel with Satan, their decision seems to have been permanent in its effect. Their condition may be described as nonviolable and nonredeemable.

All angels, good or evil, now continue in their respective states as *nonviolable*. The lines have been drawn, and their condition is unchangeable. The fact that certain angels are termed "elect" means that God intervened to confirm some in holiness. A period of probation is implied in that all angels were created in holiness and then subject to a test through the solicitation of Satan. Note the expression "the iniquity of thy traffick" (Eze 28:18), which may refer to his solicitation of other angels to his rebellious cause. "The good angels . . . evidently received, in addition to the grace with which all angels were endowed, and which was sufficient to enable them to retain their position, a special grace of perseverance, by which they were confirmed in their position."‡¹ It is obvious that God's election of angels was unto perseverance, not unto redemption. It was to confirm in holiness, not to convert from evil; for not all angels fell, nor are fallen angels capable of repentance unto salvation. All of Satan's original followers, without a doubt, are destined with him to the lake of fire (Mt 25:41). Therefore, we deduce that the "elect angels" remain fixed in holiness and that the evil angels remain fixed in wickedness.

Furthermore, we may deduce that evil angels are *nonredeemable*. Those that followed Satan in his sin, fell decisively and are permanently left in their evil state without recourse

---

‡"There has been a great deal of useless speculation about the time and character of the fall of angels. Protestant theology, however, was generally satisfied with the knowledge that the good angels retained their original state, were confirmed in their position, and are now incapable of sinning" (Berkhof, p. 145).

or even the possibility of redemption. They are irrevocably consigned to the lake of fire (Mt 25:41).

What evidence is there for such a position? First, there is no record of any angel ever being delivered from sin. True, this is an argument from silence, which is never too strong; but if Christ's redemption extended to angels, we could rightly expect some mention of it in God's revelation of the grace of His Son's work. We read of many other accomplishments of the death of Christ besides the redemption of man, but nothing of the salvation of angels. We read of His cross as their judgment (Jn 16:11; Col 2:14-15), but it is never presented as their blessing in any sense.

Second, there is the definite statement that Christ did not take hold of angels to save them, but only of believing man (Heb 2:16). He passed by angels to help man.

Third, it is implied in Hebrews 2:14-17 and is evident from the very nature of angels, that Christ did not and could not take upon Himself the nature of angels. Hebrews tells us that Christ saves those who are His "brethren" (2:11). He had to be made like them, in fact one of them, to save them; so He took upon Himself "flesh and blood" (2:14). This means that He entered into the race of men by the virgin birth, retaining His deity in essence (though not always its expression) and adding to His person sinless but genuine humanity. As the God-man He is a genuine representative of the race because He is truly human, as well as divine. On the cross, Christ was the effective Mediator between God and men because He was the God-man, representing both God and man in the settlement of our debt of sin. For man He suffered the penalty as a genuine substitute, since He genuinely participated in our humanity.

Christ could not lay hold on angels in like fashion to represent and to redeem them. Their very nature forbids it. Angels are not a race to which genuine additions may enter. They are individually separate creations of God, and they do not procreate (Mt 22:28-30). Christ could not become their Kinsman-Redeemer by birth or creation and so represent angels as a class before God.

But since Christ did become the last Adam, the Head of a new race of men reborn by faith in Christ, we have a song no angel can sing—of Jesus the God-man and His saving grace (Jn 1:12-13; Heb 2:9-12).

We must reject any teaching of universal restoration of all men, or even of Satan, to God. Only humans can be saved, and only those who trust Christ in this life will be saved. So taught Christ who died and rose again (Mt 25:41; Jn 5:29; 8:24). The lake of fire is an eternal torment for wicked men and angels (Rev 14:10-11; 19:20; 20:11-15).

4. Conflict. The division of elect and evil angels came as the result of a rebellion. Separation of some from God introduced spiritual enmity and warfare. We read of conflict between the good and evil angels as they battle behind the scenes of human governments and the course of world events (Dan 10:13; 12:1; implied in Is 14:4-17; Eze 28:12-19). We read of a conflict in the future tribulation period between Michael and his angels and the devil and his angels (Rev 12:7-9). This is warfare in the angelic sphere.

There is also warfare in the human sphere. The devil and his demons wrestle with God's people on earth to discourage and to defeat spiritual advance in the individual and in the church. The reality of this warfare and the believer's resource and victory are set forth in Ephesians 6:11-18.

III. POWERS

The power of angels is very great. Originated and limited by God, angelic power manifests itself in several relationships.

A. SOURCE OF POWER

1. Granted by God. The angelic creatures themselves recognize God as the source of their beings and powers when they cry, "HOLY, HOLY, HOLY, IS THE LORD GOD, THE ALMIGHTY. . . . Thou didst create all things, and because of Thy will they existed, and were created" (Rev 4:8, 11, NASB). Hodge writes, "The power of angels is, therefore, (1) Dependent and derived. (2) It must be exercised in accordance with the laws of the material and spiritual world. (3) Their intervention is not optional, but permitted or commanded by God, and at his pleasure.[2]

2. *Governed by God*. Hodge has already hinted at the limitation of angelic power. The Scripture presents this limitation as due not only to God's creation but also to God's control.

Angelic power is *exercised* by God's will. God sent two angels to destroy the wretched city of Sodom, and by their power they also delivered Lot from the judgment (Gen 19:12-16). When David sinned in numbering Israel and Judah, God sent an angel to smite Jerusalem with a pestilence as chastisement (2 Sa 24:14-17). The many judgments found in the book of Revelation are under the control of Christ, who opens the book that contains the judgments described in the seals, the trumpets, and the bowls. The angels involved in the administration of these, therefore, are subservient to Christ (cf. Rev 6-16).

Angelic power is *excluded* by God's will. God limits the exercise of angelic potential in the case of both good and evil angels. When God's angel would have completed the destruction of Jerusalem, God's merciful will stopped him (2 Sa 24:13-16). During the Great Tribulation to come, angelic messengers of judgment withhold their destruction until the will of God is accomplished in protecting His own (Rev 7:1-3). Even Satan, who seems to be the greatest of all angels, was limited by God in his affliction of Job (Job 1:12; 2:6). Satan's forces are restrained by good angels acting in the will of God and are finally defeated (Rev 12:7-9).

How comforting for the believer to know that angelic power, great as it is, is under God's good and gracious control. In our weakness, we can only trust in our Father's grace and power.

B. SPHERES OF POWER

We can best understand the extent of angelic power as we

note what the Bible presents about their power in certain relationships or areas of influence.

1. In relation to the human world. Angels may *express human functions.* The story of Abraham entertaining three strangers (Gen 18:1—19:1) seems to identify these three in the appearance of men as really angels (18:1-2, 22; 19:1), though one may have been an appearance of Jehovah Himself (18:1, 13, 22). From this we learn that angels may appear in the form of men (cf. Lk 24:4), walk as men (Gen 18:2, 16; 19: 1), talk as men (18:9), and eat as men (18:8). These functions, we understand, do not belong to them normally, but are assumed to accomplish their mission.

Angelic power is known to *excel human forces.* David calls on angels to praise God: "Bless the LORD, ye his angels, that excel in strength" (Ps 103:20). Peter says that though false human teachers speak evil of dignities, angels, "which are greater in power and might" (2 Pe 2:11, cf. vv. 10-11), do not accuse them before the Lord.

God's angels exercise power over humans in gathering believers at Christ's return to earth (Mt 24:30-31). An angel entered a locked prison and released Peter who was bound with chains (Ac 12:7-11). Great strength was manifest by the angel who rolled away the huge stone that sealed the tomb of Christ (Mt 28:2; Mk 16:3-4).

Angels are used by God to *exclude human wickedness.* Angels may be powerful instruments in the hand of God to restrain evil. Angels restrained the wickedness of the men of Sodom. Two of the angels that had spoken to Abraham went to Sodom, where they found Lot in the midst of a wretched and perverted people. In face of danger, they rescued Lot and smote the wicked men with blindness, preventing their evil intentions (Gen 18:22; 19:1, 10-11). An angel of God prevented Balaam from pursuing his selfish and destructive intent against Israel (Num 22:22-35).

God also uses angels to *execute human judgment.* The Lord may use angels *to chastise God's own people* on the occasion of some great sin. Consider David's sin of confidence in the flesh when he numbered the fighting men in Israel. Though provoked by Satan (1 Ch 21:1) and permitted by God (2 Sa 24:1), the sin was King David's (24:10). Rather than famine or the enemies' sword, David chose to receive pestilence at the hand of God. When His angel would have destroyed Jerusalem, God in mercy stayed His angel (24:13-16), lest the chastisement be excessive.

Angels execute judgment *to punish God's enemies.* They may inflict bodily sickness and even death upon those who oppose God's people and presume to take to themselves the honor due God, as in the case of Herod (Ac 12:23). God sent angels to destroy the cities of Sodom and Gomorrah (Gen 19:1, 13, 24-25). An angel caused great destruction of the enemies of Israel. God defended His people against the blasphemous leader of Assyria and sent His angel who slew 185,000 men of war (2 Ki 19:35).

The superhuman power of angels extends to *exercise human deliverance.* Angels rescued Lot (Gen. 19:10, 16), released Peter (Ac 12:7-11), and preserved the three Hebrew children in the fiery furnace (Dan 3:28).

2. · *In relation to the material world.* With startling power *they control, in certain instances, the elements of nature.* Four angels are described as "holding the four winds of the earth, that the wind should not blow on the earth (Rev 7:2-3). One angel receives power over the scorching heat of the sun to plague men during the Great Tribulation (Rev 16:8-9). In certain cases, *they destroy natural resources,* as during the worldwide catastrophes of the Great Tribulation. Then, according to Revelation 8 and 9, they will in accord with God's wrath destroy a third of earth's vegetation, salt and fresh waters, and water life (with men and ships).

3. *In relation to the angelic world.* With respect to their own persons, angels exercise certain powers. Among them are the powers of choice and active obedience or rebellion, as noted before. They also have the power of communication.

Satan shared his purposes, it seems, with other angels and enticed them to follow him (Eze 28:16; Rev 12:3-4). God's angels relay messages to other angels (Rev 6:5; 7:1-3).

With respect to their peers, angels command other angels (Rev 7:1-3; 14:17-18) and battle opposing angels (Dan 10:13; Rev 12:7-8). In God's purpose and power, one great angel will, at the coming of Christ to rule on earth, lay hold of Satan and bind him for one thousand years (Rev 20:1-3).

SUMMARY

Though the power of angels is great, it is derived from God and limited by Him. Says Hodge, "These limitations are of the greatest practical importance. We are not to regard angels as intervening between us and God, or to attribute to them the effects which the Bible everywhere refers to the providential agency of God."[3]

4

THE POSITION OF ANGELS

WHAT IS THE POSITION of angels relative to the Son of God and to man? Clarification of this question will give us further insight into the proper respect and estimation of angels.

I. IN RELATION TO THE SON OF GOD

There are some who suppose, by prejudice of mind or by ignorance of the Scriptures, that Christ, the Son of God, is the first and highest of all God's angelic creatures. This tragic error is degrading to the Son and deceptive to the saints. The Scriptures set forth an obvious and extensive contrast between Christ and angels.

A. CONTRAST IN ESSENCE

The Bible clearly contrasts the nature of Christ and of angels.

1. Statements of Christ's nature. He is the eternal God, and they are created by Him. John 1:1-3 declares clearly and forcibly that Christ is equally God with the Father and that He is the Creator of all things. Note five compact statements that declare to us the identity and essential nature of the Son of God: (1) "In the beginning was the Word"—Christ's continued existence before creation of the world; (2) "and the Word was with God"—His existence in God's presence as a distinct person; (3) "and the Word was God"—His essential equality with God the Father; (4) "The same was in the beginning with God"—His eternal fellowship with the Father; and (5) "All things were made by him; and without him was not any thing made that was made"—His all-inclusive creatorship. To no angel are any of these great statements attributed.

Some play on the construction of the Greek language in the statement, "the Word was God." They say since there is no definite article with the word *God,* the translation should be, "the Word was *a* God," and so find grounds for classifying Christ as an angel. Actually, nothing could be further from John's intent or the truth as set forth in the rest of Scripture. The absence of the article in Greek puts the emphasis not on indefiniteness (as in the use of the English indefinite articles *a* and *an*), but on quality or essence. Thus, John is asserting that the Word (Christ, cf. Jn 1:1, 14) in His basic or essential nature was *God.* Christ's deity is clearly attested in both Testaments (Is 9:6; Mic 5:2; Col 2:8-9; 1 Ti 3:16).

2. *Significance of Christ's names.* Christ is titled God's "only begotten Son" (Jn 1:14, 18; 3:16; 1 Jn 4:9), whereas the angels are called "the sons of God" as of a large class (Job 1:6; 2:1). Christ is unique, eternally begotten of the Father, without beginning (Mic 5:2; Rev 1:8-18). An angel is one of many of the same class. Christ *is* the image of God in that He is the exact likeness and counterpart of God, corresponding in every point to what God is (Col 1:15; Heb 1:3); whereas angels were created in the image of God, reflecting Him only in that they were created persons with holiness. Christ is titled "the firstborn of all creation" (Col 1:15, NASB). This means that Christ is prior to and sovereign over all creation, including His created angels (Col 1:15-16). Angels and men are to worship Him who is the fullness of the Godhead in bodily form (Col 2:9; Heb 1:6).

We are called upon to confess Jesus as Jehovah (Is 42:8; 45:23; Ro 10:9, 13), not to confuse Him with angels (Heb 1:4).

B. CONTRAST IN POSITION

The book of Hebrews, in presenting the perfection of Christ and His superiority to all the Old Testament system and revered personages, begins with an argument for the superiority of

Christ to angels, who were held in high regard by the Jews. The emphasis in Hebrews 1 and 2 is on Christ's superior person and position.

After presenting Him as the fullness of God's glory, the exact likeness of God's person, the Creator of all, and the great Redeemer, the author speaks of the Son as "having become as much better than the angels, as He has inherited a more excellent name than they" (Heb 1:4, NASB). The name that God gave Him that indicates His superior position and dignity is "my Son" and "God" (Heb 1:5, 8). Such qualifies Him to be the unexcelled and complete personal revelation of God (cf. Jn 1:18). We trust and worship one who said, "He that hath seen me hath seen the Father" (Jn 14:9). This He could say because "in Him all the fulness of Deity dwells in bodily form" (Col 2:9, NASB).

1. The dignity of the God-man. In Hebrews 1:5-14 there are seven quotations from the Old Testament to demonstrate that Christ is superior to angels. These are prefaced by the question, "For unto which of the angels said he [God] at any time?" The answer is made clear in the following context: no angel can qualify for the position and dignity ascribed to the Son of God.

(a) His dignity as the eternal Son. "Thou art my Son, this day have I begotten thee" (v. 5; Ps 2:7) refers to Christ's eternal dignity as the eternally begotten Son of God.

(b) His dignity as the Son of David. "I will be to him a Father, and he shall be to me a Son" (v. 5) is taken from David's covenant (2 Sa 7:14) and emphasizes His continued dignity as the divine inheritor and fulfiller of the kingly promise.

(c) His dignity as the reigning Son. The American Standard Version and New American Standard Bible make verse 6 a reference to Christ's second coming: "And when He again brings the first-born into the world, He says, 'AND LET ALL THE ANGELS OF GOD WORSHIP HIM' " (NASB). Here is His future millennial dignity as the ruling Son of man. (Note Deu 32:43

in the Septuagint; cf. Ps 97:7.) Only God, no angel is to be worshiped.

(d) His superiority to angels. Hebrews 1:7 quotes Psalm 104:4 concerning the nature and service of angels. The Son is superior to them because they are spirit beings created to serve God with the speed of wind and fervency of fire. They serve the Son also.

(e) His dignity as eternal Deity and Messiah. Verses 8-9 state that the Son is eternal, not created as the angels, and is truly God. The quotation from Psalm 45:6-7 pictures God the Father addressing the Son as God. This one addressed, "O God" (v. 8) is "anointed" (from the same root as *Christ*) by one called "thy God" (v. 9). While the words *sceptre, anointed,* and *fellows* call attention to the humanity of Messiah, yet the stress in Hebrews 1 is that He is superior to the angels as the *God*-man, because He is the eternal Son.

(f) His dignity as the eternal, immutable Creator. Further contrasting the Son with angels, Hebrews 1:10-12 quotes Psalm 102:25-27. There the reigning "Jehovah in Zion" (Christ reigning in Jerusalem's future kingdom) is Jehovah the Creator of heaven and earth who abides eternally, never aging and never changing. Though all creation may wax old and perish, yet "THOU REMAINEST. . . . BUT THOU ART THE SAME, AND THY YEARS WILL NOT COME TO AN END (Heb 1:11-12, NASB).

(g) His dignity as the victorious King-Priest. Hebrews 1:13-14 make a final contrast. Not to any angel but to the Son the Father said, "SIT AT MY RIGHT HAND, UNTIL I MAKE THINE ENEMIES A FOOTSTOOL FOR THY FEET" (v. 13, NASB). This quotation from Psalm 110:1 pictures Christ as having completed His work of redemption and taking His rest at the right hand of God, the place of exaltation. He sits there as a high priest according to the order of Melchizedek, replacing all Old Testament priests. He is presently awaiting final subjection of all to Himself. Meanwhile, angels are "all ministering spirits, sent out to render service for the sake of those who will inherit salvation" (v. 14, NASB). Angels do spiritual service to Christ as God, and to those who have trusted Christ as Saviour. This

present service is designed to deliver us and preserve us "unto his heavenly kingdom" (2 Ti 4:18) and our final salvation and enjoyment of our eternal inheritance in the future kingdom.

Nothing in the angelic class can lay claim to any of the above ascriptions of positional dignity. These belong only to God's unique Son, eternally begotten, born into David's line, destined to reign on David's throne forever.

2. The dominion of the God-man. While Hebrews 1 presents Christ superior to angels as the Son of God, chapter 2 presents Him superior to angels as the Son of man. As God-*man* He is ruler of the future kingdom of God on earth, and as such will rule the world of men and angels.

Angels are not assigned dominion of the coming kingdom. The earth was originally subjected to man as God's representative ruler. Even though man was made a little lower than the angels, yet God crowned him with glory and honor and put him over God's creation on earth (v. 7; Gen 1:26-31). Though all things are not now under man's control due to sin (v. 8; Gen 3), yet the eternal Son became the God-man and is now crowned with glory and honor (v. 9). It is the God-*man* who shall reign when God's kingdom shall come to earth (Mt 25:31-34). The righteous, perfect man, Christ Jesus, shall reign with a new race of men reborn by faith in Him; and He shall reign over an earth where the curse is lifted and righteousness permanently dwells (Is 11:1-9; 55:3-4, 13; 60:21; 2 Pe 3:13). Christ is the Sovereign, not angels.

3. The deliverance of the God-man. Not only is Christ superior to angels as the Sovereign, but He is superior to angels as the Saviour. He is the Redeemer of those to whom He is related by flesh and by faith. The process of bringing many sons to glory first necessitated His going to the cross (Heb 2:9-10). As the Redeemer, He did not identify Himself with angels, but He took on Himself humanity . This He did to undo Satan, the greatest of all angels, and to deliver man from fear of death (vv. 14-15). In His incarnation, the Son bypassed angels to lay hold on man, who was made a little lower than they, and to raise believing men above angels (2:16, ASV).

The redemption accomplished by Christ on the cross shows Him superior to all angels as the God-*man*.

4. The defeat by the God-man. We understand something of the moral power of angels when we consider that the Son of God alone could overcome Satan and his armies in the battle for the souls of men and the purpose of God. However, the power of angels provides a measure for the exceeding power of Christ and gives us further insight into the greater position of Christ.

He is the victor over sin and Satan through the cross. In His death He not only blotted out the condemnation of the law against us, but He made a public spectacle of angelic rulers and authorities. This effective and far-reaching defeat of the forces of Satan and demons is portrayed in historic Roman style. The apostle Paul says that Christ first stripped them of their weapons and then paraded them to public view as He led them captive in His triumphant procession (Col 2:15). The point is forcibly clear: the God-man defeated and judged all the evil angelic forces arrayed against God by His death on the cross (cf. Jn 12:31-33; 16:11; Heb 2:14).

5. The designation of the God-man as Lord over all. Christ's death and resurrection won the victory over sin, death, and Satan. Evidence of this victory is found in Christ's exaltation to the right hand of God in heaven. To the God-man has been accorded the name designated as "the name which is above every name, that at the name of Jesus every knee should bow, of those who are in heaven, and on earth, and under the earth, and that every tongue should confess that Jesus Christ is Lord, to the glory of God the Father" (Phil 2:9-11, NASB).

Not only was this exaltation a personal honor for the God-man for His voluntary humbling and obedience in death (Phil 2:8-11), but it was a public heralding of His victory over His angelic opponents. The present position of the man Christ Jesus in heaven in His resurrected body proclaims the present sovereign position of our Kinsman-Redeemer over all angels, both holy and evil (1 Pe 3:22).

Behold such dignity accorded Jesus the Son of God when

He passed through the heavens and sat down on the right hand of the Majesty on high (Heb 1:3; 4:14)! Behold such power which God wrought in Christ in this action! It was overcoming power, resurrection power, exaltation power, and subjection power (Eph 1:20-22). God's power and authority are now accorded the exalted Christ since He "seated Him at His right hand in the heavenly places, far above all rule and authority and power and dominion [angelic designations], and every name that is named, not only in this age, but also in the one to come" (Eph 1:20-21, NASB).

Measured by the dignity and authority of all angels, our Saviour is "far above all."

II. In Relation to Man

Though the words *angelos* (Gk.) and *malak* (Heb.) may be used of human messengers as well as angelic, it is obvious that there are two separate kinds of beings.

A. Distinction Between Men and Angels

1. Distinct station. We have previously spoken of the nature of angels as distinct from human nature, but distinction may also be supported by the distinct stations accorded to men and angels by creation. Psalm 8:4-6 is quoted in Hebrews 2:5-7 and describes mankind as "a little lower than the angels" and so distinguishes men from angels. This is the main point we seek to make here.

However, there are several questions that bear on the matter of the relation of men and angels to be considered. First, what is the meaning of "a little lower"? The American Standard Version margin has "a little while lower," indicating that man and/or Christ is ultimately above angels in the plan of God. This certainly is not without support in the context of Hebrews 2 with the reference to the future age (v. 5) and the note of expectation in "not yet" (v. 8). Furthermore, there is the reference to the temporary state of humiliation of Christ (2:9) and the design of bringing men to glory (2:10). The "little while" could refer to man's temporary condition of being lower than angels in the rule of this world, looking forward to the day when he will rule angels (1 Co 6:2-3). Or it could refer to the time of Christ's humiliation in contrast to His exaltation. Or it could refer to a combination of man and Christ, as man in Christ rules with Christ in the future.

Nevertheless, there are strong reasons for holding that "a little lower" refers to the original constitution and station God gave to man in the creation. Though we admit there is reference to the future dominion of man and Christ on earth in Hebrews 2, yet it seems that the original intent of the psalmist in Psalm 8:4-6 was to relate man to God and angels and to the creation placed under man. The writer looks at the heavens with their display of God's supernatural wisdom and power and is reminded of his own frailty and limitations. At the same time he is reminded of the dignity and authority granted to man as God's representative ruler on earth. In the psalm there is no indication of a temporary condition with future expectation of elevation; instead, there is a marveling at the station accorded to man by God in creation and in the governing of the world. The emphasis, it seems then, is on the fact that man is constitutionally a little lower than God or angels and yet is in command of God's earth. The psalm is reminiscent of the creation account of Genesis 1:26-27 where the same two truths are presented concerning the constitution and station of man. Man was made in the image of God and was appointed to rule for God. Man is then a little lower than God because "he is a being in the image of God, and, therefore, nearly a divine being."[1] Man is short of and lesser than Deity because he is a product of Deity and related to Deity by His image.

Did angels have part in the creation of man? Some hold, as Delitzsch, that God connects Himself with angels in the statement "Let us make man in our image after our likeness."[2] While it may be true that angels are also created in the image of God,* it seems unlikely that God would call upon angels to create with Him other creations. There is no indication in the Scriptures that angels can create life as does God. It may be that

---

*See chap. 3 on the description of angels' personality.

they were involved in the forming of man from the ground, but there is not a shred of evidence for this. Angels have the power of animation, as does Satan in his deceptive program (cf. 2 Th 2:9-10; Rev 13:11-15); but nowhere do we find them having the power of creation. In fact, it is the breathing of God into the earthy form of man that caused man to become a living soul and so distinguished him from the animal creation. The statements of John 1:3, Colossians 1:16, and Revelation 4:11 seem to exclude from the act of creation all but God Himself.

The second question related to our subject is the interpretation of psalmist's original Hebrew statement, "a little lower than *Elohim* (Ps 8:5). *Elohim* is one of the common names for God in the Old Testament. It is plural in form and speaks of strength or might. (For instance, it is used of God the omnipotent Creator in Gen 1.) However, in Hebrews 2:7 the word for angels (*angelos*) is used. What is the significance of this change?

The writer to the Hebrews uses the Septuagint and so quotes Psalm 8 which uses the word *angelos*. Obviously the writer and the Holy Spirit had a point in quoting this Greek version because it fits his subject in the context of Hebrews, the fact that the Son of God is superior to angels.

How then do we explain, within our accepted confines of verbal inspiration of the Scriptures, that *angelos* is an accepted alternate in this place for *elohim?* Of course, *angelos* is not an acceptable translation in many cases, but it may be that this is the best translation to use for Hebrews 2. The subject is angels, and it seems that *elohim* is used of God Himself or of God and angels as belonging to that category of supernatural beings above man.† (*Elohim* may be used of false gods, often associated with evil angels or demons, as in Ps 86:8 and in Ps 97:7, which the Septuagint translates "angels." It may also

†Davidson says of angels: "They are called *Elohim,* or *sons of Elohim; Elim,* or *sons of Elim.* . . . The name *Elohim* is used both for God and for angels. The angels are *Elohim;* and as a family or class they are 'sons of Elohim' " (A. B. Davidson, *The Theology of the Old Testament* [Edinburgh: T. & T. Clark, 1904], p. 293).

be used of human judges who act for God, as in Ps 82:1, 6; cf. Jn 10:34-35.) It may be that in Psalm 8 the intent centered upon the fact that man was lesser in nature than God or that he had in mind that man was frail and limited in comparison to supernatural beings such as God and angels. In any case, the writer of Hebrews does not use an expression foreign to the original thought. Man is certainly constitutionally less than God and less than angels as well. The emphasis in Hebrews 2 is that the Son of God became "a little lower than angels," that is, He took on Himself human nature with its frailties, limitations, and mortality, that He might as the God-man take man's place in suffering death as the penalty for sin. Thus He freed man to rule with Him for God, in the coming glory, over the world and angels.

"The angels, therefore, in contrast with the human race, belong to the class of Elohim."[3] Man, then, is "a little lower than angels" in that his nature is weaker, not strong like *elohim,* and subject to death, unlike angels.

2. Distinct service. The distinction between men and angels may be supported further by the fact that angels are presented as a class of beings sent forth from God's presence to minister to redeemed men who are to be inheritors of God's salvation. In that day of final salvation connected with Christ's second coming and kingdom, redeemed man in Christ will inherit all that God purchased for man in Christ (Heb 1:14). To man, on the other hand, is given the responsibility of preaching the gospel of salvation accomplished and offered in Christ. This is a ministry not granted to angels. Furthermore, in the coming kingdom, man will rule over angels. Thus men and angels are distinct, as seen in their services.

B. SIMILARITY OF MEN AND ANGELS

Distinct as they are, angels and men are alike in some respects. Both are creatures limited by time and space. Both are dependent upon God for existence and well-being. Both of them have responsibilities to God and are accountable to God (Jn 16:11; 1 Co 6:3; Heb 9:27). It may be that both are "sons of God" by creation (Job 1:6; 2:1; also Lk 3:38, where Adam is called "son of God"). Both are persons created in the image of God (Gen 1:27; cf. study above on personality of angels). Just as no two men are alike in personal characteristics, so we may suppose the same to be true of angels. If we consider God's wisdom and originality in lifeless snowflakes, why not in angels?

C. DIFFERENCES BETWEEN MEN AND ANGELS

Man differs from angels in many particulars, not just in class of being. Angels are essentially spirit (Heb 1:14), while men are both spirit and material body (Ja 2:26). While angels may have a body or something other than earthy material, their normal state is invisible even though they may manifest themselves in a visible manner. Angels are not a race; they are not related as are men, because they do not procreate (Mt 22:28-30). They were individually created by God. Angels are greater in intelligence, strength, and swiftness (2 Pe 2:11), whereas man is "a little lower than angels." Man is subject to death, whereas angels are not (Lk 20:36). However, glorified man will judge angels (1 Co 6:3).

Obviously, angels do not become human; nor do humans become angels. Though there are likeness, there is a definite distinction in nature and many differences in particulars.

SUMMARY

Angels are lesser than Christ in essence and position. He is the eternal Creator and Sovereign; they are creatures and servants. Even as the incarnate God-man, Jesus, He is superior to them.

Man is a little lower than angels in that he is weaker and subject to death. However, believers in Christ are positionally above angels since they are "in Christ." In the glory of resurrection, believers shall rule over angels with Christ.

Though there are similarities between men and angels, they are never confused in the Scriptures.

5

NAMES, CLASSIFICATIONS, AND ABODE

THE NAMES AND CLASSIFICATIONS of angels enrich our understanding of their nature and ministry. By reflection upon these, we gain insight into the wonders of God's person, power, and program.

I. GENERAL NAMES

The names of angels are further evidence that they are persons with peculiar nature and special relationships to God and to man.

A. NAMES REVEALING ANGELS' MINISTRIES

1. Angel is the transliteration of the Greek word *angelos* and is the word used in many cases to translate the Hebrew *malak*. The basic meaning of both words is "messenger." Depending on the context, these words may be used of a human messenger (1 Sa 6:21; Is 44:26; Mt 11:10; Lk 7:24; Ja 2:25) or of a supernatural, spiritual, heavenly being who attends upon God and is employed as His messenger to make known His purposes (Lk 1:11) or to execute them (Ps 104:4; Mt 4:6; Rev 16:1). This latter sense is by far the most frequent use in Scripture. This is certainly the sense in Hebrews 1:7, which states that angels are spirit beings created to serve God with the speed of wind and the fervency of fire.

2. Minister is a related concept referring to angels. The Greek word is *leitourgos,* a servant or minister, especially in connection with religious duties, as a priest (Ro 13:6; 15:16; Phil 2:25; Heb 8:2). The related Hebrew word is *mishrathim* (pl.), which is used in much the same way as the Greek word

58

(Ex 24:13; 1 Ki 8:11; 2 Ki 4:43; 1 Ch 27:1). It is used of angels in Psalm 104:4. With such a name, angels are viewed as those who minister for and in the presence of God in spiritual service.

3. *Host* pictures God's heavenly angels as His army, and is the translation of the Hebrew *sava*. In Psalm 103:20-21, angels are called upon to bless the Lord. In these verses, angels termed *malakim* and *mishrathim* are also termed *sava* (v. 21, cf. Ps 148:2). This term encompasses the whole array of God's heavenly army and sees them employed as a military force to accomplish His will and do His battles. As such, they are an extension of His power and providence. The name for God, Jehovah of Hosts, pictures God as the sovereign commander of a great heavenly army, who works all His pleasure in heaven and in earth (cf. 1 Sa 17:45; Ps 89:6, 8).

4. *Chariots* applies to angels in the sense that they are part of God's host or army that accomplish His purpose. Psalm 68:17 refers to angelic intervention that enabled victory over kings and armies that opposed Israel (cf. Ps 68:12, 14). This term is used also in 2 Kings 6:16-17, where Elisha and his servant were protected by an angelic task force of horses and chariots. Zechariah's visions included four chariots which carried out God's military judgments on the nations surrounding Israel. These are further described as "four spirits of the heavens, which go forth from standing before the Lord of all the earth" (Zec 6:5).

5. *Watchers* (Dan 4:13, 17) denotes angels as supervisors and agents under God employed by Him in the control of world government. They may be involved in decision making and execution of decrees that affect world affairs.

B. NAMES REVEALING ANGELS' NATURE

1. *Sons of the Mighty (benê elim)* occurs in Psalm 89:6 and is translated, "O ye mighty," in Psalm 29:1. The Hebrew expression is descriptive of the great strength of angels (cf. Ps 103:20). Often the expression "son(s) of" is descriptive of a class of persons. The prophets were *nebi'im* or *sons of nebi'im*,

indicating their classification. Some reckless or lawless persons were termed *sons of Belial,* which simply means a worthless person (cf .1 Sa 2:12; 25:17, 25). This is probably the classifying connotation in Jesus' surnaming James and John "sons of thunder" (Mk 3:17). *Elim* speaks of strength so that *benê elim* refers to angels as a class of mighty ones.[1]

2. *Sons of God (benê elohim)* by the Hebrew idiom refers to angels as belonging to a class of mights or powers. "In contrast with man, angels belong to the class of Elohim."[2] This term is used of angels in Job 1:6; 2:1; 38:7, and includes Satan. This term does not reflect the holy nature of angels—because Satan, the evil one, is classed among them—but it does speak of their might. In Job, the *benê elohim* are pictured as assembling before God, ministering to Him and answering to Him. Payne, with others, says that this term is used also of the elect of mankind;[3] however, close inspection of the passages usually listed (Deu 14:1; Is 46:3; Ho 1:10; 11:1) will disclose that they do not use the exact term, which seems to be a technical term to classify angels. This is probably the sense in which "the sons of God" in Genesis 6 is used.[4]

3. *Elohim* by itself is sometimes applied to angels. "The name *Elohim* is used both for God and for angels. The angels are *elohim;* and as a family or class they are 'sons of Elohim.' "[5] This is the understanding, evidently, of the writer to the Hebrews (as well as the translators of the Septuagint) when he takes "a little lower than *elohim*" as a little lower than angels (Heb 2:7; cf. Ps 8:5). This term pictures angels along with God as a supernatural class of beings of great strength and higher than weak and mortal man. "Moses . . . described Jacob's experience at Bethel by saying that *'Elohim* were revealed [plural verb] unto him' (Gen. 35:7). He thus indicated that God and His angels, when envisioned together, may be called *Elohim,* supernatural beings."[6] As the created servants of God, angels are reflective of God's great power and immortality.

4. *Holy ones* in Psalm 89:6-7 refers to God's angels. It is a translation of *kadoshim,* which means separated ones, those

set apart to God, and "The 'assembly of the saints [holy ones]' . . . is best understood as referring to angels."[7] The same expression is used in Job 5:1; 15:15, Daniel 8:13, and Zechariah 14:5; and in each case it probably refers to angels. This term reflects their holy character and activities as those devoted to God.

5. *Stars,* used symbolically of angels, denotes their heavenly nature and abode. God speaks to Job about the wonders of creation and the time when "the morning stars sang together, and all the sons of God [*benê elohim*] shouted for joy" (38:7). It is rather natural that stars and angels be compared as heavenly creations that reflect the power and wisdom of God. They are often mentioned in the same context (cf. Ps 148:1-5). Both angels and stars are called "the host of heaven" (Deu 4: 19; 17:3; 1 Ki 22:19; Neh 9:6; Ps 33:6). In fact, astrology is connected to demon worship though this term (Jer 19:13; Ac 7:42; particularly 2 Ki 23:5, 10, 24). Divination and worship of the stars is condemned by the Scripture (cf. Deu 18: 10-14)[8] as connected with demonological elements.[9] It is not strange, then, to note that Satan is described in his rebellion and warfare against God as a "wonder in heaven . . . a great red dragon . . . and his tail drew the third part of the stars of heaven, and did cast them to the earth" (Rev 12:3-4). This force of spirit beings is later called "Satan . . . and his angels" (Rev 12:9). Stars, then, speak symbolically of heavenly spirits created by God.

II. SPECIAL CLASSIFICATIONS

The Scriptures reveal that there are several special classes or orders of angels. Each class has its special distinguishing characteristics which seem to be part of a created constitution.

A. CHERUBIM

Cherubim (Heb. pl. of *cherub*) seem to be angelic beings of the highest order or class, created with indescribable powers and beauty. As is the case with many heavenly realities, their character and appearance is so far beyond human imagination and present comprehension that they must be described in earthly terms obviously designed to convey something surpassingly supernatural (Eze 1:5-14; 28:12-13, 17).

1. Description. God made the visible appearances of the cherubim to differ, as each occasion might best be served.[10] However, certain basic descriptions may be traced through the Bible. The first biblical reference to angels is to the cherubim of Genesis 3:24 who were placed at the gate of the Garden of Eden after man was expelled. They were stationed with flaming swords to protect the way to the tree of life, lest sinful man should intrude into God's presence or presume to partake of the tree of life. They teach us that sin and paradise are incompatible. Sinful man cannot approach God without the righteousness granted to those who trust Christ.

Cherubim appear next in connection with the designated dwelling place of God in the tabernacle. They appear in the form of golden images upon the mercy seat, the lid on the ark of the covenant in the Old Testament worship tent (Ex 25: 17-22). The ark and mercy seat with its symbolic cherubim were kept in the innermost sanctuary of the tabernacle where God's shekinah glory was manifest. In this connection they are designated "the cherubim of glory" (Heb 9:5), probably as associated with the glory of God. "The *cherubim* are one of the most important symbols of the Mosaic worship. Figures of them appear also on the tapestry of the tabernacle, and, at a later time, on the walls of Solomon's temple, and in the vision of the new temple, Ezek. xli."[11]

The cherubim on the mercy seat seem to be represented as having one face and two wings each. They sat on opposite ends of the mercy seat facing each other and stretching out their wings so as to cover the mercy seat. They seem to be looking down at the lid of the ark rather than at one another.

During Ezekiel's captivity in Babylon, he received a vision of the glory of God which involved the presence of "four living creatures" (Eze 1:1, 28). Later references to this vision identify these creatures as cherubim (10:4, 18-22). They were, along with "the glory of God," associated with the golden images on the mercy seat, "The seat of the image of jealousy" (8:3).

The cherubim of Ezekiel's vision were complex creatures. Each one had four faces and four wings and the overall appearance could be likened to a man (1:5-6), "not that of the mythological winged sphinx of Assyrian-type lion, as is claimed by liberal historicism."[12] They had hands of a man under their wings (v. 8). The four faces of each of them are compared with the faces of a man, a lion, an ox, and an eagle (v. 10). They had the appearance of polished brass and bright coals of fire, and their movements flashed as lightning (vv. 7, 13-14).

2. Design and duties. What purpose do cherubim serve and in what activities are they engaged? Though it seems obvious that they are an angelic class, they are never termed "angels." Perhaps this is because they are not *messengers (malakim)* in their duties. They seem never to carry revelation or instruction from God to men.

Their main purpose and activity might be summarized in this way: they are *proclaimers* and *protectors of God's glorious presence, His sovereignty, and His holiness.* This characterization may be substantiated by reference to their various appearances and connections in Scripture.

Since they are nowhere sent from God's presence but are "confined to the seat of the divine habitation and the manifestation of the Divine Being,"[13] they *designate the place of abode of the presence of God* as in the Garden of Eden, the inner room of the tabernacle, and later of the temple.[14] Psalm 80:1 and Psalm 99:1 refer to the Shekinah glory as representing God who is "enthroned *above* the cherubim" (NASB).

In one sense they *proclaim to men the transcendent and unapproachable God,* since they forbid entrance to Paradise and protect and shade the ark.[15] But in another sense, they *speak of the revelation of God's glory to man,* since they are associated with the visible form of the glory of God and present themselves in the form of earthly living creatures and men.[16]

From the vision in Ezekiel 1, the cherubim *indicate the intervention of a sovereign God in the affairs of men.* In this

vision they were positioned under the four corners of a platform on which was seated the glory of God in the appearance
of a man upon His throne (1:22-23, 26). Under each of the
cherubim were four peculiar wheels composed of two wheels
each, probably at right angles to each other and of the same
size and centered upon the same vertical diameter. The impres-
sion is that these wheels could run in any direction immediately
without taking any space or time to turn around as would single
wheels. The platform with its throne was propelled by the
powerful wings of the cherubim with a great rushing noise (perhaps as jet engines? 1:9, 24). The whole vision speaks of the
glory of God moving swiftly and sovereignly upon the earth and
in the heaven to accomplish His holy purposes and judgments.
From a survey of the book of Ezekiel, we may see the glory
of God, associated with the cherubim, judging the sin of Israel,
the sin of the nations, and intervening on behalf of Israel to
bring about the accomplishments of God's promised ultimate
blessing upon His chosen nation in the millennial kingdom.

A final interesting point might be noted concerning the
cherubim. It seems clear that they emphasize God's presence
and holiness in their symbolic form upon the mercy seat, the lid
of the ark of the covenant. These things were kept in the innermost sanctuary of the tabernacle where God's shekinah glory
was pleased to dwell with His people. There God met sinful
man on the basis of blood sacrifice and through a God-given
priesthood. In the ark were kept a golden pot of manna, Aaron's
rod that budded, and the tables of the law (Heb 9:4). These
contents were reminders of God's gracious provisions scorned
and rejected by man. When the high priest would enter once
a year to sprinkle the blood of the atonement for sin on the
mercy seat, the blood would grant entrance to God and atone
for sins (Lev 17:11). Thus, the cherubim, proclaimers of God's
holiness, would symbolically look down and see the sprinkled
blood on the mercy seat covering the sins of the people as
symbolized by the three items under the lid of the ark. All
this God-designed imagery pointed forward to Christ, who
would shed His blood not just to cover sins but to put them

away by the sacrifice of Himself (Heb 9:6-14, 25-26). In witnessing the sprinkling of the divinely provided blood, "the cherubim of glory" (Heb 9:5) were not only protectors of God's glory but *proclaimers of the grace of God* that provides salvation and access for man, both in the Old Testament symbolism and in the New Testament reality in Christ.

B. SERAPHIM

Another special class of angels are the seraphim. They also, as the cherubim, are closely associated with the glory of God and are probably related closely in class to them.

1. Description. The Hebrew term (*seraphim*) means "burning ones." This probably speaks of their consuming devotion to God rather than of their outward ministry. Oehler says that "they are evidently represented in human form; for faces, hands, and feet are spoken of."[17] They each have six wings. Oehler writes:

> The *symbolism of their appearance* is very simple. With two wings they cover their faces,—to indicate that even the most exalted spirits cannot bear the full vision of the Divine glory; with two they cover their feet,—to symbolize their reverence [speaking of hesitancy to tread uninvited upon holy ground];—with two they fly,—to express the swiftness with which they execute the Divine commands.[18]

It seems that the seraphim were hovering above on both sides of Jehovah on His throne. They were crying to each other, as antiphonal choirs, "Holy, holy, holy, is Jehovah of hosts; the whole earth is full of his glory" (Is 6:3). Whether there were only two seraphim or two rows of several seraphim, it is difficult to determine. The force of their voices was such that the supports of the throne room shook (v. 4). The altar mentioned probably corresponds to the golden altar of incense in the tabernacle. It stood before the veil closing off the holiest place and was used when the high priest would enter into the symbolic presence of God. Incense placed upon coals taken from the altar would fill the holiest place with smoke, signifying that sinful man could not look directly upon the holiness of God. Note that in Isaiah's vision "the house was filled with smoke" (v. 4).

2. Design and duties. Seraphim are angelic type beings who perform a priestly type service for God. Succinctly put, their purpose is to show forth Jehovah's holiness and ethical transcendence.[19] This may be substantiated by their name and activities.

The very name *seraphim* speaks of their consuming devotion to God. They are afire with adoration of the holy God. Their great cry is in praise of the perfect holiness of God. To ascribe the term "holy" to God three times means, according to Hebrew idiom, to recognize God as extremely, perfectly holy. Therefore, they *praise and proclaim the perfect holiness of God*.

The seraphim also express the holiness of God in that they *proclaim that man must be cleansed* of sin's moral defilement before he can stand before God and serve Him. One of them, upon Isaiah's confession of sinfulness and uncleanness (reminiscent of the leper's cry, Lev 13:45), flew with a live coal from the altar near Jehovah and touched Isaiah's lips to purge his sin (Is 6:6-7). The action was symbolic of cleansing, but the cleansing was real. This priestly type service for God speaks of God's holy standard and demand that the believer be cleansed before service. Isaiah's lips, once unclean, are now cleansed and ready to speak God's message to men (vv. 8-9).

C. LIVING CREATURES (BEASTS, KJV)

1. Identity. If the living creatures (*hayoth*) of Ezekiel 1 are cherubim, what are the four living creatures (*zoa*) of Revelation 4:6-9 (ASV)? Are they also cherubim? There are likenesses in the two appearances. There is reference to faces like a lion, a calf, a man, and an eagle, and to multiple wings and to many eyes. However, there are striking differences. In Ezekiel each living creature had four faces, whereas in Revelation each has only one. In Ezekiel each one had four wings; in Revelation each has six. In Ezekiel the eyes were pictured as in the wheels associated with the living creatures; in Revelation the creatures had eyes round about themselves and within. Of their identity we are not certain. It may be that those of Revelation were seraphim, who also have six wings and also cry, as do they, "Holy, holy, holy" (Is 6:1-3).

2. Activities. What are the functions of the living creatures of the book of Revelation? We see them *worshiping God* in chapters 4, 5, 7, and 19, and witness the worship of God by redeemed men in chapter 14. Again we see them *directing the judgments of God* during the tribulation period, as in chapter 6 they each in turn call for the execution of the judgments associated with the first four seals of the scroll, and as in chapter 15 one of them gave to seven other angels the seven bowls of the wrath of God to be poured out upon the earth. If we allow that the purging of Isaiah by fire and the punishment of the earth by judgments both are expressions of a ministry of purgation by a holy God, then we may have additional grounds for identifying the living creatures as seraphim.

III. SPECIAL NAMES

It is noteworthy that of all the angels, only two are designated by name in our canonical books, and these are not mentioned until after the Babylonian captivity of Israel. Michael and Gabriel are given places of great importance among angels in the ministries of God, and both are mentioned in the Old and New Testaments. In emphasis, Michael seems to be the greater. He might be characterized as the military leader, while Gabriel is the leading messenger.

A. MICHAEL

1. Designations. The name *Michael* is significant. There is among some a question as to its meaning, but it is probably to be taken as a question, "Who is like God?" This name would call attention humbly to the incomparableness of God. It would speak of his devotedness to God and His will, and would be in stark contrast with Satan who in his pride declared, "I will be like the most High" (Is 14:14).

However, others take the name to be a statement and declaration that its bearer is God Himself and should be understood as, "Who is like me, who am God."[20] Oehler writes, "It is certainly true that the later Jewish theology identified Michael with the shekhina, . . . while among moderns Hengstenberg identifies him with the Logos."[21] Nevertheless, it seems clear that Michael is clearly a created angel and not God himself. The name appears fairly frequently in the Old Testament as the name of a man from Numbers 13:13 to Ezra 8:8.[22] Furthermore, he is designated an archangel and is classified as "one of the chief princes" (Dan 10:13), as if belonging to a group of comparable ones among angels. He is further assigned to the welfare of the nation Israel as others are assigned to other nations by God or by Satan (cf. Dan 10:13, 20). In contrast, the Logos (preincarnate designation for Christ) is termed *monogenes* (only begotten, unique), is the creator of all angels (Col 1:16), and is the Lord of all nations (Rev 19:13-16).

Michael is further designated as "the archangel" (Jude 9). This title immediately sets him above some others of the angels, and indeed we see him as the military leader of an army of angels in battle with Satan (Rev 12:7). The definite article with *archangel* does not necessarily limit the class of archangel to Michael. The article may be one of identification as the well-known archangel instead of limitation as the only archangel. There may be others of the same class or rank, since he is described as "one of the chief princes" (Dan 10:13). Perhaps he is the archangel among the chief angelic rulers of God. He may possibly be of the cherub class, as is Satan with whom he is seen contending and battling (Eze 28:14-16; Rev 12:7). In this case, he might be the only cherub who leaves the presence of God on a mission.

We conclude, then, that Michael is a created angelic being of the rank of archangel and perhaps belonging to the class of cherubim. He alone, however, is specifically termed *archangel*.

2. Duties. We see Michael endued with authority from God, standing for God's people Israel, and opposing God's enemies.

In the mysterious angelic sphere there is obviously even now warfare between God's angels and Satan's (cf. 2Co 11:13-15;

Eph 6:10-12). It was so in Daniel's day also. An angel, seemingly lesser in rank and power than Michael, speaks of "the prince of the kingdom of Persia" withstanding him (Dan 10:13, cf. vv. 10-14). In that case, Michael came to help the angel. He was assigned by God to Daniel's people, the nation of Israel. Thus he is also called "Michael your prince" (Dan 10:21). Other nations may have their angelic princes, good or evil, but Michael is the defender of Israel.

We read of him as "the great prince which standeth for the children of thy people" in the time of the coming Great Tribulation (Dan 12:1; cf. also Mt 24:15, 21-22). As the specially appointed guardian of Israel, Michael will defend them in "the time of Jacob's trouble" (Jer 30:7), when Israel will be persecuted by the kingdoms of the world and the satanic host in the unprecedented time of trial and wrath that comes upon the whole world immediately before Christ's second coming (Rev 12:3-17). Under God, Michael and his army will be victorious over Satan (Rev 12:8-9), a token of the total victory of Christ the coming King (12:10).

3. Deferment. Despite his greatness and power, Michael, when disputing with Satan about the body of Moses, dared not blasphemously accuse Satan. But deferring to God he said, "The Lord rebuke thee" (Jude 9). If one so great as Michael, the head of all the angelic armies of God, does not rely on his own strength in opposing Satan but respects his evil power, how much more must we rely upon God (cf. Eph 6:10-12; 2 Pe 2:11).

B. GABRIEL

1. Designations. The name Gabriel means "mighty one of God," and speaks of his great strength endowed by God. The fact that he was "caused to fly swiftly" to Daniel reveals his great strength demonstrated in unusual speed (cf. Dan 9:21). He is further designated "the man Gabriel" (Dan 9:21), reflecting his form; and "the angel Gabriel" (Lk 1:26), revealing his nature as angelic. He is self-described as, "I am Gabriel, that stand in the presence of God" (Lk 1:19). A special and important messenger of God, he has permanent access to God's presence.

2. Description. We have noted that Gabriel is obviously an angelic being presented in human form on occasions. Daniel says, "There came again . . . one like the appearance of a man" (10:18). This one spoke with a man's voice (10:17-18) and had the power of touch, much as a man's (8:18; 10:18). This angel could stand in one particular spot as he appeared to Zacharias, and his appearance caused him to be troubled with great fear (Lk 1:11-12). When Mary saw him, she seemed not so much troubled with his appearance as with what he had to say about her supernatural offspring, Jesus (Lk 1:26-29).

3. Duties. Whereas Michael is God's special champion for Israel in her warfare, Gabriel seems to be God's special messenger of His kingdom program in each of the four times he appears in the Bible record. He stands in the presence of God ready to do His bidding (Lk 1:19) and quickly obeys to accomplish His purpose (Dan 9:21). He reveals and interprets God's purpose and program concerning Messiah and His kingdom to the prophets and people of Israel.

He brought to Daniel an interpretation of the vision of the ram and the rough goat. He revealed that the two-horned ram represented the Medo-Persian Empire, and that the great horned goat represented the Grecian Empire under Alexander, whose kingdom was later split into four parts (Dan 8:15-22). Gabriel is also the interpretive messenger of the "seventy sevens" of years that God has planned for Israel under the domination of Gentile world powers. This remarkable prediction pinpointed the date of Messiah's first coming to 483 years (69 sevens of years) after the decree to rebuild the wall and city of Jerusalem (probably that of Artaxerxes, cf. Ezra 7:7). The separately treated seventieth "week" of years (Dan 9:27) refers to another literal seven-year period yet to come after God's parenthetical program of the Church. This will involve the time of tribulation planned for Israel (Jer 30:7; Dan 12:1-2; Mt 24:15-21) that immediately precedes Christ's second coming (Mt 24:29-31).

Gabriel is also the messenger that appeared to Zacharias announcing the birth of John the Baptist, the official forerunner of the King, Jesus Christ (Lk 1:13-17, 19). He appears once more to Mary, the virgin mother of the human nature of Christ. He announces the virgin birth to her as the means of bringing the eternal Son of God into the human race to become the promised God-man, the seed of David, who should reign on David's throne over the nations of the world (Lk 1:26, 31-35). His kingdom will be established at His second coming (Mt 25:31-34).

It seems clear, then, that wherever Gabriel appears in Scripture, he is the special messenger of God to communicate revelation and interpretation concerning God's theocratic kingdom program, particularly concerning Israel and Messiah. He sets an example before us, who stand before God in the grace of Christ (Ro 5:1-2), as one who is swift to carry God's message to His people.

IV. Special Designations

There are a few other angels that are not personally named but are described by certain designations associated with their service.

A. Messengers of the Seven Churches

In Revelation 1:20, Christ designates that, "The seven stars are the angels of the seven churches," to whom John was commissioned to write. The word *angel* means "messenger," and can be used of either human or supernatural messengers in the Scriptures. It was used of John the Baptist (Mk 1:2), John's messengers (Lk 7:24), Jesus' messengers (Lk 9:52), and the spies who hid in Rahab's house (Ja 2:25). However, the more usual meaning of the word is angelic, supernatural creatures. The books of Daniel and Revelation use the term this latter way especially. Except for Revelation 2 and 3, the term is used this way exclusively.

The evidence is not sufficient to come to a firm decision as to whether the messengers to the seven churches were men or

angels. In favor of the view that they are angels is the usual
use in the New Testament and particularly in the books of
Daniel and Revelation. Some point out that the responsibilities laid upon the angels were too great for a man and that human leadership had not yet advanced to the point where one
man could be considered the leader for each church at the
time of the writing. On the other hand, in favor of human
messengers or leaders, it might be said that John was commissioned to write to the messengers letters that dealt with concrete problems men were facing. The concept of writing to
an angel does not seem the direct way of dealing with the problems. Furthermore, the angel or messenger seems to be addressed in each of the seven letters as participating in the life
and problems of the church as found in genuinely human problems. If we were to favor one view over another, the view
that these "angels" were human messengers who led and
guarded the churches seems more acceptable to the context.

B. Special Groups of Angels

The book of Revelation contains reference to several groups
of angels that are noteworthy. We will touch upon some at
this point.

*1. Four angels who stand on the four corners of the earth
and control the four winds of the earth.* We should not construe
this (Rev 1:7) to say that the earth is four-cornered; the concept is that angelic control (used but not needed by God) is
complete in this case and extends to controlling the elements.

2. "Seven angels who stand before God." To them were
given seven trumpets to call for judgment on the earth (Rev
8:2, NASB). They are messengers of God's judgment during
the tribulation period that immediately precedes Christ's second coming. As each sounds his trumpet, great plagues fall
upon the earth successively.

3. Seven angels who administrate the seven last plagues.
These plagues complete the outpouring of the wrath of God in
the Great Tribulation (Rev 15:1). To them were given "seven
golden bowls full of the wrath of God" (15:7, NASB). These,

as the other seven, poured out their bowls of wrath in successive fashion bringing great destruction upon the earth. These angels came out of the temple, the symbolic dwelling place of God (15:6). We do not have sufficient evidence to say whether they are the same or different angels than the seven mentioned in the previous series of judgments (Rev 8).

4. Twenty-four elders of Revelation 4 and 5. There are two views of this passage. Some say that the elders represent the true Church of Christ as it appears in heaven during the tribulation period. To support this its advocates cite the use of *elders* in the New Testament as referring to officers and representatives in the church and the mention of crowns and of ruling or thrones in the book of Revelation as referring to believers' rewards and privileges.[23] Others hold that the twenty-four elders are angelic beings that attend in priestly fashion the throne of God along with the "living creatures," who seem definitely angelic beings.[24] Advocates of this view point out that the elders join with the four living creatures to praise God for the redemption of mankind in expression that seems to exclude themselves. Many significant biblical manuscripts omit "us" in Revelation 5:9 and read "them" and "they" instead of "us" and "we" in 4:10 (cf. ASV). This would allow the twenty-four to be angels who do at times appear in white robes and may act as God's appointed heavenly representatives for His redeemed people on earth (cf. Dan 12:1; Mt 18:10; Lk 1:19; Rev 8:3). The number twenty-four may correspond to the twenty-four courses of priests established by King David (1 Ch 24) and to the sum of the twelve tribes and the twelve apostles.

There is not sufficient evidence to determine whether the twenty-four elders be men or angels.

C. ANGELS OF SPECIAL RESPONSIBILITIES

Certain angels are designated by the activity they are assigned. There is the "angel, the one who has power over fire" (Rev 14:18, NASB). Another is called "the angel of the waters" (Rev 16:5). An unusual one is designated as "the angel of the abyss" (Rev 9:11, NASB). He is also specifically named as Abaddon in the Hebrew, and as Apollyon in the Greek. Both names signify the activity of destruction. There is one called a star from heaven which had fallen to the earth (Rev 9:1), and to him was given the key of the shaft of the abyss. Since he had already fallen and had authority—signified by the key—over the abyss (see also v. 11) and was called the Destroyer, some identify this one as Satan.[25] Finally, there is one described in Revelation 20:1 as "an angel coming down from heaven, having the keys of the abyss and a great chain in his hand" (NASB). This one will bind Satan for the millennial reign of Christ (Rev 20:2-3).

All the unseen and awesome angelic activity around us now and scheduled for the future falls under the control of our Saviour, who works all things to accomplish His good and perfect purpose for His people and the glory of God (Mt 28: 19; Eph 1:11; Rev 1:18).

D. NONCANONICAL ANGELS

We have mentioned those angels within the bounds of holy Scripture, our only reliable source of truth about the unseen spiritual world. However, in the apocryphal writings, mention is made of three angels not mentioned in the Bible: Raphael, Uriel, and Jeremiel. We cannot attest to their reality, nor to the reality of the many angels of mythologies.[26]

V. ABODE

Since angels were all created in the state of holiness before the material creation (Job 38:4-7), it follows logically that their original dwelling place was with God in heaven. However, since the fall of some angels, the question of abode is a bit more complicated.

A. HOLY ANGELS

Opinions vary as to where the holy angels actually abide. Some say heaven, the dwelling place of God, while others prefer to say the second heaven. Perhaps there are some in each.

1. In heaven, the abode of God. Some angels are definitely pictured in the presence of God in a rather permanent sense. This seems to be the case of the seraphim (Is 6:1-6), of the living creatures (Rev 4:6-11), and of the angel Gabriel, "who stands in the presence of God" (Lk 1:19, NASB). To this agrees, it seems, the references to angels in heaven (Mt 22:30; Mk 12:25) and to "an angel from heaven" (Gal 1:8). Perhaps angels rejoice in the presence of God over sinners who repent (Lk 15:10).

2. In second heaven. The reasoning for this choice as the abode of at least some angels is: (1) there is more than one heaven, and at most three (2 Co 12:2), supposedly the atmosphere, the stellar heaven, and the presence of God; (2) Jesus passed through the heavens (plural) into God's presence (Heb 4:14, NASB); (3) Jesus is seated above all angelic principalities and powers (Eph 3:10; cf. 1 Pe 3:22); (4) therefore, angels do not abide in the third heaven. They abide, according to this view, in the second heaven and possibly have access to the third. This view also appeals to Satan's desire to ascend into heaven, that is, to the place of God (Is 14:13).

Some angels may permanently abide in the presence of God while others abide in the second heaven with possible access to the third, God's presence. We might question the significance of "above" in referring to Christ's position with reference to angels. The force of the passages seems to indicate position of authority rather than of locality. However, locality cannot be totally ruled out in the total consideration. The connection of angels with stars (Job 38:6-7; Rev 9:1) and the term "host of heaven" (Ps 148:1-5) may indicate angels as abiding in the second or stellar heaven.

3. In the. heavenlies. The heavenlies ("heavenly places") apparently refer to a spiritual sphere of position and activity that involves Christ and the believer (Eph 1:3; 2:6), holy angels (Eph 3:10), and evil angels and Satan (Eph 6:12). Whether this is a place of abode for angels or merely a place of activity for and against God and His own, is not quite certain. If it is a spatial location, then since it involves believers on earth, it must refer to an area included in the first or atmospheric heavens. It seems, however, that the primary reference is to a spiritual sphere that must also include the earth's atmosphere. Certainly elect and evil angels both are declared to have invaded our realm of space and sense, where they are affected by and also affect men.

B. EVIL ANGELS

Since the fall, evil angels have been cast out of heaven and are now found in various places.

1. In the heavenlies. As noted above, Christians struggle against wicked spirit beings in the heavenlies (Eph 6:12). These are most likely the demons, Satan's henchmen who seek to hinder God's purpose and people on earth. They may also live and move in the stellar heavens.

2. In the abyss. Revelation 9:1-11 pictures a star from heaven which had fallen to earth. He had a key to the bottomless pit ("shaft of the abyss," v. 1, NASB margin). When he opened the abyss or pit, out came monstrous creatures who had an angel king over them (v. 11). These creatures appear to be demons or wicked angelic spirits who had been imprisoned for some time. This abyss may be the same place to which certain demons asked not to be sent by Christ during His ministry on earth (Lk 8:31). It is a place of temporary confinement for certain wicked angels now and for Satan during the future kingdom for one thousand years (note Rev 11:7; 17:8; 20:1-3).

3. In the earth, bound. At least four great angels are bound or will be bound at the river Euphrates (Rev 9:14). They may be leaders of great angelic armies involved in the destruction of one-third of mankind (Rev 9:15-18). These angelic armies may also be bound with the four great angels. This place of retention seems to be a different location from the abyss.

4. In eternal bonds under darkness. Some angels are described by Jude 6 as those who did not keep their own domain, but abandoned their proper abode" (NASB). These God "has kept in eternal bonds under darkness for the judgment of the great day." Their release from these bonds is only for entrance into the lake of fire (Mt 25:41). These words parallel what 2 Peter 2:4 says about angels that sinned peculiarly and are cast into *tartarus* ("hell," KJV), peculiar place of retention. The larger contexts of Jude and 2 Peter 2 indicates that these are the same angels and the same place. The sin here mentioned is probably not the original rebellion, since all those involved were imprisoned. This would not allow for some fallen angels to be free or in other places.

SUMMARY

The names of angels are significant, giving insight into their nature and ministries. The special classes of cherubim and seraphim involve creatures of complex constitutions and important ministries associated with God's presence and holiness. The living creatures are also angelic type beings associated with God's presence. In Ezekiel they are cherubim. In Revelation they may be seraphim.

Michael and Gabriel are the only angels besides Satan identified by personal names. Michael is the only designated archangel. He is particularly assigned to defend the nation Israel. Gabriel is God's special messenger to reveal truth about Messiah and His Kingdom.

There are certain groups of angels. Among them are the messengers of the seven churches of Revelation who by some are considered angels but probably are men. The twenty-four elders of Revelation seem to be angels who surround the throne of God.

Some angels abide in God's presence, but most seem to have the stellar heavens as their abode. Evil angels cannot live in God's presence. Free evil angels may be in the stellar heavens or the heavenlies, attacking men and opposing God. Some fallen angels are bound, either in the abyss, in tartarus, or in the earth.

6

THE ANGEL OF JEHOVAH

THIS ANGEL carries with him an air of mystery. Who is he?
He seems far more than an ordinary angel. Some identify him
with Jehovah and even with Christ. If this is so, then the angel
is a theophany, a manifestation of God in visible and bodily
form before the incarnation of Christ.

I. HIS IDENTITY

What evidence is there that his angel might be Jehovah or
even the eternal Son of God, our Lord?

A. HIS IDENTITY WITH JEHOVAH

The Angel of Jehovah acts as a unique messenger of God in
Old Testament times. His appearances extend from the time
of Abraham to the time of Zechariah.

1. His peculiar title. The title *Elohim* ("the mighty one")
was used of both the true God and the gods of the heathen.
But the title *Jehovah* (Heb., *Yaweh*) was reserved for the God
of Israel, the eternally self-existent One who made heaven and
earth and who entered into covenant relationship with His people. The angels in general are called "the sons of God" *(benê
elohim)*, but never "the sons of Jehovah." Therefore, since this
one has the singular and peculiar title "the Angel of Jehovah"
(malak Yaweh), we may suspect that he was more than an
angel, perhaps Jehovah Himself.

2. His personal identification. From a number of appearances throughout biblical history, we notice this angel consistently presented as Jehovah.

This angel found Hagar (Gen 16:7) and promised to do

78

himself what God alone can do (v. 10). Moses, the writer, identifies the angel as "Jehovah that spake unto her" (v. 13, ASV).

When this angel appeared to Moses "in a flame of fire out of the midst of a bush" (Ex 3:2), verse 4 says, "God called unto him out of the midst of the bush." The one who spoke with Moses is called the God of Abraham, Isaac, and Jacob; and with this announcement, Moses hid his face for fear of looking upon God (v. 6). The one who continued to speak is called "Jehovah" (3:7, ASV). Upon this historic occasion, God revealed His name as I AM THAT I AM (v. 14), the eternal, unchanging One. Would God entrust this unique personal revelation to a mere angelic creature?

The record of Gideon's commission identifies the one who spoke to him as "the angel of Jehovah" (Judg 6:12, ASV) and as "Jehovah" (v. 14, ASV) without any notice of change of speaker. Manoah and his wife saw the Angel of Jehovah; and upon recognizing him, Manoah feared they would die because they had seen God (Judg 13: 21-22).

That this angel was Jehovah is also implied in the vision of Zechariah when the angel in 3:1 seems clearly called Jehovah in the next verse (v. 2).

Most likely, the Angel of Jehovah was a theophany, a manifestation of God in visible and bodily form before the incarnation. His appearances were evidences of God's grace in revealing His person and purpose to His people.

B. HIS DISTINCTION FROM JEHOVAH

The same person is most likely in view in every mention of the singular and peculiar title, the Angel of Jehovah. Yet this angel, while identified as Jehovah is presented as distinct from Jehovah.

1. He intercedes to Jehovah. In Zechariah 1:9-11 we see that the man among the myrtle trees was the Angel of Jehovah, and that Jehovah had sent the horsemen who were to report to this angel. Their separate identity also appears in verses 12-13 where the Angel of Jehovah intercedes for Jerusalem as he speaks to Jehovah.

2. He calls upon Jehovah. In the visions of the cleansing of Joshua, Zechariah saw the Angel of Jehovah defending this priestly leader of Israel against the accusations of Satan in the presence of Jehovah (3:1-2). The angel (v. 1) is called Jehovah: "And Jehovah said unto Satan, Jehovah rebuke thee, O Satan; yea, Jehovah that hath chosen Jerusalem rebuke thee" (3:2, ASV). The angel called Jehovah was speaking to a separate person called Jehovah. How can there be more than one person called Jehovah?

C. HIS IDENTITY WITH CHRIST

1. Christ's essential nature. To those not recognizing the deity of Christ and not able to welcome the truth of the Scriptures, the problem is irreconcilable. But to those who recognize Christ as God's eternal Son and truly God, the problem is easily resolved. Christ, the eternal Son, is Jehovah in essence, yet a distinct person within the Trinity (note Is 6:3; 40:3; Mt 3:3; Jn 1:1-2; 12:36-41; Heb 1:8-9).

2. Christ's economic function. In the outworking of the purpose of the great triune God (Father, Son, and Holy Spirit; see Mt 28:19-20), the Son of God voluntarily took upon Himself the assignment of certain responsibilities. Thinking along this line, there are four considerations that help to identify the Angel of Jehovah as Christ in preincarnate appearances. (1) The second person of the Trinity, the Son, is the visible God of the New Testament (Jn 1:14, 18; Col 2:8-9). Accordingly, the Son was the visible manifestation of God in the Old Testament also. (2) The Angel of Jehovah no longer appeared after Christ's incarnation. A reference such as Matthew 1:20 does not identify the angel and should be understood as an angel of the Lord. (3) They both were sent by God and had similar ministries such as revealing, guiding, and judging. The Father was never sent. (4) This angel could not be the Father or the Spirit. They never take bodily form (Jn 1:18; 3:8).

The Angel of Jehovah, then, according to all the evidence,

seems to be the preincarnate Son. His appearances evidence His eternal existence.

II. HIS MINISTRIES

The ministries of the Angel of Jehovah were many and varied. He was obviously God's special representative to His people in the Old Testament, just as Christ was in the New Testament. Their ministries were surprisingly parallel and argue further for the identification of the angel with Christ.

A. PARALLELS WITH CHRIST'S MINISTRIES

1. Revelation. Outstanding in this angel's ministries of revelation was that of disclosing God's name, Jehovah (Ex 3:2, 4, 6, 14). To him was given this unique privilege above all angels. Jesus Christ is the permanent revelation of God in bodily form (Jn 1:14, 18; Col 2:9), and He also revealed God's name (Jn 17:6) by word and in person.

2. Commission. On the same occasion, the angel commissioned Moses to deliver God's people fom Egyptian bondage and to lead them to the promised land (Ex 3:7-8). He called and commissioned Gideon to go in God's might against the Midianites (Judg 6:11-23). He called and commissioned Samson through his parents (Judg 13:1-21). Jesus Christ called and commissioned His disciples and us to deliver men from sin with the gospel (Mt 28:19-20; Jn 20:21).

3. Deliverance. He was the angel of deliverance as well, for in each of the above cases, he acted to deliver God's people from servitude to their enemies. Jesus Christ delivers from fear and death and sin's guilt for those who trust Him now (Eph 1:7; Heb 2:14-15) and for Israel (Ro 11:25-26).

4. Protection. His protecting ministry was renown in David's days. Psalm 34:7 declares, "The angel of Jehovah encampeth round about them that fear him, and delivereth them" (ASV). Hezekiah knew spectacular deliverance from the Assyrian army (2 Ki 19:35). Jesus Christ is our Protector today. We need not fear man because "He hath said, I will never leave thee, nor forsake thee" (Heb 13:5).

5. *Intercession*. The Angel of Jehovah interceded for Israel when they were oppressed by their enemies. He asked God to act to deliver them (Zec 1:12-13). Our High Priest ever lives to intercede for us (Heb 7:25).

6. *Advocacy*. Zechariah pictures the angel as the advocate of God's imperfect believers, defending them against the accusations of Satan (Zec 3:1-7). Jesus Christ the righteous is our Advocate defending our position gained by His work on Calvary that satisfied God for our sins (1 Jn 2:1-2).

7. *Confirmation of the covenant*. The angel confirmed the covenant with Abraham (Gen 22:11-18). God had previously promised Abraham great personal, national, and universal blessings (Gen 12:1-3). Abraham had believed God (15:5-6), and God "cut a covenant" unconditionally with Abraham (15:8-21). So great was his faith that he would have sacrificed Isaac, his only son; but the Angel of Jehovah stopped him and confirmed God's promises (22:15-18). It is in this connection that the angel is identified with Jehovah as He who made an unbreakable covenant with Israel (Judg 2:1). Christ was sent to confirm the promises to Israel for their deliverance, and the forgiveness of sins for all (Mt 26:28; Ro 15:8-9; Heb 9:15).

8. *Comfort*. The Angel of Jehovah found and comforted the outcast slavewoman Hagar, promising her safety and a great progeny (Gen 16:7-13). Christ came with comfort and blessing (Lk 4:16-19) and ministered to the outcast (Jn 9:35-38; 16:1-4).

9. *Judgment*. At times the angel brought judgment. When Satan had provoked David to number Israel to revel in his military might, God was displeased and sent the Angel of Jehovah to partially destroy Jerusalem (1 Ch 21:1, 14-15). David saw him with a drawn sword in his hand stretched out over Jerusalem, and fell on his face in repentance and intercession (vv. 16-17). Then the angel commanded him to build an altar, which later became the site of the Solomonic Temple (21:18, 24-29; 22:1, 6). During the Great Tribulation, the Lord Jesus shall judge His people Israel along with unbelieving earth-dwellers (Mt 24:44-51; 25:32-42; 2 Th 1:5-10; Rev 5:5; 6:

1-17). The purging done, the temple will be rebuilt for worship (Eze 20:37-42; 43:2-5, 12).

B. POSSIBLE OTHER MINISTRIES

Other passages seem to refer to the Angel of Jehovah, even though his name is not specifically mentioned. If this is the case, he has other possible ministries. Some of the following overlap, but we are seeking the emphasis in each reference.

1. Calling to faith and commitment. The angel received intercession from Abraham (Gen 18:22-33). He called Jacob to faith in Jehovah (Gen 31:11-13). Later he brought Jacob to submission, granted him a new name, and left him with a new walk (Gen 32:24-32). These actions picture the Lord Jesus.

2. Provision and safekeeping. In blessing Joseph's sons, Jacob spoke of "the God which fed me all my life long unto this day, The Angel which redeemed me from all evil" (Gen 48:15-16). His Hebraistic parallel statements may equate the angel with God, and he is credited with provision and protection.

3. Forgiveness and direction. In Exodus 3:20-21 God promised to send an angel before Moses and Israel to keep them on their journey and to bring them to the promised land. They were to obey him and not provoke him. This angel could forgive sin, which only God can do, because God's name (signifying His character and authority) was in him. Here is another preview of our Lord Jesus who will keep us along life's way and deliver us to our destination, forgiving us our daily sins by God's authority.

4. Representative of God's presence. In the wilderness journey, Moses interceded for Israel after their first breach of the law. God responded by promising, "Behold, mine Angel shall go before thee." Immediately afterward, God said, "I will not go up in the midst of thee." Moses pleaded further, and God responded, "My presence shall go with thee, and I will give thee rest" (Ex 32:34—33:3, 14-15). This presents a distinction between an ordinary angel and the angel who was said to carry with him God's presence (Ex 23:20-21). The Angel of Jehovah seems to be "the angel of his presence" (Is 63:9).

5. *Associated with the glory cloud.* The fiery, cloudy pillar that led Israel in the wilderness is associated with the angel of God (Ex 13:21-22; 14-19). If this is the Angel of Jehovah, then this unique angel guided and protected God's people along their pilgrim pathway (note Num 9:15-23).

6. *Heavenly leader of God's armies.* If the one who appeared to Joshua just before Israel's initial move to conquer Palestine was the Angel of Jehovah, then he was styled "the captain of the host of Jehovah" (Jos 5:13-15). He leads God's people to victory over their enemies (see Eph 6:10-18).

SUMMARY

The Angel of Jehovah has been shown to be equal in essence with Jehovah and yet distinct from Jehovah. The only answer to this seeming contradiction is that he is a preincarnate appearance of our Lord Jesus, the eternal Son. Indeed, he is the most frequent Christophany in the Old Testament. His ministries are varied and extensive and well known in Old Testament times from the days of Abraham to Zechariah. Some of his ministries are those that only God Himself can do and are so extensively parallel with Christ's ministries that they argue further for his identity as the preincarnate Christ.

7

NUMBER, ORGANIZATION, AND RANK

THE SCRIPTURES GIVE interesting insight, though perhaps not all we would wish to know, into the number and organization of angels.

I. NUMBER

Medieval scholastics reportedly argued over how many angels could dance on the head of a pin. But we do not speculate when we consider in reverent fashion the insights the Bible gives into the great number of angelic beings.

A. NUMBERED IN MULTITUDES AND LEGIONS

At the birth of Christ, there appeared a "multitude" of angels praising God. This great grouping was only part of the heavenly host (Lk 2:13-15). The title "Jehovah of hosts" (Ps 46: 7, 11) indicates that God is the head of armies (hosts) of angels.

At His betrayal, Christ could have called upon God for twelve legions of angels (Mt 26:53). In the time of Augustus Caesar, a legion numbered about 6,000 men, usually backed by an equal number of auxiliary troups. If there is a parallel in the number of troops and of angels, Christ may have called for 72,000 angels or as many as 144,000 angels. Actually, He could have called the whole heavenly army if needed.

B. NUMBERED BY MEN AND STARS

Perhaps we could compare the total number of angels with the total number of humans in all history (as might be indicated in Mt 18:10). The number of angels might be compared with the number of stars in the heavens, for angels are associated with the stars (Job 38:7; Ps 148:1-3; Rev 9:1-2; 12:3-4, 7-9). If so, their number would exceed that of stars visible to the human eye—about six thousand during a year. Some scientists estimate that the total number of stars in the galaxies may run into the billions.

C. BEYOND NUMBERING

The apostle John saw in a vision an exceedingly great number of angels: "ten thousand times ten thousand, and thousands of thousands" (Rev 5:11). Taken literally, this would be over two-hundred million, and these may be only a part of the heavenly host. This expression, however, may not be an exact number but an indication of a multitude beyond comprehension. So we read in Hebrews 12:22 of "an innumerable company of angels."

This immense number reflects the vastness of God's power and wisdom. The heavens and their hosts declare the glory of God. They are all His handiwork. They are His individual creations whose number is fixed, since they do not procreate or die (Mt 22:28-30).

II. ORGANIZATION

God is the Author of order and organization, not of confusion (1 Co 14:33). This characteristic is reflected in His creatures to a greater or lesser degree. Angels manifest this characteristic in that both the elect and the evil are well organized.

A. EVIDENCED IN MANY ASSEMBLIES

Organization is implied when we read of an appointed time "when the sons of God came to present themselves before the LORD" (Job 1:6). Possibly there are regular, periodic assemblies of the angels, for the incident is repeated (2:1). They were evidently gathered in order at the creation of the world (Job 38:7). A hint of other assemblies of angels comes from

Psalm 89:5-6 (ASV): "And the heavens shall praise thy wonders, O Jehovah; thy faithfulness also in the assembly of the holy ones. For who in the skies can be compared unto Jehovah? Who among the sons of the mighty is like unto Jehovah?" Here, because of Hebrew poetic parallelism, we may associate "the holy ones" with "the sons of the mighty." Because of the reference to the heavens and skies, angels, not men, are most likely in view. There are, then, stated assemblies among the angels of God in heaven, when they meet to praise God and report their service to Him, for they are accountable to Him.

B. Evidenced in Military Administration

God's angels are undoubtedly organized under the archangel Michael. He leads an army of angels in order against Satan's angels in the coming Great Tribulation (Rev 12:7-9). Their strength and organization backed by God bring victory over the forces of Satan. Satan's armies are also well organized. In what seems an obvious description of demon activity in the tribulation age, the powerful demons have "a king over them, which is the angel of the bottomless pit," named Apollyon, meaning "destroyer" (Rev 9:11).

C. Evidenced in Meaningful Appelations

Various levels in the organization of angels are seen in the several titles ascribed to them by eight Greek terms: *thrones, dominions, principalities, authorities, powers, angels, world rulers, wicked spirits* (Ro 8:38; 1 Co 15:24; Eph 1:21; 3:10; 6:12; Col 1:16; 2:10, 15).

III. Rank

Rank among angels is a fascinating subject. There is enough evidence to say that there are distinct and graded ranks, but not enough evidence to make a complete comparison or organizational chart. Remember that these facts reflect God's orderly and creative ingenuity and skill.

A. RANKING BY CLASSES

There seem to be larger categories of angels that we may term *classes*. Their basic or essential nature, or at least its details, differs from class to class. Here we might consider cherubim, seraphim, and living creatures (which were treated in a previous chapter). Within classes there seems to be various ranks obtained by appointment from God.

Cherubim seem to hold the highest position, since they are consistently presented as the highest class, associated as they are with God's presence and glory.

Among the cherubim, Satan held the highest rank, for he was described as "the sum, full of wisdom, and perfect in beauty," and was appointed as "the anointed cherub that covereth," and again as "covering* cherub" (Eze 28:12, 14, 16). With him, Michael the archangel would not dispute (Jude 9), most likely due to his high rank and power. This indicates that Satan and his angels still retain some of their dignity and rank even after their fall into sin.

B. RANKING BY TITLES

1. Significance of titles. Certain titles imply rank by their very meaning. Consider the title *archangel*. The etymology of it implies a rank first among angels, since *arche* (Gr.) means first. This title is applied directly only to Michael (Jude 9). He, however, is also called "one of the chief princes" (Dan 10:13). This implies that there are others of high rank, but whether they also are archangels we cannot say definitely.

2. Significance of sequence. If the order of listing implies rank (for which there is good evidence), then a comparison of the various listings seems to indicate that among what we might call governmental rulers the descending ranks are *thrones, principalities, authorities, powers, world rulers, wicked spirits* and *angels*. It may be that the last two listed are equal, wicked spirits describing evil angels. The rank of *dominions* is listed last in Ephesians 1:21 and second, after *thrones*, in Colossians 1:16, so its place is more uncertain than the others.

*"Guardian," NASB margin.

Some of the titles apply to both good and evil angels, and only the biblical context can determine which kind they are. The rule of angels is often manifest through earthly rulers. It may be that those called *world rulers* are particularly responsible in this activity (see Dan 10:13, 21; 12:1; Eph 6:12).

The rather consistent order in listing, or the sequence of the names, evidences order of rank among good and evil angels.

SUMMARY

The unimaginably vast number of angels are highly organized and ranked according to their class and position.

8

THE MINISTRY OF ANGELS

THE EXTENSIVE AND VARIED ministries of angels carry us even deeper into the world of spirits. They minister in heaven and on earth, for the most part beyond the observation of man. Again, only the Bible accurately discloses such things.

I. IN RELATION TO GOD

The most important ministry is that of service to God. Some of these ministries are quite clearly revealed.

A. MINISTERS OF WORSHIP

Angels' primary ministry seems to be that of worship and praise of God. Consider Isaiah's awesome vision of seraphim hovering above on either side of Jehovah as they cry antiphonally, "Holy, holy, holy, is Jehovah of hosts: the whole earth is full of his glory" (Is 6:3, ASV, cf. vv. 1-3). Here they ascribe holiness and sovereignty to God.

Revelation 4:6-11 pictures the four angelic creatures around the throne of God who "rest not day and night, saying, Holy, holy, holy, Lord God Almighty, which was, and is, and is to come. . . . Thou art worthy, O Lord, to receive glory and honour and power: for thou hast created all things, and for thy pleasure they are and were created" (vv. 8, 11). Here angels ascribe to God holiness, worthiness, and omnipotence as the sovereign Creator.

In Revelation 5:8-13, these angelic creatures join others to sing the new song of redemption that excels Moses' old song (Ex 15; Deu 32). In this case, angels ascribe worthiness and grace to God and to Christ for accomplishing redemption.

Angels seem to always sing their praise. Song is a most fitting and expressive means of giving God the praise due His name (Job 38:7; Rev 5:8-9). Such worship suggests the indescribable majesty and glory of God which unfallen angels understand better than do fallen men. Because of God's infinite worthiness, such beautiful and excellent worship continues forever without ceasing.

B. MINISTERS OF SERVICE

The attitude of worship leads to the activity of service. Two specific types of service need attention here.

1. Priestly ministers. In Hebrews 1:7 the term *ministers* (Gr., *leitourgous*) is generally used of a priestly service for God. It does not suggest that angels represent men before God or that men should pray to angels, an act strictly forbidden (Col 2:18; Rev 22:8-9). It may refer to service carried on in God's presence. Hebrews 1:7 also suggests that all the angelic hosts serve Him quickly as winds and fervently as fire.

2. Personal messengers. We should suspect that since the word *angel* means "messenger" in both Hebrew and Greek, we should see angels playing a large role in messenger service for God. Angels hasten to carry out God's orders, harkening to the voice of His commandments (Ps 103:20). Some stand in the presence of God, ready to carry His messages to men. Such is the case of Gabriel, who was sent with good news to Zacharias (Lk 1:19) and to Mary, the mother of Jesus (Lk 1:26-33). An angel informed the shepherds about Christ's birth. He was supported by a multitude of other angels in this role (Lk 2:8-14).

C. AGENTS OF GOD'S GOVERNMENT

Angels minister to God by carrying out certain aspects of His government. God is the sovereign Ruler of the universe, controlling all things, directing all things for His glory and for the good of His subjects (see Is 46:8-11; Ro 11:36; Eph 1:11). This is the theme of Psalm 103:19-20, where God's kingdom rule is connected with the service of His angelic creatures. In verse

19 we read, "The LORD hath prepared his throne in the heavens; and his kingdom ruleth over all." Because He is pleased sometimes to use His creatures to carry out His works, we read in verse 20, "Bless the LORD ye his angels, that excel in strength, that do his commandments, hearkening unto the voice of his word."

1. In controlling nature. Angels are at times involved in the control of nature's elements, such as the winds (Rev 7:1), the seas (Rev 16:3), and even the heat of the sun (Rev 16: 8-9). These refer to the future tribulation, but the principle of their control is established. Angels may be active in nature now.

2. In controlling nations. Behind the human scene, angels busily exercise influence and engage in battle. Individually or collectively they may guide the governments of the earth. God's angels oppose Satan and his angels (Dan 10:13, 21; 12:1). Note the activity of evil angels in Revelation 12:7-9; 13:1-7; 16:13-14. They may influence governments to oppose the gospel and God's people. For our needs we have the armor of God (Eph 6:10-13) and the angels of God (2 Ki 6:17; Heb 1:14).

D. PROTECTORS OF GOD'S PEOPLE

Angels minister to God by protecting His people. Their object is to glorify God's name. They may harass our enemies (Ps 35:4-5) and deliver us from their wicked works (Ps 34:7; Is 63:9). They are probably involved in physically preserving God's own for their future inheritance in His presence and kingdom (Heb 1:14).

E. EXECUTORS OF GOD'S JUDGMENTS

Angels were involved in the destruction of Sodom and Gomorrah (Gen 19:1, 12-13). God used angels in bringing the plagues on Egypt (Ps 78:43, 49) and sent the destroying angel to execute the firstborn in Egypt at the Passover (Ex 12:13, 23).

An angel chastised God's own people, as with David and

Israel (1 Ch 21:15-18). One angel utterly destroyed the 185,000 Assyrians in answer to Hezekiah's prayer (2 Ki 19:35).

Future judgments include administering the wrath of God during the Great Tribulation. The four living creatures summon judgment (Rev 6:1ff), as does another angel later (14:17-18). Seven angels sound the trumpet judgments (Rev 8:1-6), and these are followed by another seven who pour out bowls of God's wrath on the earth (15:1; 16:1-21). During the tribulation, Michael and his angels execute judgment in war against Satan and his angels (Rev 12:7-9).

II. IN RELATION TO CHRIST

Christ receives the ministry of angels—as does God in the description above—yet He is specifically connected to them in several aspects.

A. AT HIS BIRTH

1. Predicted His birth. The angel Gabriel was sent to predict the unique birth of Christ to the virgin Mary, assuring her that this was God's special intervention to produce a holy offspring, the God-man, our Saviour (Lk 1:26-28). An angel also appeared to Joseph in a dream to assure him, as he was about to dissolve their bethrothal. He confirmed that the pregnancy was a direct act of the Holy Spirit and that she would bear a son, the Saviour, according to the prophesied virgin birth (Mt 1:18-23).

2. Announced His birth. Certain shepherds first heard the good news of the Saviour's birth from an angel. He identified the baby as Christ the Lord and gave them an identifying sign. To substantiate his message, there suddenly appeared a multitude of holy angels praising God (Lk 2:8-15).

B. DURING HIS EARTHLY LIFE

1. Protected Christ. When He was yet an infant, an angel warned His parents to flee to Egypt to escape the wrath of Herod (Mt 2:13-15). Later, an angel directed Joseph to return to Israel after Herod's death (Mt 2:19-21).

2. Strengthened Christ. Angels carried out the Father's loving ministrations to the Son during His earthly trials. After the ordeal of the temptation by Satan, "Angels came and ministered unto him" (Mt 4:11). In Gethsemane, when His soul shrank from the horrible prospect of bearing the full weight of God's wrath for our sins, an angel came from heaven to strengthen Him (Lk 22:43).

3. Stood ready for Christ's defense. When He was betrayed and taken prisoner, Christ could have called twelve legions of angels so deliver Him, but He willingly went to the cross to do God's will (Mt 26:53).

C. AFTER HIS RESURRECTION

1. Announced His resurrection. An angel rolled away the stone from the door of the tomb (Mt 28:1-2). He did not remove the stone that Christ might exit, but to show that He was no longer in the tomb. They specifically announced the good news of Christ's resurrection to those who came to the empty tomb, and reminded them of His prediction (Mt 28:6; Lk 24:5-8).

2. Subjected to Him. The resurrection and exaltation of the God-man put a man in authority over angels. As Peter states, the resurrection of Christ placed Him "at the right hand of God, having gone into heaven, after angels and authorities and powers had been subjected to Him" (1 Pe 3:22, NASB, cf. Eph 1:20-21).

3. Intrigued with His salvation. Angels must marvel at the grace shown when God's own Son stooped to ransom lowly sinners. They desire to stoop and peer into our salvation (1 Pe 1:10-12). They also rejoice or view God's rejoicing when Christ saves a repentant sinner (Lk 15:10).

4. Ministering to the restored Sovereign. The Son once voluntarily gave up the independent use of His sovereign rights and the enjoyment of glory. He did this when He became a servant in human form (Phil 2:5-8). But now, following resurrection, He is restored to His original glory (Jn 17:4-5). In His restored glory, He again exercises full rights as the Sovereign and enjoys the full ministration of all His angels, as does the Father. Today, angels worship the God-man in heaven (Rev 5:11-12).

D. About His Second Coming

1. Predicted His return. Angels predicted not only Christ's birth, but also His second advent. At the ascension, they said He would personally, bodily, visibly come again to earth (Ac 1:11).

2. Accompany His return. The holy angels, said Christ, will accompany the God-man as He returns in the glory of His Father (Mt 25:31). They may be the "holy ones" mentioned in Jude 14.

3. Worship Him at His return. This is the sense of Hebrews 1:6: "And when He again brings the first-born into the world, He says, 'AND LET ALL THE ANGELS OF GOD WORSHIP HIM' " (NASB).

4. Gather groups of men at His return. Angels serve the returning King of kings in gathering His elect from all parts of the earth. This may primarily refer to His elect from the nation Israel, but may extend to Gentiles also (Mt 24:31).

Angels will also gather the wicked for Christ's pre-Kingdom judgment so that they may be cast into fire (Mt 13:39-43; 2 Th 1:7-10).

III. In Relation to Epochs

Another method of considering angelic ministry is to notice their presence at the beginning of new eras or at great events.

A. At Creation

God asked Job, "Where were you when I laid the foundation of the earth! Tell Me, if you have understanding. . . . Or who laid its cornerstone, when the morning stars sang together, and all the sons of God shouted for joy?" (Job 38:4, 6-7, NASB). Obviously no man was present at creation, but the angels were. The terms "the morning stars" and "the sons of God" refer to them.* They had no part in creation, for God alone creates (Heb 3:4). The Father created all things through His Agent, His equal, the Lord Jesus (Jn 1:3). Angels were first created by Christ, and then they rejoiced to behold His power and artistry in the material creation (Col 1:16).

B. AT THE GIVING OF THE LAW

At Mount Sinai, God obviously used angels to deliver the Law to Moses. Three New Testament references help us to understand something of what was involved. The Law came through angels into the hands of Moses and then to the people (Gal 3:19). The Jews correctly regarded the Law as ordained by angels, and yet they failed to keep it (Ac 7:38, 52-53). The words of the Law, at least in part if not the whole, are regarded as spoken through angels (Heb 2:2). These statements may refer to the tablets of Law containing the Ten Commandments which Moses said were "written by the finger of God" (Ex 31: 18; Deu 9:10). It seems that God's intervention came through the agency of angels who actually engraved the first and second editions of the tablets. This helps us to understand the Jews' high regard for angels and why the writer of Hebrews takes two chapters to show the superiority of Christ to angels and His replacing of Mosaic Law (Heb 1, 2).

C. MAJOR EVENTS IN CHRIST'S PROGRAM

Though we have noticed their presence on these occasions in the previous section,† we round out angel's presence at the epochs in summary form here.

1. At Christ's birth. The privilege fell to them to announce the birth of Messiah, the entrance of the eternal Son into humanity (Lk 2:8-15).

2. At Christ's resurrection. At this great historic event, angels rolled away the tombstone, announced that Christ was no longer dead but alive, and instructed the disciples to meet Him in Galilee (Mt 28:2-7; Mk 16:5-8; Lk 24:3-7).

---

*See treatment on pp. 59-61.
†Note their ministry to Christ, pp. 93-95.

3. At Christ's ascension. While Jesus was being lifted up into heaven, two angels delivered God's guarantee that Christ would come again in the same fashion (Ac 1:11).

4. At Christ's return. Angels will add their solemn presence and glory to the glory of the Son of God when He comes again to earth (Mt 25:31).

III. IN RELATION TO BELIEVERS

The Bible presents a wide range of angelic ministry to men. They minister to those whom God loves, for they are interested in God's concerns. This is reflected in the angel's address: "O Daniel, a man greatly beloved" (Dan 10:11). Their ministry shows God's love, for they are "sent forth to minister for them who shall be heirs of salvation" (Heb 1:14). This ministry takes many forms.

A. REVEALING

God has used angels to communicate His will and word to men. As noted, angels were involved in the revelation of the Law to Moses (Ac 7:52-53; Gal 3:19). An angel whom Zechariah calls "The angel that talked with me," interpreted visions from God (Zec 4:1; 5:5; 6:5). An angel predicted birth of John the Baptist (Lk 1:11-20), and the virgin birth of Christ to Mary and Joseph (Mt 1:20-25; Lk 1:26-35). One revealed to the shepherds the time and place of Jesus' birth (Lk 2:8-12).

Much of the books of Daniel and Revelation came through angels' mediation. They interpreted extensively two visions given to Daniel regarding the course of world kingdoms (Dan 7:15-27; 8:13-26). Through Gabriel came the famous prophecy of the seventy sevens of years involved in God's program for Israel (Dan 9:20-27). The entire prophecy of Daniel 10:1—12:13 came through an angel who described the course of Israel's future in the intertestamental period and in the days just before the return of Christ and His subsequent Kingdom. The greatest part of the book of Revelation was given by an angel (Rev 1:1; 22:6, 8).

B. GUIDING

On several occasions angels were used by God to direct men. One told Joseph to take Mary as his wife and the virgin-born Jesus as his own son (Mt 1:20-21). The women who came to Jesus' empty tomb were instructed and directed by an angel.

Twice in the apostolic age God used angels in the work of winning men to Christ. One directed Philip to go south to the road between Jerusalem and Gaza (Ac 8:26). This led to a contact with the Ethiopian treasurer, a strategic person for the spread of the gospel. Note that the angel gave the general direction, but the Holy Spirit pointed out the exact person (8:29). Cornelius was directed by an angel to send for Peter who would inform him how to be saved (Ac 10:1-8; 11:13-14). But again specific instruction came to Peter by the Holy Spirit (10:19; 11:12).

C. PROVIDING

Angels have ministered to physical needs, such as providing food in several instances. An angel, who encouraged Hagar and her son, seems also to have provided water to keep them alive (Gen 21:17-20). Psalm 78:23-25 speaks of God's provision of manna for Israel in the wilderness wanderings and calls the manna angels' food. It was food from angels for man.

When Elijah had fled from Jezebel, he despaired of life and lay down to die. But an angel awakened him and provided him with "a cake baken on the coals, and a cruse of water" (1 Ki 19:6, cf. vv. 5-7). It may be that food was part of the angels' ministering to Christ after His forty days of fasting and His gruelling temptation by Satan (Mt 4:11). They must have marveled at the privilege of serving food to the One who for so long had provided life for all.

D. PROTECTING

Angels often guard God's people and keep them from physical danger. Jacob may have had the protection of angels as he traveled with his family to meet Esau (Gen 32:1-32). Daniel knew that God had sent His angel to shut the lions' mouths, an evidence of Daniel's innocency and of God's power and faithfulness (Dan 6:20-23). The three Hebrew youths seem to have had an angel keeping them from harm in the fiery furnace (Dan 3:24-28).

When Israel's king sent an army to capture Elisha at Dothan, the prophet told his fearful servant, "Fear not: for they that be with us are more than they that be with them" (2 Ki 6:16, cf. vv. 13-17). He then prayed, and God revealed an angelic army surrounding and protecting God's men.

E. DELIVERING

The concepts of protecting and delivering are closely related. The supernatural protection from an angel provides deliverance from physical harm for the 144,000 Israelites who will witness to the gospel of Christ during the tribulation period. They are preserved to complete their job, and as a result many from all nations will be saved in that day (Rev 7:1-14).

In apostolic days, angels delivered believers from harm. When the Jewish leaders put the apostles in prison, an angel of the Lord opened the doors and led them out, commissioning them to preach again (Ac 5:17-20). Similarly, Peter was delivered from prison. An angel caused his chains to fall off and the prison doors to open before Peter, and he walked out (Ac 12:5-10).

F. STRENGTHENING AND ENCOURAGING

Not only did angels strengthen Christ Himself (Mt 4:11; Lk 22:43), but angels have encouraged and strengthened His messengers. After freeing the apostles from prison, an angel encouraged them to continue preaching (Ac 5:19-20).

Another encouraged Paul, predicting that he would be preserved from death at sea for ministry in Rome. With this word Paul encouraged others: "Wherefore, sirs, be of good cheer: for I believe God, that it shall be even as it was told me" (Ac 27:25).

G. AGENTS IN ANSWERING PRAYER

Twice angels were sent in response to Daniel's prayers. When he prayed for his nation's restoration, Gabriel was caused to fly swiftly to instruct him of Israel's future and final restoration (Dan 9:20-24). Again when Daniel fasted and prayed for three weeks, an angel came to give him strength and instruction in answer to his concern for his nation (Dan 10:10-12).

In the days of the early church, when Herod cast Peter into prison, the church prayed for him without ceasing. Then God sent an angel to deliver him. The answer was so quick and spectacular that it astonished those praying; they hardly believed it (Ac 12:1-17).

In John's view into heaven, he saw an angel attending the altar of incense (Rev 8:2-4), as did the priest in the tabernacle (Ex 30:1-10). The angel was given incense to offer with the prayers of the saints. When he placed the incense upon the live coals on the altar, smoke ascended with the prayers of the saints before God. The angel then took coals in his censer and cast them upon earth, as if in prelude to the coming judgments. It seems that God's people were praying for God to judge the wicked world. The prayers were answered as the angel brought them before God and as seven angels then sounded their judgments. Angelic intervention came in answer to the prayer.

H. ATTENDANTS UPON THE RIGHTEOUS DEAD

The Lord Jesus spoke of angels carrying Lazarus' spirit to Abraham's bosom upon death (Lk 16:22). Moses' body was the concern of the archangel Michael in his dispute with Satan (Jude 9). Note also that Michael is mentioned in connection with the day of resurrection for Israel's righteous dead, though his specific duties with regard to the dead are not mentioned (Dan 12:1-3).

SUMMARY

The ministry of angels to God, Christ, and believers is wide and varied. They are primarily servants and messengers of

God to accomplish His purposes. "Scripture makes it clear that God is in no way dependent upon these His subservient creatures (Job 4:18; 15:15)."[1]

Scripture indicates that the ministry of angels to men is primarily external and physical, whereas the ministry of the Holy Spirit is internal and spiritual. Angels minister *for* us; the Holy Spirit ministers *in* us (Jn 14:16-17; Heb 1:13-14). They guard our bodies and pathway; He guards our spirits and guides us in the right way. They may be agents to answer prayer, but He is the Prompter and Director of our prayers (Ro 8:26-27; Jude 20).

9

DEVELOPMENT AND DESTINY OF ANGELS

ANGELS OBSERVE AND LEARN from the work of God and men on earth in this present age. The Bible also reveals their future activities and destiny.

I. IN THIS PRESENT AGE

In addition to their ministries and warfare previously described,* the angels of God, perfect though they are in their creaturely state, are capable of learning and developing. One way they learn is by observing earthly activities.

A. OBSERVING SALVATION

It is worth considering this fact again from the standpoint of the personal development of angelic personalities. They are intensely desirous to stoop down and peer into our wonderful salvation in Christ. This is the emphasis of 1 Peter 1:10-12. Angels marvel at the grace of God designed to come upon us in this age. With reverent curiosity they desire to learn more of God and Christ from their work of salvation. As they learn, they develop; and thus they may be able to worship and serve God with more devotion and understanding.

B. OBSERVING WORSHIP

Angels evidently observe with interest worship and order in the local church. In a chapter where Paul emphasizes order and dignity in the assembly and the relative position of men and women, angels seem to look for evidence of woman's sub-

*See chapter 8.

jection to man (1 Co 11:1-10). The symbol on the woman's head was an evidence in that culture of the condition of her heart. It appears contradictory to them that a woman who is not subject to her husband could be subject to God and worship Him properly (1 Co 11:3).

C. OBSERVING WORK AND WITNESS

The ministry of the Church is of interest to the angels, it seems. Their presence and observation is implicit in Paul's charge to Timothy. In regard to prayer and impartial administration of the church, Paul said, "I solemnly charge you in the presence of God and of Christ Jesus and of His chosen angels" (1 Ti 5:21, NASB).

Paul pictured the apostles as public spectacles, appointed by God as gladiators in a life-and-death struggle as they carried on their witness for Christ. The whole intelligent universe played the part of the spectators. All mankind, hostile or sympathetic, and all angels, elect or evil, watched the humble apostles in their ministry (1 Co 4:9-13). When there is response to the gospel and a sinner repents, it seems that the angels rejoice from their "grandstand" in heaven (Lk 15:10).

Angels will hear Christ confessing or denying those who have confessed or denied Him before men (Lk 12:8-9), and will probably witness the rewarding of believers (Mt 16:27).

D. OBSERVING POSITION AND PURPOSE

The particular place and function of the Church in God's plan of the ages is to demonstrate the manifold wisdom of God to angelic principalities and powers in the heavenlies (Eph 3:9-10). In God's administrational sequence, He dealt first with the Jews. Now, in this age, He is dealing in a new and different way in the Church. Now with the Jewish rejection of Messiah, the death of Messiah has ended the rule of the Mosaic Law and abolished the difference between Jew and Gentile (Eph 2:11-22). Now Gentiles are received with equal status as the Jews in the Church so that all are equal members of Christ's new body, the Church (Eph 2:15; 3:5-6). This rare jewel, hidden in the plan of God from past ages and generations, is now revealed to all as a magnificent creation of the grace of God in Christ (Eph 3:9-10). Romans 9-11 makes clear that God will again deal with the nation Israel after He completes the Church. This whole grand theme of God's wisdom in redemption's plan causes Paul to marvel greatly (Ro 11:25-36). Angels marvel as well.

It may be that God has revealed these angelic observations to us to cause us to walk soberly in dedication, dependence, and dignity. If we are sobered by the sense of unseen angelic witness to our life and service, how much more the fact that God sees all!

II. IN THE GREAT TRIBULATION

At this point, because of our limitation in purpose and space, let us assume, rather than prove, that order of events in God's plan of the ages called premillennial and pretribulational. That means the order would be first the rapture of the Church into heaven (1 Co 15:51-52; Phil 3:20; 1 Th 4:13-18); second, the Great Tribulation, a period of unprecedented, unparalleled distress upon earth due to the wicked activities of men and the wrath of God (Mt 24:9-22; Lk 21:20-26; 1 Th 5:1-10; Rev 6-19); third, the second coming of Christ (Mt 25:29-31; Lk 21:25-31; Rev 19:11-21); fourth, the millennial Kingdom of Christ on earth (Mt 25:31-34; Lk 22:16, 30; Rev 20:1-6); fifth, the new heavens and new earth (2 Pe 3:10-13; Rev 21-22).

Angels have an active and prolific part in the Great Tribulation that immediately precedes Christ's return to earth. A view into heaven during this period finds them worshiping God as the great Sovereign (Rev 4:1-11) and worshiping Christ as the great Saviour (5:8-13).

They will control the elements of nature (7:1; 14:18). They will seal the 144,000 of Israel to protect them in their worldwide gospel witness (7:2-10).

Christ is the Lamb who will open the sealed book of God's

judgment on earth (5:5; 6:1ff.). When the seventh seal is opened, Christ delegates further judgments to His angels. Seven angels sound their judgments upon trumpets (8:1—11: 15). To seven angels one of the four living creatures gives seven "bowls full of the wrath of God" (15:6-7; 16:1-21). By these trumpets and bowls, God carries out His judgment upon an unbelieving world and prepares for His Son's glorious coming to rule the earth (11:15).

An angel looses a great horde of locusts to afflict men (Rev 9:1-11). These are probably demons locked in the abyss, who have an evil angel over them (9:1, 11).

As the Tribulation nears completion, an angel announces that the time for wrapping up God's program is now short (10: 5-6). Another declares the good news that God's judgment is soon to end (14:6-7).

III. IN CHRIST'S COMING AND KINGDOM

After the Tribulation, Christ will return, and angels will enjoy the privilege of coming with Him in glory (Mt 25:31; Lk 9:26). They will participate in taking vengeance on those who have not submitted to Christ (2 Th 1:7-9). They will gather the nations for judgment before Christ and will carry out His judgment by casting unbelievers into the lake of fire (Mt 13:41-42; 25:31-32, 41). Angels will also gather Christ's own people into His earthly Kingdom (Mt 13:43; 24:31; 25: 31-34).

God's angel binds Satan before the millennial Kingdom for its thousand-year duration (Rev 20:1-3). During the Kingdom, the elect angels will associate with elect men in the New Jerusalem (Heb 12:22-23; Rev 21:1-11). It may be that elect angels also continue to help administrate God's program during the Kingdom.

After the Millennium, Satan will be loosed to deceive the nations in one final, worldwide rebellion of unconverted sinners born during the Millennium. He meets judgment at the hand of Christ and is cast with his angels into the lake of fire (Mt 25:

41; Rev 20:7-10). Then Christ will reign forever over men and angels in the new heavens and new earth (1 Co 15:24-25; Phil 2:9-11; Rev 21-22).

SUMMARY

Presently angels are developing by observing men in salvation, in worship, and in service. They are intrigued by God's grace operating in men.

Scripture describes their destiny in the Tribulation and in the second coming and Kingdom. In the new heaven and new earth, elect angels will associate with Christ and believers, but evil angels will suffer eternal judgment in the lake of fire.

10

OUR RELATIONSHIPS WITH ANGELS

THERE ARE SOME POINTS of biblical teaching that bear upon our personal association and attitude toward angels. Any study of angels would be incomplete without considering these. One outstanding point to keep in mind is that our position in Christ vitally affects our relation to angels.

When we trust Christ for salvation, we are placed by the Spirit into Christ (Ro 6:1-10; Gal 3:26-27). Our position as a result is termed *in Christ,* and we are sharers in His position and wealth before God. We died with Christ, rose and ascended with Christ (Eph 2:5-6). Not only are we perfectly accepted before God, but our position in Christ also puts us above angels (Eph 1:20-21), since no angel could be in Christ through the grace of salvation. This bears upon what follows about our relation to angels.

I. OUR ASSOCIATION WITH ANGELS

Our association with angels has both present and future aspects.

A. OUR PRESENT POSITION

The writer of Hebrews presents the perfect position the believer has in Christ by virtue of His perfect salvation. He argues that Christ is better than angels (chaps. 1-2), better than Moses (chap. 3), and better than Aaron and his sacrifices (chaps. 4-10). In one final and descriptive word about our exalted position in Christ, he declares that we have not come to fiery, cloudy Mount Sinai from which thundered the Law of Moses, but we have "come unto mount Sion, and unto the city of the living God, the heavenly Jerusalem, and to an innumerable company of angels" (12:22).

This New Jerusalem is the residence of the glorified Church and Old Testament saints, of God, and of Christ. It will descend from heaven to earth, it seems, for the future millennial Kingdom as possibly indicated in Revelation 19:7-9, 14; 20:4; 21:10-11. But it certainly will come to earth for the eternal state in the new heavens and the new earth (Rev 21:1-3).

We have come to this new and heavenly Jerusalem now positionally, just as we are now exalted with Christ and glorified positionally (Ro 8:30; Eph 2:5-6). Right now our position links us with the innumerable company of elect angels. We all belong to God's larger elect company, and He is our Father, both of angels and of men who belong to Christ. We shall come to the New Jerusalem in personal presence when we share with Christ in His glorious kingdom at His second coming. Then we shall join Old Testament saints and the elect angels in praise to God for His marvelous salvation of sinners.

B. Our Future Rule with Angels

During the millennial reign of Christ, the saints will live and reign with Him (Rev 20:4-6). The apostles will sit on twelve thrones, judging the twelve tribes of Israel when Christ sits upon the throne of His glory (Mt 19:28). Then we also shall rule with Christ over the world (1 Co 6:2). Angels probably will continue in their ministry of carrying out Christ's rule.

However, we shall also judge or rule over angels (1 Co 6:3). When Christ, who was made a little lower than angels, finally brings His sons into glory, He will have raised us over elect and evil angels to share in the exercise of His position and authority (Eph 1:19-21; Heb 2:5-10). Paul argues that if we shall judge angels, we should be able to settle agreeably matters of this life now (1 Co 6:3).

II. Our Attitude Toward Angels

A study of angels makes us aware of spiritual realities beyond our usual experience and our limited world of sense. But we must be balanced in our thinking and teaching. Some would go so far as to say that the creation and salvation of man and God's whole program for the world was to prove to angels that He is sovereign and wise. Certainly God does instruct angels through this, but His primary purpose is to glorify Himself among all His creatures and to express His glorious attributes in action to satisfy the desires and purposes of the persons of the Godhead. Others would relegate angels to a place of little importance in God's plan, if indeed their existence and activity is allowed. This is the other extreme. What is a biblically based, balanced approach?

A. We May Wonder at Angels

1. Respect their persons. The Bible portrays men of God bowing in fear and awe in the presence of angels as God's messengers (Dan 8:16-17; 10:1-18). We also may be in awe of their marvelous personalities, constitution, and powers.

2. Appreciate their ministries. Angels do us good for God. They are His ministers to us and are involved much more in our earthly welfare than we may dare to think (Heb 1:14).

3. Admire their example. Their incessant worship, their unswerving allegiance, and their urgent obedience challenge us.

B. We May Not Worship Angels

Though angels are exalted and awesome, God forbids us to worship them.

1. Forbidden by their example. The holy angels worship God alone. Isaiah pictures great seraphim worshiping Jehovah (6:1-4). John saw the angelic "living creatures" constantly worshiping God as the Creator of all, even angels (Rev 4:6-11). He also saw millions of angels worshiping Christ as the Lamb of God (Rev 5:8-14). These instances imply that angels consider only members of the Trinity to be worthy of worship. To this we add that nowhere in Scripture are angels worshiped, nor are we ever commanded to worship them.

2. Forbidden by revelation. There are specific statements in God's Word that specifically forbid the worship of angels. The first Commandment restricts worship to God alone (Ex 20:1-6). No creature may usurp what rightly belongs to the infinite Creator.

Paul pointedly writes, "Let no one keep defrauding you of your prize by delighting in self-abasement and the worship of the angels, taking his stand on visions he has seen inflated without cause by his fleshly mind" (Col 2:18, NASB). Paul wrote this to combat a false view of Christ that heretics had brought to Colosse. An early form of gnosticism, it taught a salvation through secret knowledge of truth. It had its roots in Jewish legalism and asceticism combined with oriental philosophy of dualism. The heresy held that physical matter was evil and spirit was good. The human body was regarded as evil. Thus, Christ could not be truly God and truly man, for God would not be contaminated with evil matter. So they regarded Christ as some sort of angelic being, an intermediate god (one of the overflowings of God) who was neither God nor man. God was to be approached through angels in the spirit world. But Paul declares that Christ created all angels (Col 1:15-17) and is completely God in human bodily form (2:9). All knowledge about God resides in Him (2:1-3).

We must beware of present heretical sects and isms that teach much the same concepts. We are to exalt Christ and worship Him, not angels or spirits.

3. Forbidden by angels themselves. When John saw the future heavenly Jerusalem and the glory of God, he fell down in his awe at all these things to worship the angel who had shown them to him. But the angel forbade his worship saying, "Do not do that; I am a fellowservant of yours and of your brethren the prophets and of those who heed the words of this book: worship God" (Rev 22:9, NASB). The same restriction was put on him in Revelation 19:10.

We are not to worship angels themselves or to worship God through angels. All creatures are to worship only the triune

God, and there is but one Mediator between God and man, Christ Jesus, Himself man (1 Ti 2:5-6).

SUMMARY

Because believers are "in Christ," they are exalted above angels. We shall associate with angels in heaven and in the Kingdom on earth. We shall rule over angels.

Though we are to respect and may admire angels, we are not to worship them or give them undue attention. They, too, are servants of Christ.

Part II
SATAN AND DEMONS

11

THE REALITY AND PERSONALITY
OF SATAN

THERE IS A VAST AMOUNT of scriptural evidence that Satan actually exists and that he is a person, not just a symbol of evil or a figure of speech. He is an angelic being of wide and powful influence, a major character on the moral stage of God's universe. He is an enemy of man and of believers, one whom we should know, respect, and resist in the faith and in the power of the Lord Jesus.

1. EXISTENCE OF SATAN

Consider the evidence from the Scriptures and from the Saviour.

A. EVIDENCE IN THE OLD TESTAMENT

The Old Testament assumes the existence of Satan, much as it does the existence of God. There is no formal proof presented for either one, but the story unfolds depending for its vitality upon their reality.

The whole plot of the book of Genesis depends upon the reality of Satan working through the serpent to cause the fall of mankind into sin (chap. 3). The basic facts of the creation and the fall lay the foundation for the whole battle between good and evil throughout the Bible and history and for the whole redemptive plan of God centered in the God-man who overcomes Satan.

The whole story of the tragedy and triumph of Job is based in the first two chapters upon the personal challenges and battle between God and Satan.

115

A crucial judgment upon Israel in which seventy thousand men fell is linked directly to Satan moving David to number Israel in 1 Chronicles 21. To stay the plague of God, David was ordered to offer sacrifice upon the threshing floor of Ornan, which later became the site of the tabernacle and temple.

The concepts of demons behind idolatry and an adversary like Satan are found in Psalms 106:36-37 and 109:6. It is difficult to explain seemingly superhuman powers behind the king of Babylon in Isaiah 14:12-17 and the king of Tyre in Ezekiel 28:1-19 without the recognition of a personal Satan.

Zechariah 3 could not be understood properly without the reality of Satan opposing and accusing Israel. Here Satan is presented as a definite person who is opposed by the Angel of Jehovah, the preincarnate Son of God.*

We conclude that there are some books of the Old Testament that make little sense historically or exegetically without the reality of Satan's existence and influence as a person.

B. EVIDENCE IN THE NEW TESTAMENT

Satan's existence is recognized by every writer of the New Testament, though not necessarily by every book. In fact, nineteen of the twenty-seven books mention Satan by one of his names. Even of the eight that do not specifically mention him, four imply his existence by the mention of evil angels or demons. The evidence in the New Testament is extensive.

C. EVIDENCE FROM CHRIST HIMSELF

In the gospels there are twenty-nine references to Satan. In twenty-five of these, it is Christ who speaks of Satan as actually existing as a person. The report of the temptation of the wilderness could have come from none other than the Lord Himself, as He described the person-to-person encounter He had with Satan. The essence of the testings and the details of the conversations seem to have been related directly by the Lord to the disciples for their information and later writings. When Christ speaks on a subject, the reverent receive it as truth.

*See chapter 6 on the Angel of Jehovah.

II. Constitution of Satan

Here we consider the evidence for Satan's personality and the kind of being he is.

A. His Person

What further evidence is there that Satan is a genuine person and not just a figment of imagination or personification of evil? Consider three lines of evidence.

1. Traits of personality. An accepted proof of personality consists of demonstrating that one possesses intellect, emotion, and will. Satan has these. His intellect is obvious in his scheming to deceive (2 Co 11:3) and in his communication through speech to other persons (Lk 4:1-12).

His emotions are clearly involved in his rebellious desire to oppose God (Is 14:12-17) and conquer Christ (Lk 4:1-12).

We see Satan's will in operation appealing to the will of Christ in commands (Lk 4:3, 9) and in his determined and indefatigable rebellion against God (Rev 20:7-9).

2. Personal pronouns. The Scripture uses the personal pronouns of him, God says of him, "You were the anointed cherub who covers; And I placed you there. . . . . And you sinned." (Eze 28:14, 16, NASB). Paul writes, "Satan disguises himself as an angel of light. Therefore it is not surprising if his servants also disguise themselves as servants of righteousness" (2 Co 11: 14-15, NASB). James commands, "Submit yourselves therefore to God. Resist the devil, and he will flee from you" (Ja 4:7). In the last two instances, note the association with other persons.

3. Moral responsibility. Neither impersonal animals nor forces are held morally accountable, but only persons who reflect the moral image of their Creator. Judgment has come and will further come upon Satan and his angels (Mt 25:41; Jn 16:11).

We conclude that Satan is a person in a genuine sense. This is observable from the evidence and was determined when he was made in God's image.†

†See p. 32 regarding angels made in God's image.

B. His Nature

Certain facts are clear about Satan's basic makeup.

1. Creature. Satan was created by God, not in his present corrupt form, but wonderfully constituted and holy. God describes him: "You were blameless in your ways from the day you were created, until unrighteousness was found in you" (Eze 28:15, NASB). Colossians 1:16 includes Satan as one created by Christ, since he is one of the invisible powers that owe their existence to the Son. As a creature, he is infinitely less than God.

2. Spirit being. As other angels, with whom he is constantly associated (Is 14:12-13; Mt 25:41; Rev 12:9), Satan is in essence a spirit, finite and limited.‡ This means he is incorporeal and invisible (Col 1:16), though at times he may manifest his his presence in temporary, visible form.

3. Cherubim class. Satan is called by God, "the anointed cherub" and "O covering cherub" (Eze 28:14, 16). This seems to be the highest classification of angelic being.§ Cherubim speak of God's presence, glory, holiness, and sovereignty. They were created for this specific ministry. This makes the defection of Satan all the more heinous and reprehensible.

4. First in rank among all creatures. The terms "the anointed cherub" and "covering cherub" indicate that before he fell, Satan was a high-stationed guardian for God. "Anointed" indicates that he had a special position, just as anointed kings had special position. The further description in Ezekiel 28 leaves little room for a greater creature: "You had the seal of perfection, full of wisdom and perfect in beauty. . . . Every precious stone was your covering" (vv. 12-13, NASB).

Satan still retains some of the dignity he had before he fell into sin. He is regarded as the leader of the fallen angels, one without equal in their ranks (Mt 25:41; Rev 12:4, 7). Michael the archangel respected his authority and dignity when disputing with him over the body of Moses (Jude 8-9). It is

‡See properties of angels, p. 33.
§See Cherubim, pp. 61-65.

most likely that Satan is equivalent to an archangel among the evil angels or demons.

SUMMARY

Satan was created a person of the angelic class of cherubim, probably first in position among all created spirit beings. Great beauty and power were his from God. Today, after his fall, he is still powerful, but his power is limited and resisted by God the infinite Creator and Sovereign. He retains some of his dignity, but he is no longer beautiful, since he lost his holiness in his fall. We need to remember that God is in complete control, and no creature can overthrow God or any of His purposes.

12

NAMES OF SATAN

THERE MAY BE as many as forty different titles referring to Satan. We will consider a few of the most significant, since they tell us about God's enemy and ours.

I. NAMES DESCRIBING POSITION

A. ANOINTED CHERUB WHO COVERS (EZE 28:14)

This title, treated in the previous chapter, describes Satan's original exalted position. He was probably the highest rank of the highest class of angelic beings.

B. THE PRINCE OF THIS WORLD (JN 12:31; 16:11)

Satan rules a world (Gr., *cosmos,* ordered system) that includes men and angels who are separated from God and are His enemies by nature (Mt 12:24; Ro 8:7-8). This *cosmos* is Satan's counterpart to God's rule and kingdom.* His desire to be like God (Is 14:14) caused him to sin, and now he rules over all rebels who have like him fallen into sin. This world engulfs false religionists (Jn 8:44) and threatens to defeat the true children of God (1 Jn 2:15-17).

C. THE PRINCE OF THE POWER OF THE AIR (EPH 2:2)

This title might be rendered "the ruler of the empire of this atmosphere." It pictures Satan's position and activity as a dominating leader operating in a kingdom that centers in the atmosphere of the earth. It is a limited empire, but it includes all fallen men and angels. It is closely associated in Ephesians 2:2

---

*For satanic and demonic activity in the world system, see chapters 14 and 19.

with the *cosmos,* and is probably another description of the same entity.

D. THE GOD OF THIS AGE (2 Co 4:4)

This title has been translated "the god of this world" (KJV). However, the term is not *cosmos,* but *aiōn.* The emphasis is on a system of philosophy or a spirit of the age that expresses a creature-centered manner of life and religion that rejects the true God and sets up a counterfeit life and substitute religion. Men walk according to the course (*aiōn*) of this world (*cosmos*); that is, they are governed and dominated by it. It partakes of its leader's characteristics, and so it is termed "this present evil age" (Gal 1:4, NASB). From this sphere we have been delivered by the redemption in Christ.

E. THE PRINCE OF DEMONS (Mt 12:24; Lk 11:15)

Christ was accused of casting out demons by "Beelzebul, the ruler of the demons" (Lk 11:15, NASB). Since Christ's enemies could not deny His miracles, to avoid admitting that His power came from God, they attributed His power over demons to Beelzebul, their ruler. Christ understood that they said He was in league with Satan and refuted the charge publicly in unanswerable fashion. He claimed instead that He cast them out by the power of the Holy Spirit and this was evidence of His Messiahship (Mt 12:25-29).

The title Beelzebul, from the better Greek texts, comes from the Hebrew *Baalzebul,* "lord of flies," or "lord of the dwelling." "It was the title given to one of the gods of the Philistines, and had been brought over into Judaism as a title of Satan."[1] Second Kings 1:3, 6, and 16 mention Baal-zebub as the god of Ekron, a northern city of Philistia. Another opinion is that *Baalzebub* ("lord of flies") may be an intentional Hebrew alteration of the Canaanite *Baalzebul* ("lord of the high place," or "exalted Baal").[2] In this case, it would be a Hebraistic insult to a false god. Using this name as a source of Christ's power, the Jewish leaders were indeed blaspheming God's Son and the Holy Spirit.

This title, then, describes Satan's position as the ruler of a demonic host involved in bringing men into spiritual bondage through lust and idolatry.

II. NAMES REFLECTING CHARACTER

A. LUCIFER (Is 14:12)

There is some question as to who is called Lucifer in Isaiah 14:12, whether he is the king of Babylon or Satan as the power behind him.† Assuming here that it refers to Satan, this title refers to him in his original state, as a shining one (Heb., *Helel*). The New American Standard Bible renders it "O star of the morning," and the further description that follows as "son of the dawn."

This title may connect Satan with the other angels, pictured as stars, and may indicate that he is the first among them. It speaks of the light that was his character and his abode before the blackness of sin invaded and surrounded him.

B. SATAN (ZEC 3:1; REV 12:9)

This common title is used fifty-two times in the Bible. Taken from the Hebrew *satan,* it means adversary or opposer; and it designates this person as self-proposed rival of God whose purpose it is to set up a counterfeit and rival kingdom. In his opposition to God, he also opposes God's people (Zech 3:1-2; Lk 22:31-32). However, our Advocate, Christ the Lord, defends us against him successfully.

C. DEVIL (LK 4:2, 13; REV 12:9)

Another common title, "devil" is used thirty-five times. The Greek *diabolos* means slanderer or one who trips up. It pictures this person as uttering maliciously false reports that tend to injure the reputation of another. The devil seeks to defame God and Christ and Their purpose. He seeks also to defame believers.

D. OLD SERPENT (REV 12:9)

This name recalls the first reference to Satan in the Bible

†See pp. 129-32.

as he stalked Eve in Genesis 3 and caused the fall of man. "Old" indicates that he has been around a long time and is well known. There was no need for Paul to clarify his use of "serpent" as referring to Satan. To the Corinthians he wrote, "But I am afraid, lest as the serpent deceived Eve by his craftiness, your minds should be led astray from the simplicity and purity of devotion to Christ" (2 Co 11:3, NASB). Later in the same passage he refers to false apostles who are the servants of Satan (vv. 13-15). The identification of the serpent with Satan is obvious. The characteristic that stands out is crafty deception.

E. GREAT DRAGON (REV 12:3, 7, 9)

The crafty serpent's true character becomes clear. He is with this title portrayed as a terrifying, destructive beast whose wrath against God and His people seeks their total devastation. Besides "great dragon," he is also called "great red dragon" and "dragon" (Rev 12:3-4). As such, he has an army of angels that join him in his war of destruction against Christ and His people (Rev 12:4, 9, 17). Note the reversion to the name "serpent" in Revelation 12:15.

F. THE EVIL ONE (JN 17:15; 1 JN 5:18)

The Greek term *ho ponēros* refers to one intrinsically wicked who is not content to be corrupt in himself but must seek to corrupt others. Christ and the apostle John connect this term with Satan's character and influence, extending to the world (*cosmos*) that is under Satan's influence and control. The article *ho* limits the name to a specific person who is well known, not just the concept of evil. Christ prayed that believers might be kept from the power of the evil one (Jn 17:15), in which the whole world lies (1 Jn 5:19). Several translations take 1 John 5:18 as saying the same thing as John 17:15, that the Son who was born of God keeps all those born of God from the power of the evil one, Satan.‡

‡See, for example, New American Standard Bible; W. F. Beck; C. B. Williams.

G. Destroyer (Rev 9:11)

The text tells of grotesque locust-like demons who "have as king over them, the angel of the abyss; his name in Hebrew is Abaddon, and in the Greek he has the name Apollyon." Both the Hebrew and the Greek names mean "destroyer." In the context, the demons torment and kill great numbers of mankind. Satan is not only a destroyer of physical life, but of spiritual life. The end of rebellion against God is self-destruction and the destruction of others.

In summary, the above names paint an awesome and gruesome character whose beauty was changed into scheming, seething, destructive wickedness when he revolted against the holy God.

III. Names Indicating Activity

A. Tempter (Mt 4:3; 1 Th 3:5)

Matthew, telling Christ's own story, gives three names to the one who tempted Christ: "the devil" (4:1), "the tempter" (4:3), and "Satan" (4:10). As the tempter, Satan tries men in moral combat, enticing them to evil. The title is a present participle in the Greek, indicating a continuous and characterizing activity. Satan is devoted to this as his job. First it was Adam and Eve, and then the whole race he worked on. He even sought to entice the last Adam, but was overcome by Him.

B. Accuser (Rev 12:10)

The full title and activity is found in a context of his defeat by Christ: "For the accuser of our brethren has been thrown down, who accuses them before our God day and night" (Rev 12:10, NASB). Satan has always done this. He accused Job before God and brought about a spiritual battle in which the grace of God and the uprightness of Job were demonstrated to the defeat of Satan (Job 1:9-11; 2:4-5). Satan accused Joshua and Israel, but the Angel of the Lord defended them (Zec 3:1-2). Satan's incessant activity involves access to God's presence (until the time indicated by the text during the Great Tribulation) and opposition to believers. The Father never takes Satan's side, nor should the believer. We stand secure in the grace of God through Christ's sacrifice (1 Jn 2:1-2) so our consciences should not condemn us (Ro 8:33-39). Neither should we accuse and condemn the brethren.

C. DECEIVER (REV 12:9; 20:3)

Currently Satan is the one "who deceives the whole world," or inhabited earth (Rev 12:9, NASB). Again the present participle in Greek indicates that he is characterized by this continuous action. It continues until he is bound during the millennial reign of Christ and resumes again upon his release for a short time (Rev 20:3, 7-8). This deception involves a wide range of scheming from hiding his own existence to actively promoting false philosophies, religions, and outright perversions of behavior and morals.§ Too many Christians are ignorant of "the wiles of the devil" (Eph 6:11). His schemes or deceits are very successful with many. Three factors that make him a master of trickery are his constitutional superiority as a cherub, his extensive experience and knowledge, and his ability to transform himself in a variety of ways.[3]

D. THE SPIRIT THAT NOW WORKS IN THE SONS OF DISOBEDIENCE (EPH 2:2)

This phrase may be a title of Satan or a reference to an attitude that characterizes unbelievers. Some translations (e.g., ASV, NASB) reflect the Greek genitive construction by reading "of the spirit." In this case, it would not be a title of Satan, but a parallel phrase with "of the power of the air." Satan would then be described as "the ruler of the power of the air, of the spirit that is now working in the sons of disobedience." This would make Satan the ruler of the worldly influence that fills unsaved men.

In either case, whether a title or description of his realm and

§See chapter 15.

type of activity, this phrase further describes the ruler opposed to God constantly energizing other rebels.

SUMMARY

These names of Satan do not exhaust the list, but they do represent the scope of his titles and present the multifaceted aspects of his power, character, and activity.

13

ORIGINAL STATE AND FALL OF SATAN

ALL ANGELS were created by God through His Son, the Lord Jesus (Col 1:16-17). There is no creature that was not created by Him (Jn 1:3). God cannot be directly involved in the creation of evil, for He is holy. So it is obvious from reason and from the Bible that all angels were created in a holy state, each a direct creation of God and all at or near the same time.

Satan fell from his originally holy state when he tragically rebelled against God, incurring his own condemnation (1 Ti 3:6) and enticing perhaps a third of the angels to defect with him (Mt 25:41; Rev 12:4). Now Satan and his angels are permanently wicked and opposed to God and His program and people.*

Two major passages are usually connected with Satan's original state and fall which we will consider: Ezekiel 28:12-19 and Isaiah 14:12-17.

I. HIS PRIVILEGES AND PERVERSION

Ezekiel 28:1-9 speaks of God's judgment on a rebellious ruler or rulers. Few conservative scholars reject this passage as referring to Satan's original condition and fall.

A. IDENTIFICATION OF PERSONS

Some would say that the whole pronouncement of judgment in 28:1-19 speaks to the one person called the prince of Tyre (v. 2) and the king of Tyre (v. 12). We would support the view that two persons are addressed: the human leader (vv.

---

*See pp. 40-41. The devil was never an angel, says Barth, for angels cannot sin. A proper angel does not do such a thing, but Satan was a murderer from the beginning. (See Karl Barth, *Church Dogmatics,* 3, pp. 620-22.)

1-10) and behind him the superhuman leader, Satan (vv. 11-19).

Support for this second view include the following: (1) different titles, "prince" (leader) and "king"; (2) different natures, "man" (vv. 2, 9), and "the anointed cherub" (v. 14), "O covering cherub" (v. 16); (3) the superlatives used of the king, "full of wisdom and perfect in beauty" (v. 12); (4) the perfection of the king, "You were blameless in your ways from the day you were created" (v. 15, NASB). For these reasons we take Ezekiel 28:12-19 to refer to Satan.

B. Initial Privileges

Before his fall, Satan seems to have had the greatest privileges ever accorded to a creature.

1. Nature. Satan belongs to the cherub class of angelic being. These are probably of the great class and highest order.† Among them he was the anointed one, a privilege given to a God-appointed leader (v. 14). The expressions, "You had the seal of perfection," and "Full of wisdom and perfect in beauty" (v. 13, NASB), indicate that he was the greatest of all creatures. The figurative language of this verse speaks of his exquisite perfections.

2. Position. Not only was he an anointed leader, but twice was called a guardian (covering) cherub. This could refer to his role as a guardian and proclaimer of God's glorious presence and holiness.

3. Habitation. "You were in Eden, the garden of God" (v. 13, NASB) probably refers in earthly terms to God's paradise in heaven. Within the paradise was "the mountain of God," from which abode he was cast (vv. 14, 16). So he seems to have been in the very presence of God, for he "walked in the midst of the stones of fire" (v. 14, NASB).

4. Perfection. This term summarizes his personal and moral qualities. He "had the seal of perfection" and was "perfect in beauty" (v. 12, NASB). He was perfect or blameless in his ways from the day he was created until his first sin (v. 15).

†See pp. 61-65.

C. INCEPTION OF PERVERSION

Without explaining how it happened, God says, "Iniquity was found in thee" (v. 15). The only clue as to what occurred in Satan's mind is found in verse 17: "Your heart was lifted up because of your beauty; you corrupted your wisdom by reason of your splendor" (NASB). His sin is obviously a proud heart and self-occupation. Reflecting upon his God-endowed beauty, he became enthralled with himself and was lifted up with pride (1 Ti 3:6).

He also perverted other angels from God's way. The words *merchandise* (v. 16) and *traffick* (v. 18) may refer it to a soliciting to his evil cause a large group of fellow angels (cf. Mt 25: 41; Rev 12:4, 9). His habitation was defiled by his sin also: "By the multitude of your iniquities, in the unrighteousness of your trade, you profaned your sanctuaries" (v. 18, NASB).

D. INDICTMENT AND PUNISHMENT

Because of Satan's sin of arrogance and violence, God cast him from his privileged position near the throne of God ("out of the mountain of God," v. 16). He may have been cast to the earth after his original sin ("I cast you to the ground," v. 17, NASB). So God accused him of flagrant and unwarranted rebellion and banished him from His presence. His ultimate punishment is the lake of fire, said Christ (Mt 25:41).

II. HIS PECULIAR SIN

Isaiah 14:12-17 is a passage of disputed reference to Satan. We cannot treat all the factors to be considered, but will refer to the variant views and some of the supports. Then we will see what it contributes to Satanology.

A. IDENTIFYING THE PERSONS

As in Ezekiel 28, some hold that the whole passage of Isaiah 14:3-21 announces judgment against the king of Babylon mentioned by name in verse 4. They explain the unusual language in verses 12-17 as containing allusions to Canaanite Ugaritic mythology which are applied to the pagan king. Others see two persons addressed, the first being the king and the second being Satan, called Lucifer (14:12-17).

Those who say that this is not a reference to Satan at all point to similar language in pagan literature referring to their idolatrous and astrological worship.‡ They also note that Lucifer (v. 12) is also called a man (v. 16), and that he is compared with other kings of earth (v. 18).

According to this view, to fall from heaven (v. 12) is to fall from a great political height as in pagan literature. (There also may be a parallel in Daniel 8:10 in reference to Antiochus causing stars to fall from heaven.) The name "son of the dawn" (v. 12, NASB) could be a reference to a pagan deity. "The mount of the assembly" (v. 13, NASB) may refer to a mountain about twenty-five or thirty miles northeast of Ugarit, a place where the gods were supposed to gather.[1]

> The Babylonian king had desired to be above God, and so fell from heaven. He falls to Sheol, and his power is done away. Not so Satan. His fall was against God, but he continues yet his tyrannical acts against God's people. "His doom is sure," for Christ has died, but not until the final judgment will he be confined to the lake of fire. Inasmuch, then as this passage describes a king's downfall and removal from the scene, it cannot apply to Satan.[2]

‡Delitzsch, Gray, and Young support this. Says Young, "The pagan mythology best known to the Hebrews would be the Canaanitish. Hence Isaiah places in the mouth of the king the language of Canaanitish paganism and polytheism that the men of Judah may learn the extent of his boastful pretensions. This would seem to militate against Babylon as the place of composition of Isa. 14. The boasting typifies that of the man of sin, 2 Thess. 2:4" (E. J. Young, in *The New International Critical Commentary* [Grand Rapids: Eerdmans, 1965], 1:441).

Delitzsch writes,

> Lucifer, as a name given to the devil, was derived from this passage, which the fathers . . . interpreted without any warrant whatever, as relating to the apostasy and punishment of the angelic leaders. The appellation is a perfectly appropriate one for the king of Babel, on account of the early date of the Babylonian culture, which reached back as far as the grey twilight of primeval times, and also because of its predominant astrological character. . . . A retrospective glance is now cast at the self-deification of the king of Babylon, in which he was the antitype of the devil and the type of antichrist (Dan. xi. 36; 2 Thess. ii. 4) and which had met with its reward (Franz Delitzsch, *Biblical Commentary on the Prophecies of Isaiah* [Grand Rapids: Eerdmans, 1949], 1:311-12).

See also George B. Gray on Isaiah in *The International Critical Commentary* (Edinburgh: T. & T. Clark, 1912), 1:256-57.

There are those who hold that Isaiah 14:12-17 refers to Satan only. They cite the unusual language as far beyond applying to a human king. In favor of this view is the repetition in these verses of what has basically been said in Isaiah 14:4-11. Even some of the specific terms are repeated. Then, too, the assertions of rebellion and pride fit what is known about Satan.

Perhaps the view that best answers the biblical evidence is that there is a dual reference. Verses 4-11 seem to refer to a future "king of Babylon," or the coming Antichrist associated with Babylon, a politico-religious system existing just before the second coming of Christ. This one is pictured in Revelation 13, 17, and 18, and is described in 2 Thessalonians 2. There seems also to be an inclusion of Satan in verses 12-17 to retrace Satan's sin as analogous with Antichrist's character and actions in the future. We must remember that the Antichrist is empowered by Satan (2 Th 2:8-10). According to this view, Isaiah reveals the true nature of the Antichrist and his ultimate defeat, even though he is empowered by the highest of all heavenly creatures. Satan will be defeated and all his heavenly and earthly hosts.

To support this view, we note first that the whole passage, as determined by the opening verses (1-4) looks forward to that day when God shall have restored the nation Israel to its land and leadership among the nations. The nation shall enjoy rest when all her enemies are defeated by the Lord Jesus, who returns to earth to reign in His Kingdom. Then Israel will rule over her oppressors. Babylon is singled out as representative of all Israel's enemies and of the future Antichrist who is empowered by Satan (Dan 7:23-27; 9:26-27; 11:36-45; 2 Th 2:8-10; Rev 13:4). In these passages there is terminology very similar to that used in Isaiah 14:12-17. It seems, then, that Isaiah would not be referring to the historic king of Babylon as the primary oppressor of Israel, but rather the future one with Satan behind him.

Second, the language especially befits Satan, who is pictured here and elsewhere as fallen from his high station in heaven

(Lk 10:18) and cast down to earth (Eze 28:13-14, 17; Rev 12:7-9). He seems to be first among other heavenly beings, for he is the "star of the morning" and would rule over "the stars of God," a term which does describe angels.§ His character and actions certainly compare to those described here.

Third, the pattern here parallels the pattern set in Ezekiel 28 where the king of Tyre is first addressed, and then Satan, the highest cherub, is addressed as the power behind him (as noted earlier in this chapter).

B. IDENTIFYING THE SIN

The basic sin of Satan seems to be pride, as we previously noted from Ezekiel 28:17. Pride or conceit is specifically labeled by Paul as the reason for "the condemnation incurred by the devil" (1 Ti 3:6, NASB). Isaiah pictures his pride expressed in determined rebellion. Note the five occurrences of "I will" in verses 13-14. This fits the description of the future Antichrist, pictured by Paul as a proud rebel (2 Th 2:3-4).

C. EXPRESSION OF SIN

The five statements of "I will" specifically express Satan's self-assertion and rebellion. These statements are probably flashbacks to his original intentions in his original situation just before he was cast out of the presence of God. This seems to fit the indictment (probably by God) in 14:13: "But you said in your heart" (NASB). So at the time of Satan's future defeat in the defeat of Antichrist, God reminds him of his original scheme and how it has come to complete failure.

The five assertions speak of Satan's desire to rise above the sphere in which he was created and placed.[3] He asserted his own will against the beneficent will of the Most High.

1. "I will ascend to heaven." Since Satan had access to the very presence of God as the leading cherub (Eze 28:13-14), this assertion does not mean he would visit, but abide there. It means that he desired to occupy the abode of God, probably desiring equal recognition with God.

§See p. 61.

2. *"I will raise my throne above the stars of God."* The stars, as we have seen, are references to angels. Satan already was the greatest angelic being, and it may be that all angels took orders from him as the chief administrator under God. Angels would recognize that orders through him came directly from God. Lucifer now seems to desire to be an independent ruler and to receive the recognition that belonged to God. He may be saying, "I will usurp God's rule over all the angels."

3. *"I will sit on the mount of assembly."* According to Isaiah 2:2 and Psalm 48:2, the mount of the assembly is the center of God's Kingdom rule. It seems asscciated with Messiah's earthly rule from Jerusalem. Satan would also, then, seek to rule over all human affairs, usurping the place of Messiah.

4. *"I will ascend above the heights of the clouds."* The atmospheric clouds are hardly in view here. Isaiah's pattern helps us to understand the figurative use of clouds. *Stars* refer here to angels, *mount* to a place of rule; now *clouds* are associated with the glory of God. (Note the connection of clouds with God in Ex 13:21; 40:28-34; Job 37:15-16; Mt 26:64; Rev 14:14-16.) Lucifer had in him a great glory that reflected his Creator. Now he desired a glory equal to or above God's glory.

5. *"I will make myself like the Most High."* This is the climax of all self-assertion and defiance of God! Why did Lucifer choose this title among all the titles of God? Because it refers to God as the "possessor of heaven and earth" (Gen 14:18-19). Two points are worth noting here. First, Satan did not want to be unlike God. He respected God's power and authority, and he wanted it for himself. He would usurp God's authority rather than be submissive to it, for no one can be like God and still let God be God; for there is none like Him (Is 42:8; 43:10; 44:6; 45:5-6, 21-33). God will not share His glory or position with any other.

Second, Satan would be like God primarily in the matter of authority and control. He originally thought to replace God, but he ended up a counterfeiter, not a replacement. With rebellion there came a change in character, and all the holiness he had derived from his Creator was lost, and corruption replaced it. He could no longer be like God, even in reflection.

D. WRETCHEDNESS OF HIS SIN

Satan's sin is peculiarly heinous for several reasons. (1) There was no previous example; this was the beginning of rebellion against the most high God. (2) He was created beautiful and perfect; he lacked nothing as the greatest of all creatures. (3) His greatest of all intelligence gave him greater light and understanding of the greatness and goodness of the God against whom he sinned. (4) His highest position gave him the privilege of the greatest service to God. (5) In his perfection and holiness, he had the privilege of intimate fellowship with God.

E. RESULTS OF HIS SIN

In Isaiah 14 there are statements and intimations of what issued from Satan's fall.

1. Banishment from heaven. "How you have fallen from heaven," says God of the one who would ascend to heaven (v. 12, NASB). His privileges and position were permanently lost.

2. Corruption of character. The one whose name was Lucifer, who shone with the holy light of God, the "star of morning, son of the dawn," now has become Satan, the opposer of all that God is.

3. Perversion of power. Satan's power, once used for God's glory and the good of His creatures, is now turned to disruptive and destructive purposes. He weakened the nations (v. 12) and caused the earth and governments to tremble (v. 16). His prisoners have no relief (v. 17).

4. Retention of dignity. Though cast from his exalted position, Satan yet retains some of his great dignity. The passage indicates that his influence and power was yet felt. Even Michael the archangel "did not dare pronounce against him a railing judgment" (Jude 9, NASB).

5. Destined to the pit. God's judgment had to come in His

moral rectitude against so great a sin. He will "be thrust down to Sheol, to the recesses of the pit" (Is 14:15, NASB; cf. Rev 20:3).

III. THE TIME OF SATAN'S FALL

There is no clear revelation as to exactly when Satan fell, but there are limits to the possible time which we may deduce from biblical evidence.

If we assume that angels were part of the creation of Genesis 1:1, then their fall follows that point. However, it may be that angels were created prior to the creation of the heavens and the earth. In either case, angels were present when God "laid the foundation of the earth" and "set it measurements" (Job 38:4-5, NASB), for it was then that "the morning stars sang together, and all the sons of God shouted for joy" (Job 38:7). This involved all the angels rejoicing with God. Satan and his angels fell, then, sometime after the original creation of the heavens and the earth.

It is certain that Satan had fallen before Genesis 3 where the temptation of Adam and Eve is recorded. He fell before man fell; but whether he fell before or after man's creation, we cannot say certainly. It would be an unwarranted assumption to say that man was created to teach previously fallen angels a lesson and that angelic warfare is God's primary reason for the existence of all the rest of creation.

IV. THE FALL OF ANGELS WITH SATAN

It is obvious from the Bible that Satan has his angels. They follow his orders and fight for his cause (Mt 12:24-26; 25:41; 2 Pe 2:4; Rev 12:7). Satan solicited their following in his initial revolt against God. The expressions "the iniquity of thy traffick" (Eze 28:18), or "the unrighteousness of your trade" (NASB) may refer to Satan's selling his rebellious cause to other angels. This fits in with his plan to rule over angels (Is 14:13). Once Satan seduced these angels, they were fixed in their moral degeneration. As many as a third of the angelic creation may have followed Satan in his defection (Rev 12:4).

V. THE MORAL PROBLEM IN THE FALL OF ANGELS

It is inevitable that men would ask why a good and powerful God should allow the fall of Satan and his angels to occur. It introduced sin into the universe, affecting angels, all mankind, and even God to some extent. This is really part of the whole problem of the existence of evil. From the Bible we may deduce some possible reasons. In working toward the solution of the problem, certain factors must be kept in mind.

1. The character of God. We must remember that the same Bible that records the inception and continued existence of evil also presents God as One who is holy, righteous, and perfect in all His ways, One in whose eyes sin is exceedingly wicked and worthy of judgment (Deu 32:3-4; Ps 145:17; Is 45:21; Ro 3:4). He could not and did not promote or perpetrate the sin (Ps 5:4; Ja 1:13, 17).

2. The control of God. At the same time, the Bible presents God as both omnipotent and sovereign. He is in control of all things, and He has no potential successful rival (Is 41:4; 43: 13; 45:5; 46:8-11; Eph 1:11; Rev 4:11). Evil did not rise up apart from His control, otherwise He would no longer be God.

3. The choice of God. It seems best to say that God, for good reasons, allowed evil to come into being. Not all these reasons are evident, but a few are genuinely probable. In any case, we must confess that God is the Author of a plan, a perfect plan, that included allowing His creatures to sin (Is 45: 7; Ac 15:16). Just as a composer of a musical score may include some discords to create an overall pleasing effect, so God's ultimate purpose is best served by such a plan. Perhaps He allowed angels to sin in order that He might give a concrete example of the wretchedness and degradation of sin. Perhaps He used the test to gain a group of angels to serve Him from choice and love. Perhaps He allowed sin to enter so that He might show in specific form His hatred and judgment of sin (compare Pharaoh's case, Ro 9:17-18). It may have been necessary to allow the fall of angels to finally show the grace of God in the preserving of some angels and in the redemption of unworthy, sinful man who fell because of Satan. In man, God will magnify His grace forever before angels, particularly in the God-man and His own (Eph 1:10; 2:7).

4. *The choice of angels.* It was obviously Satan and the angels who chose to sin. They felt no pressure from God or His decree. They were conscious only of their own desires and planned their wretched rebellion in light of all they knew of the greatness and goodness of God. Everywhere in the Bible, they are treated as fully responsible.

5. *The confinement by God.* When God did allow sin into His universe, He did not allow it to run without control. He confined the expression of sin and so limited its devastating effects. It was allowed only for a finite duration between what might be termed two aspects of eternity. Further, it was controlled even within that time (Ps 11:4-7; 96:11-13; 140:12; Ro 2:1-16; 2 Th 2:6-9).

6. *The condemnation by God.* God has condemned sin in the fullest sense in accord with His righteousness. He has judged it in man through human history. He judged it in awesome dimensions in the judgment of His Son at Calvary. It cost God more than all creatures could ever suffer through the suffering and sacrifice of His eternal Son. Finally, God will forever punish the evildoers in the lake of fire and will banish forever the presence of sin from the universe when He makes all things new (Rev 20:10-15; 21:4-5).

SUMMARY

Certainly Ezekiel 28 and probably Isaiah 14 give us insight as to Satan's original privileged position as the greatest of all angels. His self-occupation and self-promotion were a deliberate attempt to overthrow God. As a result, he was banished from heaven, corrupted in character, and now opposes God and man with his perverted power. His fall occurred most likely shortly after the creation recorded in Genesis 1, and in his fall he took many angels with him. In all this, the righteousness of God and the sovereignty of God is upheld by Scripture. Satan is fully responsible for his atrocious deeds.

14

SATAN'S PRESENT CHARACTER AND POSITION

KNOWLEDGE OF THE CORRUPTION of Satan's person and the position he now occupies should help us in our battle against this enemy.

I. HIS PRESENT CHARACTER

A. MURDERER (JN 8:44)

Satan cannot truly give life; he brings only death. He caused the spiritual death of angels and of mankind in Eden. Christ said, "He was a murderer from the beginning," probably referring to all that happened in Genesis 3 and 4, including the murder of Abel.

B. LIAR (JN 8:44)

Four statements by Christ describe Satan's relation to truth: (1) he does not stand in the truth; (2) there is no truth in him; (3) he speaks lies from his own nature, for he is a liar; (4) he is the father of lies. Satan promotes outright lies and some truth for the sake of his lie (2 Co 11:13-15).

C. CONFIRMED AND PRACTICING SINNER (1 JN 3:8)

Jesus and John present the devil as continuing in sin. They also present those who continue in sinning as children of the devil. There is a universal fatherhood of Satan among unbelievers (Jn 8:44).

D. OPPOSER OF THE RIGHTEOUS (1 PE 5:8; REV 12:10)

Satan, as his name indicates, opposes God and truth. He also opposes God's people. He is "the accuser of the brethren." He accused Job before God (Job 1:9-11; 2:4-5), and he charges God's elect before God and probably in their consciences as well (Zec 3:1; Ro 8:33). Peter labels him our adversary who stalks about as a ferocious killer lion seeking whom he may next devour (1 Pe 5:8).

II. HIS PRESENT POSITION

Satan has been cast out of God's presence and removed from his former office, yet he retains in the plan of God a great position.

A. HIS DIGNITY

Satan retains under God's permission such dignity that even Michael the archangel cared not "bring against him a railing accusation, but said, The Lord rebuke thee" (Jude 9). He is a majesty in his perverted and permitted realm.

B. HIS DOMINION

1. Ruler of fallen angels (Mt 25:41; Rev 12:9). Satan rules a vast army of angels, perhaps a third of the originally created number (Rev 12:9, 40). They battle with God's angels under Michael in the Great Tribulation (Rev 12:7). Even now they wrestle with believers as the power behind all sorts of opposition, direct and indirect (Eph 6:10-13). Satan is recognized by the Jews and by Christ as the prince of demons (Mt 12:24-28).

2. Ruler of the world system (Jn 12:31; 16:11). The world (*cosmos*) includes men and angels in an organized system under Satan as its god. He is "the god of this world" (2 Co 4:4) in that he dominates, with knowing or unknowing consent, men who know not God. The whole world has been affected by him (1 Jn 5:19). This world stands in opposition to believers (Jn 17:14; 1 Jn 2:15-17).

C. His Domain

1. Abides in the heavenlies (Eph 6:11-12). The heavenlies seem to be a spiritual sphere of operation and combat. The believer sits positionally with Christ in the heavenlies (Eph 2:6), and it is the sphere of his blessings in Christ (Eph 1:3). However, the believer finds authorities and powers of Satan and Satan himself in the heavenlies. Cast from heaven, Satan seems to operate in the realms of both the earth and the heavenlies.

2 Access to heaven (Rev 12:10). God evidently allows Satan to appear before Him on limited occasions. Satan cannot, since he sinned, abide there in the holy presence of God, but he appears with other "sons of God" to assemble and answer to God (Job 1:6; 2:1). There he accuses the brethren (Zec 3:1; Rev 12:10).

3. Active on earth (1 Pe 5:8). He roves the earth, he and his cohorts, seeking to oppose and defeat believers and God's purpose in individuals and in the Church. He seeks to oppose the spreading of the gospel (Mt 13:38-39; 2 Co 4:4; Eph 6:12-19).

D. His Detention

Though Satan is not now bound, as he will be in the future (Rev 20:1-3), he is limited in his operations by God. God limits who and how much he can touch (Job 1:12; 2:6; Jn 17:15; 1 Jn 5:18).

Summary

Satan retains a great position over men and angels. But with his perverted character as a liar and murderer, he continues sinning and opposing God. God limits his place and power in the universe.

15

SATAN'S PRESENT POWER AND ACTIVITY

SATAN'S POWER is great and his activity is extensive, seen in several relationships.

I. IN RELATION TO GOD

A. THE OPPOSER OF GOD'S PERSON

As Satan desired to be like the most High, so his power and activity are directed primarily against God. Other activities are understood as stemming from this rebellious aim. His attack on Adam was really an attack on the character and control of God (Gen 3:1-5). Satan induced Cain to murder Abel, a man of God (1 Jn 3:12). The opposition to God in this is mentioned in 1 John 3:10. The opposition obviously comes from a character opposite to that of God's. Once reflecting the light from God as Lucifer, the shining one, now he is full of darkness and keeps the light from others (Ac 26:18; 2 Co 4:4; Eph 6:12). God is love and promotes love, whereas Satan is hateful and promotes hatred (1 Jn 3:7-15). God is life and creates life, whereas Satan operates in the realm of death (Heb 2:14).

B. THE OPPOSER OF GOD'S PROGRAM

1. Counterfeiting God's system of truth. In line with his purpose to like the most High, Satan promotes a system that we may call "the lie" (see Eph 2:2; 2 Th 2:8-11).

Satan's counterfeit system may be irreligious. He may deny the existence of God or His control (Ps 14:1-3). To explain the world, he substitutes evolution for creation, uniformitarian-

ism for providence, human progress for divine salvation, and
man's utopia for God's Kingdom on earth. Atheism, agnos-
ticism, pragmatism, existentialism, and relativism are his substitutes for truth.

However, Satan also promotes *counterfeit religions.* He au-
thors or encourages nonbiblical religions or distortions of the
true religion. In this latter category, we find (1) false ministers, Satan's messengers who transform themselves into messengers of light (2 Co 11:13-15). Satan may be found in the
chair of theology or the pulpit. He seeks and sometimes gets
control of a work of God (2 Co 2:9-11; Gal 1:6-9; Rev 2:9;
13-15).

Satan also promotes (2) false doctrine. These he propa-
gates through his demons, who teach works righteousness (1 Ti
4:1-3) and self-seeking through ministering in religious matters
(2 Pe 2:1, 15). Some so-called churches follow his teaching in
idolatry and intrusion into the occult (Rev 2:14, 24).

In his counterfeit religion we also find (3) false Christs, or
antichrists. In 1 John 2:18, 22, and 4:3 we read of many antichrists presently invading and deceiving the world and even
Christian communities. These are forerunners of the Antichrist
who, as Satan's man, one day will promote himself as God and
through his lying miracles deceive many (2 Th 2:3-11).

During this age we also find (4) false followers. They pro-
fess to believe in Christ, but they are Satan's counterfeits (Mt
13:38-39).

2. Counteracting God's sovereign rule. Rebellion against
God's personal and constituted authority is the essence of
Satan's every expression. A rebel at heart, he is a rebel in every
deed. He cannot, of course, step outside of God's overall sovereign control; but within the limits of his creaturely freedom,
he is totally anti-God.

The great rebel counteracted God's rule in the Garden of
Eden. He turned man's submission to God into rebellion toward God and submission to him. He has opposed God's Kingdom and Church from without and within throughout the centuries. A highlight of his opposition to God came in his attack

upon Christ, confronting Him in temptation, counteracting His ministry, and instigating His death (see Mt 4:1-11; Jn 13:26-30).

An apex of his rebellious opposition will be found in his empowering of the future Antichrist, who himself is a proud rebel who would pass himself off as God (2 Th 2:3-4). This lawless one will deceive and dominate man in an unprecedented sense (2 Th 2:9-11; Rev 13:1-18). He will assume a religious pose and use a religious system called Babylon to oppose true religion, and then he will destroy even that false religious system (Rev 17). Even now "the mystery of lawlessness at work" under the restraining influence of God (2 Th 2:6-8). Its full manifestation will come in the Tribulation.

During the Great Tribulation, Satan will be cast down from heaven. Though he knows his time is short and doom sure, yet he increases his rebellious activities persecuting God's people, Israel (Rev 12:9; 12-13). Even after he has felt defeat from Christ and has been bound for one thousand years; still, after his release, he will make one last rebellious attempt to overthrow God and Christ, but he will be defeated (Rev 20:1-10).

II. IN RELATION TO THE NATIONS

A. DECEIVING THE NATIONS

Right now Satan is deceiving the nations, leading them astray from the truth as it is in God and Christ. At the second coming of Christ he will be bound for a thousand years "that he should deceive the nations no more" (Rev 20:3). Upon release, he will deceive the nations again, to assemble them against Jerusalem and God (Rev 20:7-10).

B. INFLUENCING GOVERNMENTS OF NATIONS

Satan is "the god of this world," which includes men and angels outside the family of believers (2 Co 4:4). He offered the nations to Christ in the temptation. Christ did not dispute the legitimacy of the offer, but refused to rebel against God in submitting to Satan's method of obtaining the rule (Mt 4:8-10).

Satan uses his angels to influence the affairs of nations, particularly in their opposition to God's program with Israel or with the Church (Dan 10:13, 20; Eph 6:12; 1 Th 2:18).

Today he would use governmental authorities to hinder the spread of the gospel at home and abroad. At the time of this writing, certain African nations in their nationalistic programming are insisting on a return to animistic and idolatrous religions and are persecuting and murdering national Christians and deporting missionaries.

C. Directing the Governments of Nations

During the tribulation period, Satan will actually direct the affairs of a ten-nation coalition through his man, the Antichrist. Ten rulers will give to the Antichrist their power (Rev 17:12). This may constitute a revived Roman Empire, since it is related in Daniel's vision to the fourth world empire of the Gentiles (Dan 2:31-45; 7:1-12). This Antichrist will even control all nations at that time for at least three-and-one-half years (Rev 13:4, 7). Behind this world ruler is none other than Satan, called "the dragon" (Rev 13:2, 4). These conditions will exist just before the second coming of Christ, who will destroy these world powers and the Antichrist (Dan 2:35, 44-45; 7:8-14; Rev 19:11-21). Even now it appears that Satan is assembling the national alliance predicted for those days.

III. In Relation to the unsaved

A. Preventing Acceptance of Truth

1. Snatching away the gospel (Lk 8:12). Some who hear the gospel are prevented from understanding it, lest they believe and be saved.

2. Blinding minds to the gospel (2 Co 4:3-4). He causes a barrier to the Gospel penetrating the mind with enlightenment concerning sin, righteousness, and judgment. This is one of the reasons for the convicting work of the Holy Spirit (Jn 16:7-11). As a result of Satan's work in this line, the Gospel sounds foolish and irrelevant to the perishing (1 Co 1:18).

B. Promoting Attraction to Falsehood

1. Indoctrinating in false religion (1 Ti 4:1-3). Satan and his demons use men who knowingly or unknowingly preach his lies. Either he promotes a salvation by human works, attractive to sinners who would bypass the Saviour's work of salvation; or he persuades men that there is no need for salvation, only progress. This progress may be purely human, as in systems of ethical idealism that deny sin and evil; or it may include recourse to the spirit world, as in spiritism or oriental mysticism. So today we see a great increasing interest in the occult practices, including witchcraft and satanism. John warns us to test the spirits (1 Jn 4:1-4).

2. Ingraining a false lifestyle (Eph 2:1-3). We formerly walked in this philosophy of the age ("course of this world"). It may change expression from generation to generation, but it is still creature-centered and creature-promoting. This philosophy is based on pleasure, possessions, and position (1 Jn 2:15-17). It is opposed to our Father God. Satan is now energizing constantly "the sons of disobedience" to follow this spirit. It is basically the egocentric ambition of Satan that characterizes the world. Satisfied with these things of man and materialism, unbelievers are kept from desiring a relationship with the living God.

IV. In Relation to Christians

In general, Satan seeks to defeat believers in their individual and corporate life and service. The wise Christian does not dismiss this part of spiritual warfare as superstition. He will be aware of Satan's tactics and guard against them (2 Co 2:11). Some of his tactics are obvious from Scripture.

A. Waging Warfare (Eph 6:10-18)

What we might relegate to human opposition may indeed be Satan's interference. Our ultimate wrestling is not with "flesh and blood" but with spiritual forces of wickedness in the heavenlies. We might get an idea of what sort of attacks Satan makes by noting the type of armor provided in the wisdom of God.

B. ACCUSING AND SLANDERING (Rev 12:10)

As *devil* means slanderer, so Satan lives up to his name. He accuses us before God for our sins and imperfections. He may also work on sensitive consciences not standing firm in God's grace. To answer these accusations, we have a defense lawyer, Jesus Christ the Righteous, who satisfied God for all our sins and who stands as witness to our right standing before God, thus defeating Satan (1 Jn 2:1-2).

C. PLANTING DOUBT (GEN 3:1-5)

Satan would make us doubt God's goodness, His word, His concern for us. He emphasizes God's restrictions as unjust (Gen 3:1), His warning and word as untrue (v. 4), His interests as selfish and limiting man's development (v. 5). So he maligns God's character and challenges God's authority.

D. TEMPTING TO SIN

1. To lie (Ac 5:3). Satan is the author of lies, and he tempts others to acts against the truth. To lie is to tell a falsehood in whole or in part for personal gain and to the loss or hurt of another. It is part of the self-seeking philosophy of Satan.

2. To sex sins (1 Co 7:5). Satan promotes the philosophy of the priority of bodily satisfaction. Perversion of sex in fornication, adultery, homosexuality, or masturbation comes from preoccupation with bodily needs. The first three are specifically forbidden in God's Word, and the last is distracting and debilitating in a perverted self-gratification. God has provided marriage for the normal expression of sex, and partners must recognize their mutual responsibilities. They provide Satan with an opportunity to tempt to sexual sins when there is not satisfaction in marriage. However, there is never justification to yielding to Satan and these sins.

3. To occupation with this world (1 Jn 2:15-17; 5:19). The world is Satan's system, built up on the principle of self-promotion. Its philosophy and practice are anti-God. Satan would influence and defeat us through "the lust of the flesh" (pleasures), "the lust of the eyes" (possessions), and "the boastful pride of life" (self-promotion). This attitude affects all of us somewhat, knowingly or unknowingly. Satan is actively promoting it (Eph 2:1-3). Some have succumbed to his temptations through it (2 Ti 4:10; Ja 4:1-7).

4. *To relying upon human wisdom and strength* (2 Ch 21: 1-8; Mt 16:21-23). Satan knows that he can defeat what is purely human, since it does not conform to God's standard or rely on God's power. So he tempted David to have confidence in numbers of soldiers, and Peter to resist the Lord in human wisdom. He moved the Corinthians to judge the gospel message and ministry according to human wisdom (1 Co 1:18-25; 3:18—4:5; 2 Co 4:1-7).

5. *To pride in spiritual matters* (1 Ti 3:6). The privilege of leadership in the church has its perils. Satan attacks the leaders to affect the congregations. So Paul urged that novices not be ordained to leadership, lest being proud they fall into the condemnation also incurred by the devil. Any spiritual ability carries with it the danger of self-satisfaction and self-confidence that precludes God's best blessings and affords Satan an opportunity.

6. *To discouragement* (1 Pe 5:6-10). Satan would have us occupied with our difficulties and overcome with cares. Perhaps this is why Peter first tells us to cast all our cares upon God, assuring us of God's care, and then tells us to beware of our adversary the devil who prowls about seeking whom he may devour (1 Pe 5:7-8). He may be involved in the case of the man who, hearing the word, is then overcome by the worry of the world (Mt 13:22). Persecution, rejection, lack of appreciation, physical and spiritual difficulties may lead us from discouragement to despair, to disheartenment, to defeat (see Rev 2:9-10; 3:9-10).

E. INCITING PERSECUTION (REV 2:10)

Persecution, privation, and imprisonment may be motivated

by Satan. The Church and Israel are his primary objects of attack by this method (Rev 12:13; 13:7).

F. PREVENTING SERVICE (1 TH 2:18)

On one occasion, Satan thwarted Paul from coming to help the Thessalonians. How this was done, we are not told. Perhaps it was through a physical malady (2 Co 12:7) or through some human agency (2 Co 11:22-27).

G. INFILTRATING THE CHURCH

1. Through false teachers (2 Co 11:13-15; 2 Pe 2:1-19). Satan sends his messengers disguised as messengers of light. As deceitful workers, they oppose true ministers and promote a legalistic or humanistic form of religion. Satan may use demons in this (1 Ti 4:1-5). They can attract even sincere persons into false forms of Christianity and into the occult. John warns against "the completely open mind" policy (1 Jn 4:1-4). We must test all things by God's Word, particularly its teaching on the person and work of Christ.

2. Through false disciples (Mt 13:38-39). While God sows good seed through His messengers, the enemy, Satan, also sows evil seed. "The tares are the sons of the wicked one," and they at first look like wheat, but soon are evident as impostors. The presence and activity of the false disciples hinder the work of the Church and confuse the true nature of the Church and the gospel for those on the outside.

H. PROMOTING DIVISION (2 CO 2:10-11)

A member of the Corinthians church had been disciplined to promote holiness (compare 1 Co 5:1-11). Paul instructed the church to receive him back to fellowship. But where there is not agreement on full forgiveness, there is occasion for Satan to cause strife and division. This seems the case here. Certainly the Corinthians were influenced by Satan's promotion of worldly wisdom that had already caused other divisions among them (1 Co 1:10-11; 3:1-9; 5:2; 6:1; 8:1-13). Harboring anger gives the devil an opportunity to promote division (Eph 4:26-27).

SUMMARY

Satan's present power and activity are wide and varied, but always directed against God and His program and people primarily. He is anti-God in character, and he opposes God's program by counterfeiting His program and by counteracting God's authority. He is now deceiving the nations, influencing their governments, and will one day direct world government through the coming Antichrist. Regarding the unsaved, he prevents acceptance of the truth and attracts to falsehood in doctrine and life. Against the genuine believer he wages constant warfare, accuses, plants doubt, tempts to sin, incites persecution, prevents service, infiltrates the Church and promotes division.

The Christian's response to Satan will be treated in another chapter. But we must first be aware of his schemes and tactics.

16

THE REALITY OF DEMONS

THE BIBLE GIVES abundant evidence of the existence of demons, and their names help determine what sort of realities they are.

I. EVIDENCE OF THEIR EXISTENCE

A. PROOF FROM THE EXISTENCE OF ANGELS

Evidence for the reality of angels and the reality of demons overlaps. That is, some of the same arguments pertain to both.

1. Satan's fall. When the highest of all angelic beings fell, he became evil. His existence as an evil angel has been settled.* If this evil angel exists, then there is probability that other evil spirit beings also exist.

2. Satan's following. It is obvious that other angelic beings shared in Satan's fall and so became evil also (Eze 28:18; Mt 25:41; Rev 12:4).† It seems very probable that Satan's angels are known in Scripture as demons.

B. PROOF FROM HEATHEN RELIGIONS

Says Unger, "The history of various religions from the earliest times shows belief in Satan and demons to be universal. . . . Spells, incantations, magical texts, exorcisms, and various forms of demonological phenomena abound in archaeological discoveries from Sumeria and Babylon. Egyptian, Assyrian, Chaldean, Greek, and Roman antiquity are rich in demonic phenomena. The deities worshiped were invisible demons represented by material idols and images. . . . To an amazing degree, the history of religion is an account of demon-controlled

*See pp. 115-16.
†See pp. 121-22; 129.

religion, particularly in its clash with the Hebrew faith and later with Christianity."[1]

C. PROOF FROM HEBREW OLD TESTAMENT

The Old Testament regards demons as existing evil entities. Since man's fall, God's people have been attacked by Satan and demons. Satan may have instigated the first murder (Gen 4:1-6, cf. Jn 8:44; 1 Jn 3:12). Demons may have attacked the race in Genesis 6:1-10.

> That the *shedhim* (Deut. 32:17; Ps. 106:36-37) . . . were real demons, and not mere idols is proved by the Septuagint translation of the term by *daimonia* (demons); the Jews regarded idols as demons who allowed themselves to be worshipped by men (Bar. 4:7; LXX Ps. 95:5; I Cor. 10:20). It seems certain, moreover, that the *seirim* were also demonic conceptions (Lev. 17:7; II Chron. 11:15; Isa. 13:21; 14).[2]

Consider also the spirit who volunteered to be a "lying spirit" through false prophets speaking to Ahab (1 Ki 22:20-22). Note also the spiritual powers behind the world rulers with whom Daniel's angelic visitor wrestled (Dan 10:13, 20).

D. PROOF FROM CHRIST'S TEACHING AND MINISTRY

Christ accepted the concept that Satan was the ruler of a host of demons (Mt 12:22-28). He taught that Satan and his angels were morally responsible persons destined by God for the lake of fire (Mt 25:41). A large portion of Christ's ministry involved the casting out of demons from those possessed (Mt 12:22-29; 15:22-28; Mk 5:1-16). He gave His disciples power to cast out demons (Mt 10:1) and viewed His victory over them as over Satan (Lk 10:17-18). He spoke of their reality and power to His disciples in private (Mt 17:14-20). He never corrected anyone for believing in their existence and never gave hint that they were not real.

E. PROOF FROM NEW TESTAMENT WRITERS

There are over one hundred references to demons in the Bible, most of them occurring in the New Testament. All the writers of the synoptic gospels report several cases of demon possession to demonstrate the power of Christ over demons. We may briefly state that all the writers (though not every book) of the New Testament except the author of Hebrews mentions demons or evil angels.

II. EXPLANATION OF THEIR NAMES

A. NAMES FOR DEMONS IN THE OLD TESTAMENT

The Hebrew possesses no precise equivalent for the Greek terms *daimon* or *daimonion,* but no fewer than five different Hebrew words are translated by *daimonion* (demon).[3]

1. *Shedhim* (Deu 32:17; Ps 106:37). Always in the plural, this word has the idea of rulers or lords. It speaks of idols as lords, since the Hebrews regarded images as visible symbols of invisible demons.[4] So the Israelites committing idolatry were said to have "sacrificed to demons" (*shedhim,* Deu 32:17).

2. *Seirim* (Lev 17:7). The Hebrews were to sacrifice at the altar of the tabernacle and not to sacrifice in the desert to "he-goats" (LXX, *daimonia*). Jeroboam I appointed worship for the *seirim* (2 Ch 11:15), and Josiah "brake down the high places of the gates [shearim]," which is to be read *seirim* (2 Ki 22:8).[5] These goat-like conceptions represented demon-satyrs. Isaiah's reference to them dancing in the desolated Babylon is translated in the Septuagint by *daimonia* (Isa 13:21; 34:14).

3. *'Elilim* (Ps 96:5, LXX 95:5). This passage identifies demons with idols and suggests demonism as the dynamic of idolatry. This plural word conveys emptiness, the nothingness of idols. The demons behind them are the real existences.[6]

4. *Gad* (Is 65:11). Those that forsake Jehovah "set a table for Fortune (NASB, LXX, *daimonion*). The demon god Fortune was worshiped by the Babylonians. This idolatry was elsewhere called the worship of Baal, or Bel.[7]

5. *Qeter* (Ps 91:6; LXX 90:6). The "destruction [*qeter*] that wasteth at noonday" was regarded as an evil spirit.[8]

B. NAMES FOR DEMONS IN THE NEW TESTAMENT

1. *Daimon.* This is the word from which the English word

demon is derived. It occurs once in the critical editions of the Greek New Testament in Matthew 8:31. The Textus Receptus has it on four other occasions (Mk 5:12; Lk 8:29; Rev 16:14; 18:2). Its derivation is unsure. The early Greeks (Homeric period) equated it with god (*theos*). The emphasis was upon evil power or bad influence. In post-Homeric usage, it was used of an intermediary between the gods and men, in some cases human spirits. A third stage of Greek development began to view demons as morally imperfect beings, some good, some evil. Plato thought *daimon* came from *dao*, meaning "knowing" or "intelligent." Some modern scholars derive it from *dai*, meaning "divide," "disrupt," "distributor of destiny."[9]

The final stage of its usage is found in the New Testament, where all demons are evil and work as Satan's agents. So also many early Christian writers consider demons as evil.[10]

2. Daimonion. Once used for "gods," it came to be used to mean an inferior divinity. A. T. Robertson held that it was a diminutive of *daimon*.[11] This was an appropriate term to designate idols and pagan gods (as in the Septuagint). This is the most frequently used term in the New Testament, having sixty-three occurrences.

3. Pneumata. Forty-three times demons are termed *pneuma* or *pneumata* (spirits). The context makes clear that these spirts are demons: for instance, the demon-possessed *(daimonizomenous)* were treated by Jesus and He cast out "the spirits" *(pneumata)*. The interchange of terms "demons" and "spirits" substantiates the identification in Luke 10:17-20. "The unusual usage, 'spirits of demons,' in Revelation 16:14 is apparently intended to distinguish them from human spirits. Not only are they 'unclean spirits' (v. 13), but they are not merely human, rather supernatural—'spirits of demons' (v. 14)."[12] *deidō*, meaning, 'to fear,' and *daimōn*."[14]

4. Angels. The similar expressions, "the devil and his angels" (Mt 25:41) and "Beelzebub, prince of the devils" (Mt 12:24) seem to equate Satan's angels with demons. (Note Beelzebub refers to Satan, Mt 12:26.)

C. RELATED TERMS IN THE NEW TESTAMENT

1. Daimonizomai. This verb means "to be possessed by a demon,"[13] and is used in several forms (verb and participles) thirteen times.

2. Daimoniodes. This adjective means "demonic," indicating the character of worldly wisdom in contrast to divine (Ja 3:15).

3. Deisidaimonesterous. "This word occurs only in Acts 17:22 where Paul says that the Athenians are 'too superstitious' (A.V.), or 'very religious' (A.S.V.). It literally means that they were 'reverencing the demons (or "divine" things— "gods" in their thinking) more than usual.' It is derived from *deidō*, meaning, 'to fear,' and *daimōn.*"[14]

4. Deisidaimonia. Derived from *deidō*, meaning to fear or to reverence, and from *daimonion*, this word speaks of a reverencing of demons or divine things, gods. It occurs only in Acts 25:19 and is translated "superstition" (A.V.) or "religion" (A.S.V.).[15]

SUMMARY

Demons do exist.‡ There is proof from the existence of angels, from heathen religions, from the Old Testament, and from the New Testament. Basically, the New continues the view of the Old about demons.[16] Christ's own views and actions in casting out demons would settle the issue alone. However, every writer of the New Testament, except the author of Hebrews, mentions demons in one way or another. The names for demons in the Old and New Testaments throw light on their character and connections as well as substantiate their existence. The most common terms in the New Testament for demons are *daimonion* and *pneumata*. The translation "devils" is incorrect; it should be "demons."

‡Karl Barth holds the contrary opinion. Demons seem not to have separate and distinct existence as persons in Barth's thought. They exist only as the counterpart of God and truth. They are not to be placed on the same level as angels in being or reality. They are not separate from chaos; they are part of it and are chaos itself. The New Testament compels us to disbelieve in the demons or their danger, according to Barth (see Karl Barth, *Church Dogmatics*, 3:609-22). For an evaluative summary of Barth on angels and demons, see G. C. Berkouwer, *The Triumph of Grace in the Theology of Karl Barth* (Grand Rapids: Eerdmans, 1956), pp. 76-80.

17

THE DERIVATION OF DEMONS

THERE IS A QUESTION concerning the origin and identification of demons. Because the Bible does not specifically settle the issue, several theories have been advanced.

I. SPECULATIVE THEORIES

A. SUPERSTITIOUS DESIGNATIONS FOR CERTAIN NATURAL DISEASES

This theory dismisses the existence of demons as real personal or evil forces. It does not deal with the evidence in the Bible or in extrabiblical case experiences, but rather "clashes with all the evidence of Scripture, history, and human experience."[1] It cannot account for demons' terrible fear and animosity toward God, nor for their superhuman strength manifest through demon possession.*

B. SPIRITS OF WICKED MEN DECEASED OR MINOR DEITIES

Popular Greek belief, in animistic tradition, held demons to be the spirits of departed men. It was also used of "divine" or intermediary beings, more specifically the evil ones.[2] It has no foundation in biblical teaching. The Bible view of the wicked dead sees them confined, separated from living humans and in conscious torment from God's punishment (Lk 16:19-26).

---

*Consider the case of the demoniac in Mk 5:1-17. Note his supernatural strength; his isolation and self-mutilation; his ambivalence in coming to Christ and his fear of Christ; the conversation between him and Christ; Christ's casting out the demons; the transference from the man to the swine, leaving the man healed.

155

II. Supposed Scriptural Theories

The following theories appeal to Scripture for support but fail to produce substantial evidence for their acceptance.

A. Spirits of a Pre-Adamic Race

1. Explanation. Those who favor this view hold that Genesis 1:1 refers to the creation of a perfect earth ages ago and that Satan, then Lucifer, ruled over earth and a pre-Adamic race of men. They see a catastrophe between verses 1 and 2 as a result of God's judgment of the sin of angels and men. A great "gap" ensued before God recreated order from the chaos described in verse 2. Re-creation starts in verse 3.† In the re-creation, the spirits of these fallen men now are demons. To support this theory, its advocates say that Genesis 1:2 may be translated, "But the earth became formless and void," indicating a catastrophe resulting from judgment. They also distinguish demons, as disembodied spirits, from angels, good and evil. Angels are supposed to have spiritual bodies as do the children of the resurrection (note Lk 20:36; 1 Co 15:44; 2 Co 5:2-3). So demons seem to seek desperately some body to inhabit. "This clearly infers that at one time they had physical bodies."³ Supporters also note the Jewish distinction between angels and spirits (Ac 23:8-9). Some of them see corroboration in a Greek tradition that demons are the spirits—some good and some bad—of deceased men of a mythical age. The tradition is a supposed degeneration of a primitive pure tradition about a sinless pre-Adamic earth and the fall that resulted in its judgment.⁴

2. Evaluation. Most of the evidence seems to be conjectural. The gap theory of Genesis 1:1-2 has very little support from Hebrew scholars. The Hebrew *waw* consecutive in verse 2, "And the earth was," is a continuative storytelling device that gives no hint of a break at all. Furthermore, it is extremely doubtful that the verb in verse 2 could be translated "be-

---

†Not all who hold the gap theory use it for explaining the origin of demons. Archer holds that the race was subhuman, not possessing souls (see Gleason L. Archer, Jr., *A Survey of Old Testament Introduction*, pp. 188-89).

came.""[5] But even allowing these two points, there is still no evidence of a pre-Adamic race or that their supposed spirits are now demons. In fact, the Bible seems to argue against this in that, once men die, they do not reenter this world but are bound, awaiting the final judgment (Lk 16:26; Heb 9:22).

The rigid distinction between angels and spirits which this view demands "is highly questionable since Scripture refers to angels as spirits (Psalm 104:4; Hebrews 1:4) and sometimes uses the term 'angel' for the spirit of man (Matthew 18:10; Acts 12:15).""[6] Again, we note that demons are equated with spirits in Matthew 8:16 and in Luke 10:17-20.

The desire of demons for human bodies may be explained in that demons may regard control of humans as one of the best means to accomplish their destructive and deceptive purposes. They may gain sensual pleasure through the use of human senses as an extension of their personality in control, pleasure they could not experience without a body. The desire of some demons to enter swine may be understood "as a desperate alternative which they suggested in preference to being sent to the abyss (Lk 8:32).[7]

Finally, the classical Greek use of *demons* referring to "the good spirits of departed men of the golden age as in Hesiod, is at complete variance with the uniform New Testament usage of the word. . . . To use its originally pagan concepts as the basis of a theory is totally unwarranted."[8]

For the above reasons, we would reject this theory.

B. SPIRITS OF MONSTROUS OFFSPRING OF ANGELS AND WOMEN

1. Explanation. This theory is based upon the interpretation that "the sons of God" (*bene Elohim*) of Genesis 6 were evil angels who cohabited with certain women before the flood. The results of this unnatural union were mongrel creatures, partly human and partly angelic. They may be the *nephilim* (Heb., fallen ones) rendered giants (from Gr., *gegenes*, probably meaning earthborn).[9] Or they might be "the mighty men who were of old, men of renown" (Gen 6:4, NASB). The flood destroyed these monsters, according to theory, but their spirits became the demons who today seek to inhabit bodies and continue in sensuality.

2. *Evaluation.* Even if we should allow that "the sons of God" in Genesis 6 are fallen angels, as does Unger,[10] still there is no evidence whatever that the spirits of the unusual progeny of angels continue to freely roam earth or that they should be identified with demons. If supporters should argue that demons seek bodies and sensual experiences and that demons are distinguished from angels, we would answer as we did with the previous theory.‡

We reject this theory since it is based only on conjecture.

III. Substantial Scriptural Theory

The theory that musters the most biblical support is that demons are fallen angels.

A. Statement of the Theory

All angels were created perfect, as was Lucifer (Job 38:7; Eze 28:15).§ In Satan's original rebellion, he drew with him a great number of lesser angels, perhaps a third of all created (Eze 28:18; Rev 12:4).‖ So we read of "the devil and his angels" (Mt 25:41). Satan's angels are now called demons.

Of those who hold this point of view, some call only the free fallen angels demons.[11] Others, such as Unger, hold that both the confined and non-confined fallen angels constitute the whole company of demons.[12]

Demons, then, are Satan's subjects and helpers in his program of opposition to God and His people. Expelled from heaven with Satan, they have their abode in the second heaven. Their warfare may be carried on with elect angels there and with believers in the heavenlies. The unconfined seem free to roam the earth and carry on Satan's work here.#

‡See pp. 156-57.
§See pp. 24-26.
‖See p. 135.
#For the abode of fallen angels, see pp. 76-77.

Of the angels that followed Satan, there are two general classes, the free and the bound. Of those bound, there are two places of confinement. Some are in *tartarus* (translated "hell," 2 Pe 2:4). These seem to be confined permanently until the final judgment of angels, not because of their original rebellion with Satan, but because of some other terrible sin. If they were bound in *tartarus* because of the fall, no angel or even Satan would be free. They are thought by many scholars to be "the sons of God" of Genesis 6:1-4[13]** However, the interpretation of this term has nothing to do with the existence of demons nor with their identity as fallen angels.

Other evil angels are bound in the abyss (Lk 8:31; Rev 9: 1-3, 10). Some of those expelled from possessed persons were sent there by Christ, but possibly not all. On one occasion the Lord commanded the unclean spirit to leave a boy and not to return again (Mk 9:25). This may indicate the possibility of return. Some regarded as demons are now bound and will be released to afflict wicked men in the Tribulation period (Rev 9:1-3, 10).

B. SUPPORT OF THE THEORY

We favor the theory that demons are fallen angels for the following reasons.

1. Similar relation to Satan. Certain parallel expressions seem to identify fallen angels with demons (e.g., "the devil and his angels," Mt 25:41; "the dragon . . . and his angels," Rev 12:7; "Beelzebul the ruler of the demons," Mt 12:24, NASB). Beelzebul is interpreted by the Lord Jesus as Satan (Mt 12: 26). "Moreover, when Beelzebul is designated as 'ruler of the demons,' the word that is used is *archonti* which has the basic meaning of 'first.' As 'first of the demons' he is their ruler."[14]

In the tribulation period, certain locusts are released from the abyss. From their description, activity, and place of confinement (see Lk 8:31), many take these to be demons. They have over them an angel, Abaddon (Apollyon), who may be

---

**For consideration of the problem of the identity of "the sons of God," see Appendix.

Satan.†† If their king is an angel, then these demons may also be angels fallen with their leader, Satan.

2. Similar essence of being. Angels are termed "spirits" (Ps 104:4; Heb 1:14).‡‡ Demons are also designated as "spirits" (Mt 8:16; Lk 10:17, 20). In other places, demons are termed "unclean spirits" (Lk 11:19-26) and "evil spirits" (Lk 8:2). The latter term fits one title of Satan, "the evil one" (Jn 17: 15; 1 Jn 5:18, NASB).

3. Similar activities. Just as demons seek to enter and control men (Mt 17:14-18; Lk 11:14-15), so also may angels, such as Satan (Lk 22:3; Jn 13:27). Evil angels join their leader, Satan, in warfare against God and man (Rev 9:13-15; 12:7-17), and so do demons (Mk 9:17-26; Rev 9:1-11). The many kinds and ranks of Satan's helpers listed in Ephesians 6: 10-12 and Romans 8:38-39 may indicate the inclusion of angels as demons working against believers.

4. Sufficient identification. Every mention of Satan's angels and demons seems to be parallel and there is no sufficient reason for distinguishing the two. In fact, if they are not identical, then no other origin of demons is anywhere revealed in the Bible. We should think that God would identify our enemies and their source if we are to understand their nature and activity and combat them intelligently. And we believe that He has identified demons as fallen angels under Satan.

SUMMARY

Demons, like angels, are not the product of an overactive imagination nor the superstitious designation for certain natural diseases. Neither are they the disembodied spirits of a supposed race of men before Adam. Nor are they the monstrous offsprings of angelic cohabitation with women before the flood. There is little, if any, evidence for these views that can stand critical evaluation. However, there is solid and substantial evidence to believe that they are fallen angels. They were part of Satan's original rebellion and share in his work today.

††See pp. 123-24.
‡‡See p. 33.

18

THE DESCRIPTION OF DEMONS

As FALLEN ANGELS, demons have much in common with the nature of angels, and with the nature of Satan in his perversion of personality.

I. PERSONALITY OF DEMONS

Demons are genuine persons, not just forces or phenomena in the physical and psychological realm.

A. PARALLELS WITH ANGELS' PERSONALITY

Most of what has been traced of genuine personality in angels is applicable to demons also, except for their perversion of person and powers.* They also were created in the image of God with intellect, sensibility, and will, and with moral responsibility. Having exercised their wills against God, they fell with Satan and remain entrenched in evil and estrangement from God, being nonredeemable.

B. PARTICULARS OF DEMONS' PERSONALITY

Extensive evidence is not necessary at this point. A few representative particulars will suffice to show personality.

1. Personal pronouns. The pronouns *I, me*, and *your* are applied to demons by Christ and by the demons themselves (Lk 8:27-30).

2. Personal name. Christ once asked a demon, "What is your name?" The answer came, " 'Legion'; for many demons had entered him" (Lk 8:30, NASB).

*On personality of angels, see chap. 3.

161

3. Speech. Speech evidences personality in communication. The demons spoke to Christ, and Christ spoke to the demons (Lk 4:33-35, 41; 8:28, 30).

4. Intelligence. Demons knew who the Lord Jesus was (Mk 1:23-24; Lk 4:34; 8:28). One gave a slave girl recognition of Paul and his ministry (Ac 16:16-17). The spirit also enabled her to determine secret information through fortune telling or divination.

5. Emotion. Demons evidence emotion in fear and trembling of judgment (Lk 8:28; Ja 2:19).

6. Will. Demons exercised will in appealing to Christ not to cast them into the abyss, but to allow them to enter swine (Lk 8:32). Christ's command to them is essentially a demand of His will over theirs, a demand they had to obey (Mk 1: 27; Lk 4:35-36).

II. Properties of Demons

Again, much of what we know of angels applies also to demons.

A. Spirit Beings

Demons, as angels, are termed spirits (Mt 8:16; Lk 10:17, 20). They are contrasted with flesh and blood, or corporeal beings. We wrestle with wicked spirits (Eph 6:12). These spirit beings, since they are creatures, are finite and limited in space, time, and powers. They, as angels, shall not cease to exist (Lk 20:36).

B. Morally Perverted

1. In their persons. Since their rebellion with Satan, demons are morally and spiritually unclean. Their total capacities as persons were perverted in what we might call angelic depravity. All about them is twisted—intellect, sensibility, and will— because they used all these against God. Paul says we wrestle against "the rulers, against the powers, against the world-forces of this darkness" (Eph 6:12, NASB). Their nature and realm of operation is moral darkness, not light. Though they abide in darkness, they may transform themselves into messengers (angels) of light. They often deceive men about their true darkness of character.

They are termed "unclean spirits" (Mt 10:1; Mk 1:23; Lk 11:24) or "evil spirits" (Lk 7:21). They are also termed "spiritual forces of wickedness" (Eph 6:12, NASB). Some are more wicked in their person than others (Mt 12:45).

The terminology "unclean" and "evil" is moral. Demon's immorality is often manifest in the sensuousness of those they control or influence. "This may explain the desire of the possessed to live in a state of nudity, to have licentious thoughts (Luke 8:47), and to frequent such impure places as tombs."[1] The same concept is reflected in demon-inspired false teachers in 2 Peter 2:1-2, 10, 13-14, 18.

2. In their doctrine. Promoting Satan's system of the lie, they cause men to forsake the light of God's Word (1 Ti 4:1-3). They are deceitful and hypocritical. The demon-empowered court magicians of Pharaoh, "Jannes and Jambres opposed Moses" (2 Ti 3:8). Paul likens them to false teachers who "also oppose the truth, men of depraved mind, rejected as regards the faith." He also writes, "Among them are those who enter into households and captivate weak women weighed down with sins, led on by various impulses" (2 Ti 3:6, NASB).

Peter describes false teachers with the following terms in the New American Standard Bible: "their sensuality" (2 Pe 2:2), "their greed" (v. 3), "those who indulge the flesh in its corrupt desires" (v. 10), "revelling in their deceptions, as they carouse with you" (v. 13), "having eyes full of adultery and that never cease from sin . . . having a heart trained in greed" (v. 14), "they entice by fleshly desires, by sensuality" (v. 18). These terms are especially significant to our subject because they are compared with those that God did not spare in the days of Noah, "the angels when they sinned" (v. 4) and "the cities of Sodom and Gomorrah" (v. 6). Unclean demons promote unclean teaching and teachers.

3. In their conduct. Their unclean conduct may be seen in several connections. They join Satan, no doubt, in sowing "tares," or false disciples, and so hinder and confuse true disciples (Mt 13:37-42). They, like Satan, disguise themselves as angels of light to confuse unbelievers and believers alike (2 Co 11:13-15). They would control men in their wickedness and join forces with their own kind to work spiritual destruction in their victims (Mt 12:43-45).

An outstanding example of their unclean conduct is found in "the sons of God" cohabiting with "the daughters of men" (Gen 6:4). If we understand these to be demons,† then we see sensuality at work to fulfill wicked desires and to oppose the program of God. These fallen angels are probably described by Jude as the "angels who did not keep their own domain, but abandoned their proper abode" (Jude 6, NASB). He compares them to Sodom and Gomorrah who "in the same way as these indulged in gross immorality and went after strange flesh" (v. 7, NASB). That angels were involved in sensual sin seems obvious.

C. Invisible but Capable of Manifestation

As spirit beings, angels are normally invisible to human eyes. So also with demons. But just as angels have power given them to appear on some occasions (Gen 19:15; Lk 1:26; Jn 20:12), "likewise, evil spirits seem evidently to possess a similar power."[2] Unger argues from biblical evidence that just as Satan seems to have manifest himself on several occasions (Gen 3:1; Zec 3:1; Mt 4:9-10), so also may his demons assume visible form, even human form, should occasion so require.[3] When Scripture records their appearance, they assume hideous and fearsome forms like animals (Rev 9:7-10, 17; 16:13-16).

III. Powers of Demons

Just as angels and Satan have supernatural powers, so do demons.

A. Supernatural Intelligence

Great intelligence has always been ascribed to demons.

†See pp. 60, 158-59, and Appendix.

Those who consult the occult methods and mediums have confidence in the intelligence of the spirits. The Bible witnesses that demons are of great intelligence. Not only are they in league with Satan, who has vast intelligence (Eze 28:12), but as angels they have superior intelligence on their own (2 Sa 14:20).

Demons had supernatural insight into the identity of Christ as the Son of God (Mk 1:14, 34) and they know of His great power (Mk 5:6-7). They know their place of confinement and future judgment (Mt 8:28-29; Lk 8:31). They cleverly deceive men by withholding necessary information for salvation (1 Jn 4:1-4) and masquerading as messengers of light (2 Co 11:13-15). They know how to corrupt sound doctrine (1 Ti 4:1-3) and how to distinguish between believers and nonbelievers (Rev 9:4). They evidently have some knowledge of future or of hidden things (Ac 16:16).

The source of their knowledge is found in their superior created nature and in their vast experience, as they have lived through many thousands of years observing and collecting information.

Despite their great knowledge, they use all the resources of their intellects against God and His purposes incessantly. But their knowledge is limited, and their plans will be overthrown by God.

B. Supernatural Strength

1. In controlling men. An evil spirit inhabiting a man resisted two of the seven sons of Sceva. He "leaped on them and subdued both of them and overpowered them, so that they fled out of that house naked and wounded" (Ac 19:16, cf. vv. 14-16). The maniac of the Gerasenes (Gadarenes, KJV) was controlled by many unclean spirits, "and no one was able to bind him any more, even with a chain" (Mk 5:3, NASB, cf. vv. 1-4). He had broken all shackles and chains and was uncontrollable.

Demonic power is often manifest in viciousness. The same maniac usually was crying out and gashing himself with stones

(Mk 5:5). One man's son had the marks of an epileptic. Jesus cast out of him a demon who had thrown him often into fire and into water (Mt 17:14-20). It seems demons promote self-destruction in their victims.

The great power of demons was dramatically demonstrated when Jesus cast out the demons from the demon-possessed Gerasene. They entered into a herd of about two thousand swine and rushed them over a steep bank to perish in the sea. The whole incident, however, is a witness to the power of the Son of God over all demons.

2. In afflicting men. Certain demon-locusts are pictured as painfully tormenting men to the point of preferring death (Rev 9:1-11). Others that seem to be demon-horsemen, under the control of four evil angels, pour out fire from their lion-like mouths. By them a third of mankind is killed (Rev 9:13-19).

3. In working supernatural feats. Demons can produce deceptive "miracles." Like their leader, the devil, they may interfere in the laws of nature. Satan works "all power and signs and lying wonders" (2 Th 2:9) through the Antichrist. The false prophet who supports the Antichrist also "performs great signs, so that he even makes fire come down out of heaven to the earth in the presence of men" (Rev 13:13, NASB). He even animates an image of the Antichrist to deceive men (Rev 13:15). This may be Satan's personal work, or it may be the work of his demons.

It should be noted that in Satan's counterfeiting actions, he performs through the Antichrist works similar to those of Christ. The same three words used of Christ's miracles (Ac 2:22) and of the apostles' miracles (Heb 2:4) are used of satanic or demonic miracles (2 Th 2:9): power (*dunamis*), sign (*sēmeion*), and wonder (*teras*). Demonic "miracles" are lying (*pseudos*) and not in accord with Scripture. They are used against God, as are the "signs" of the "spirits of demons" in gathering rebels to war (Rev 16:14, NASB).

There is a limit to what supernatural feats demons and Satan can duplicate. The magicians of Egypt seemed to duplicate some of God's miracles through Moses, but were unable to match others (Ex 8:5-7, contrast vv. 16-19). Further, their feats only added to the land's misery and could not relieve it. The magicians recognzed that the greater power came from God (Ex 8:19).

Modern "miracles" are not necessarily fakes. They might be real; but they might be false, counterfeits of demons.

C. SUPERNATURAL PRESENCE

Just as angels swiftly move in space, so may demons (Dan 9:21-23; 10:10-14). Since they are not limited by material bodies, their speed may be extremely fast. However, they are limited in time and space.‡

Since there are many demons, Satan's influence may be felt in many places at once. With organization of information and cooperation in the ranks of the demons, their presence and power may be extremely efficient and effective. Only the restraining of God keeps them from the total devastation they could accomplish.

Normal physical barriers or confines of space do not limit the presence of demons. A legion of demons were dwelling in the maniac of the Gerasenes (Lk 8:30). A legion may have meant from three to six thousand soldiers with auxiliary troops. There obviously were enough in the man to drive two thousand swine into the sea.

The fact that demons enter a man's physical body indicates that they pass through physical barriers. Apports (the transference of objects through closed rooms and sealed containers by means of penetration of matter) and telekinesis (the setting of objects in motion without a visible or tangible cause) are occult manifestations of the ability of demons to move or work unhindered by certain spatial limitations or barriers.[1]

SUMMARY

Demons are persons with intellect, sensibility, and will, just as are angels. They are spirit beings who are morally perverted in their personality, in their doctrine, and in their conduct.

‡See p. 33.

Often they are called unclean spirits or evil spirits. They are normally invisible but sometimes may appear in hideous forms. They possess powers of supernatural intelligence, strength, and presence. The totality of their personalities and powers is directed against God and in accord with Satan's leadership.

19

DUTIES OF DEMONS

THE ACTIVITIES OF DEMONS are quite diverse but always directed toward the promotion of unrighteousness and ultimate destruction of that which is good.

I. PROMOTION OF SATAN'S PROGRAM

In general, demons are Satan's untiring and devoted henchmen, organized to accomplish their common purposes.

A. EXTENSION OF SATAN'S POWER

Because of his creaturely limitations, Satan must extend his power through his angels. They obey him and serve his purposes. He is their god (Mt 12:24; Jn 12:31; Rev 12:7). Of their activities for Satan, we note two important aspects.

1. Their industry. Evil spirits never cease in promoting satanic deception and wickedness. They participate in the character and devotion of their leader to his evil ends. (Note Job 1:7 and 1 Pe 5:8 as illustrations of satanic industry.)

2. Their influence. Satan is not omnipresent, omnipotent, nor omniscient. But his presence, power, and knowledge are greatly extended through his demons. Because of this, satanic power is felt in many places simultaneously and in some places constantly. Pooling their resources and millennia of experience, they multiply effects, whether in individuals, nations, or the world system. Demonic cooperation is evident several places in Scripture (Mt 12:26, 45; Lk 8:30; 1 Ti 4:1).

169

B. EXPRESSION OF SATANIC PHILOSOPHY

1. In individuals. To cause men to walk according to the philosophy of this world and according to the prince of the power of the air, demons must be actively involved in the process (Eph 2:1-2). The promotion of fleshly desires, sensual pleasures, pride, and materialism comes from a satanic-demonic world system (Jn 16:11; 1 Jn 2:16).

2. In political governments. Satan and his demons are working behind the scene in determining the philosophy, course, and actions of world powers (Dan 10:13, 20). Often governmental policies opposing the spread of the gospel can be traced to demonic influence.

3. In the world system. A spiritual world system extends Satan's influence through demons and men. To control the world, demons organize and cooperate in large-scale warfare under Satan, their leader (Mt 12:26; Jn 12:31; 14:30; 16:11; Eph 6:11-12; 1 Jn 5:19).

II. OPPOSITION TO GOD AND HIS PROGRAM

Satan and his demons are opposed primarily to God and secondarily to man. It was God's revelation that termed him Satan or "adversary."

A. PROMOTING REBELLION

After their original rebellion against God, Satan and the demons have continued to promote a spirit of rebellion among men. Satan started with the first man (Gen 3), successfully involving him in rebellion. His final man, the Antichrist, heads the list of rebels among men. He is "the man of lawlessness . . . who opposes and exalts himself above every so-called god . . . displaying himself as being God" (2 Th 2:3-4, NASB). Demons, deceiving men, gather them together to wage war against God in the Great Tribulation (Rev 16:14). They cause men to become so entrenched in rebellion that even in the face of the wrath of God through demons, they do not repent of their evil works or of worshiping demons (Rev 9:20-21).

B. POSITING SLANDER

Sharing in the character of the devil ("slanderer"), demons undoubtedly participate in his slandering work.

1. Slandering God. From the beginning, the devil slandered the goodness of God before man (Gen 3:1-5). He would yet cause men to blame God for all the restriction on free expression and for the existence of evil in the world (Ro 3:5-8; 6:15; 9:14, 19; Ja 1:13).

2. Slandering men. Satan slanders men before God (Job 1:9, 11; 2:4-5; Zec 3:1; Rev 12:10). Since Satan's angels are mentioned in the context of his slandering of the saints, it is probable that they are also involved in the process, either in gathering information or in pressing the charges (Ro 8:33, 38-39; Rev 12:9).

Since demons are able to affect the thoughts of the mind, they may cause self-incriminating and condemning thoughts. The answer to any condemnation is found in Christ's advocacy for the believer (1 Jn 2:1-2) and in genuine confession and resultant cleansing (1 Jn 1:9).

C. PROMOTING IDOLATRY

The Bible points to demons as the dynamic behind idolatry. In turning men from God, Satan and his hosts often turn them to idols. The Hebrew Old Testament clearly reveals demons promoting and receiving the worship given to idols (Lev 17:7; Deu 32:17; Ps 96:4-5; Is 65:11). Israel mingled with the nations and were infected by their practices, "And served their idols, which became a snare to them. They even sacrificed their sons and their daughters to the demons . . . whom they sacrificed to the idols of Canaan" (Ps 106:36-38, NASB). As a result, they polluted the land, became unclean in their practices, and played the harlot (vv. 38-39).

"The demonizing of heathen gods, so conspicuous in the Septuagint (Ps 91:6, LXX 90:6; 96:5, LXX 95:5; and Isa. 63:3, 11) is proof, that already in the third century B.C. demonism was recognized as the dynamic of idolatry, and idol-worship was considered but demon-worship."[1]

The same is true in the New Testament. Denying, as does the Old Testament, the reality of other gods or any genuineness of idols, Paul says "that the things which the Gentiles sacrifice, they sacrifice to demons, and not to God; and I do not want you to become sharers in demons" (1 Co 10:20, NASB). The Corinthians formerly had been "led astray to the dumb idols, however you were led" (1 Co 12:2, NASB). Demons will promote idol worship on a wide scale during the reign of Antichrist in the Great Tribulation (Rev 13:4, 15; see also Rev 9:20).

D. REJECTING GRACE

Satan and demons abhor God's grace. Incapable of repentance or of being saved themselves, they do not understand grace, nor do they want men to understand it. Therefore they hide, cloud, and twist God's grace in salvation and distract men to lies.

Satan seems to have instigated or encouraged Cain to refuse to offer the blood of a substitute sacrifice and to offer through his works the fruit of a cursed earth (Gen 4:1-7; see also 1 Jn 3:12).

Satan undoubtedly uses demons to blind the minds of the unsaved, to keep them from seeing God's salvation by grace through faith in His Son (2 Co 4:3-4). So he misconstrues the true purpose of the Mosaic Law (2 Co 3:6-7, 13-14; Gal 2:21—3:1) by "bewitching" through false teachers. Demons cause men to depart from the truth of grace and promote doctrines of works-righteousness (1 Ti 4:1-8), of self-advancement through angelic intermediaries (Col 2:18-23), and of lawlessness (2 Pe 2:1-2). All their teachings are anti-Christ, denying that the Lord Jesus is the God-man, a genuine substitute sacrifice for the condemning sin of man (1 Jn 2:22; 4:1-4).

E. PROMOTING FALSE RELIGIONS AND CULTS

In promoting his lie, Satan and demons work inside and outside true biblical religion.

1. World religions. Satan and his demons will encourage all sorts of errors to keep men from God and His grace. In primitive religions where magic, superstition, and worship of evil spirits are key factors, demons provide the power to keep men enslaved.[2] "Although the motivating factors of polytheism are complex, and in some cases remarkable men have been elevated to the rank of gods, demonism always remains the dynamic behind the zeal of idolatrous devotees,"[3] whether they worship Marduk, Ashur, Zeus, Jupiter, Apollo, Ra, or a host of lesser deities.[4]

2. Cults of Christendom. Perversions of the scriptural view of the Person of Christ, His atonement, the method of salvation, and the essence of the Christian life cause divisions among so-called Christians. John warns believers to test the spirits, whether they be of God or of Satan (1 Jn 4:1-4). We are not to have a completely open mind in religious matters. Demonism is the cause for many such divisions and cults, and sound biblicism is the cure.[5]

The New Testament warns us against heresies and cults that distort the truth while retaining some of it (2 Co 11:13, 15, 22-23; Gal 1:6-8; Col 2:18-23; 1 Ti 4:1-4).

III. Oppression of Mankind

Demons act toward men in deceptive, degrading, and destructive ways. Though at times they may seem to promote some good, they are merely distracting from the best to promote evil in the end. Love and concern are not in their vocabulary. In their opposing God and promoting Satan's program, they really oppress mankind. Some idea of this truth shows up in the previous sections of this chapter. A few specifics here demonstrate their malevolent treatment of man.

A. Distressing Through Nature

Sometimes Satan and demons may use natural phenomena to afflict men. Satan may have used demons to cause injury and death in Job's family (Job 1:12, 16, 19; 2:7).

B. Degrading Man's Nature

Through the promotion of base desires and the philosophy of self-centeredness, demons degrade men made in the image of God (Eph 2:1-3). Immorality and degradation of God-given powers follow when demons lead men from God to idolatry and corrupt humanism (Ro 1:18-32).

C. Distracting from the Truth

Demons blind men to spiritual truth in Christ and distract them to perversions of the truth (2 Co 4:3-4; 1 Ti 4:1-4; 1 Jn 4:1-4). They will often promote what seems good in religion, behavior, philosophy, science, and economics to accomplish their evil purposes. The promotion of humanism can be a form of idolatry (Ro 1:23). Occupation with worldly possessions and comforts and pleasures stems from a world-philosophy promoted by demons (Eph 2:1-3). Some benefits may come to mankind through a future ecumenical religion called Babylon (Rev 18:9-19), but its true effect upon men is destructive (Rev 18:13, 23-24, 19:2). The cause of this destruction is tied to demon activity (Rev 18:2-3).

D. Disabling the Body

Demons may cause many sorts of physical ailments and injuries.

1. Dumbness (Mt 9:32-33; 12:22; Mk 9:17-29).

2. Blindness (Mt 12:22).

3. Deformity (Lk 13:11-17). Note that her trouble was attributed to "a spirit" (v. 11) who was regarded as an agent of Satan (v. 16).

4. Epilepsy (Mt 17:15-18). The term describing the boy in Matthew is "moon-smitten," but the parallel passages describe the effects of the malady. Mark 9:20 states: "the spirit threw him into a convulsion, and falling to the ground, he began rolling about and foaming at the mouth" (NASB). Luke 9:39 says, "a spirit seizes him, and he suddenly screams, and it throws him into a convulsion with foaming at the mouth, and as it mauls him, it scarcely leaves him" (NASB).

The Bible does not attribute all physical illness to demons, but clearly distinguishes natural ailments from demonic ailments (Mt 4:24; Mk 1:32, 34; Lk 7:21; 9:1).

E. Deranging the Mind

Certain mental disorders stem from demonic influence and control. Again, not all mental illnesses result from demon activity.[6]

1. Insanity. Withdrawal, nudity, moroseness, filth, and compulsive behavior seemed to characterize the maniac of the Gerasenes (Lk 8:27-29). After Christ cast out the demons, he was "sitting down at the feet of Jesus, clothed and in his right mind" (v. 35, NASB).

2. Suicidal mania. A demon who controlled a boy from childhood often threw him "both in the fire and into the water to destroy him" (Mk 9:22, NASB). A few modern cases of suicidal tendencies are recorded by Lechler.[7]

F. Driving to Injury

One demoniac kept gashing himself with stones (Mk 5:5). Another was thrown into fire and into water for destruction (Mk 9:22). The same boy was repeatedly mauled by a demon (Lk 9:39).

G. Destroying Life

Demons may move men to destroy human life (Rev 18:2, 24), or they may directly slaughter men (Rev 9:14-19).

H. Dominating Individuals

Through demon possession, Satan's agents control certain men at will to use them in any way—in the promotion of immorality, false religions, the occult practices, and other deceptions. Some of these cases are listed above. Other examples may be found in the Antichrist (2 Th 2:7-18), Simon (Ac 8:9-24), Elymas (Ac 13:8-11), and a certain slave-girl in Philippi (Ac 16:16-19). We will treat demon possession further in the next chapter.

IV. OPPOSITION OF THE SAINTS

In opposing God, Satan and demons ply their trade also against believers. "The activity of demons is so intimately and inseparably bound up with their prince-leader that their work and his is identified rather than differentiated."[8] So when Jesus healed those who were oppressed by the devil (Ac 10:38), He was involved in delivering men from demons (Mt 4:23-24; Mk 1:32; Lk 7:21). Certain activities against believers are traced to demons.

A. AGAINST BELIEVERS IN GENERAL

We struggle "not against flesh and blood, but against the rulers, against the powers, against the world forces of this darkness, against the spiritual forces of wickedness in the heavenly places" (Eph 6:12, NASB). These forces are arrayed against us to accomplish "the schemes of the devil' (Eph 6:11, NASB). Satan and demons are constantly conniving to discourage and defeat the saints in their individual and corporate life and ministry.

Paul does not say that all our struggle with evil comes immediately from demons. Much of it stems from our own evil natures within (Ro 7:21-24; Ja 1:14-15) and the world of men about us (Eph 2:2-3; 1 Jn 2:15-17). But we must recognize the great unseen hosts of evil spirits arrayed against and prepare for battle by putting on the whole armor of God (Eph 6:10).

B. AGAINST INDIVIDUALS

1. Attacking confidence and commitment. The armor of God reflects the kind of attack we may expect. Ephesians 6:14-18 suggests that Satan and demons hit us at the basis of our usefulness for God. If confidence in God's truth and our standing in Christ can be shaken, we have no experiential ground for victory (v. 14). The shield of faith not only gives us assurance of victory, but purpose and perspective for Christian service (v. 16). It answers slanders and temptations and enables us to prepare and participate in the spreading of the gospel of peace (v. 15). We need all of God's armor.

2. Tempting to sin. Satan moved David to put confidence in human resources; so he numbered Israel (1 Ch 21:1-8). Demons may encourage the same type of thing. They appeal to the flesh of believers and encourage selfish and lustful desires (1 Co 5:1-5; Eph 2:2-3; 1 Th 4:3-5; 1 Jn 2:16). Christ warns the church in Pergamum about Satan's influence and the sin of idolatry and immorality (Rev 2:12-14). The same type of warning came to Thyatira, where demonic influence in idolatry also led to immorality (Rev 2:20-24). In general, through the world system, they tempt to pride, covetousness, and expression of passion (1 Ti 3:6; 1 Jn 2:16).

3. Inflicting maladies. Satan probably used demons to afflict Job to get him to turn against God (Job 2:7-9). Satan afflicted Paul with a "thorn in the flesh." This physical difficulty or sickness (some suggest eye trouble or malaria) Paul termed "the messenger [angel] of Satan" (2 Co 12:7). Most likely a demon caused his affliction, but only under God's permission, as with Job (see vv. 7-9).

C. AGAINST THE CHURCH

Satan and demons seek to oppose the main purposes of the Body of Christ. She is to glorify God, extend the Gospel, and edify herself in God's truth (Mt 28:18-20; Eph 4:7-11). God would demonstrate to angelic forces His wisdom in and through the Church (Eph 3:10). These "rulers and authorities in the heavenly places" (NASB) could include demons as well as the holy angels. We could expect demons to seek to frustrate these purposes.

1. Creating divisions. The Holy Spirit established the Body of Christ in unity (Eph 4:4-6). The Church is to maintain the spirit of unity in the bond of peace (Eph 4:3). Demons would divide and defeat unified effort in the Church, whether locally or universally.

Demons promote *doctrinal divisions.* They speak through false teachers or fadists (1 Ti 4:1-3). They generally deny or cloud the genuine deity, the genuine humanity, or the substitutionary sacrifice of Christ with its appropriation by faith (1 Jn

4:1-4). They hold to "a form of godliness, although they have denied its power" (2 Ti 3:5, NASB). They also oppose the truth as did the demon-inspired Jannes and Jambres, court magicians of Pharaoh (2 Ti 3:8). They may promote legalistic asceticism (1 Ti 4:3-4, 8) or promote libertinism (2 Pe 2:1-2). God's servants should gently teach and correct them and their followers that "they may come to their sense and escape from the snare of the devil" (2 Ti 2:26, cf. vv. 24-26).

Demons may promote *practical divisions.* Jealousy and selfish ambition, arrogance and false practice reflects demonic wisdom(Ja 3:14-16). Demons accomplish their purposes through their toehold in our old, sinful nature (Gal 3:19-21, 26). They cause believers in carnal wisdom to rally around God's servant and not Christ (1 Co 3:1-4). They would create hard feelings toward a sinning brother, or differences of opinion as to his treatment (2 Co 2:5-11). Resentment or lack of full forgiveness may stem from their work.

2. *Countering the gospel ministry.* Demons seek to *hide the gospel message* from lost sinners. So they blind their minds (2 Co 4:3-4) and pervert the gospel (vv. 13-15).

They seek to *hinder the gospel minister* from performing his responsibilities (1 Th 2:17-18). As a result, they sometimes promote misunderstanding (vv. 2-16). Their influence extends to controlling the attitude of local and national governments so as to resist the gospel ministry (2 Co 4:3). The title "worldrulers" may suggest this (Eph 6:12). Note a similar connection in 1 Corinthians 2:7-8. Believers are to pray for deliverance from such powers so that the message and ministry may spread rapidly and God be glorified (2 Th 3:1-2).

3. *Causing persecution.* Christ warned the church in Smyrna of satanic persecution that would imprison some of them and cause tribulation and possibly death (Rev 2:8-10). Demons would be involved in this. They often promote persecution from religious sources, such as "a synagogue of Satan" (v. 9). Some may think that in opposing true believers they are doing God a service (Jn 16:1-3). In the last great apostate ecumeni-

cal religion, demons will move men to persecute and kill true believers (Rev 18:2, 24).

V. OVERRULED BY GOD

Despite the intensions of Satan and his demons, their activity is often overruled by God to the accomplishing of His glory and our good.

A. IN DISCIPLINING THE BELIEVER

In this action, God is not doing evil that good may come. Rather, He is allowing responsible moral persons, though evil, to work their desires; and yet His sovereignty so limits and controls them and their effects that His good purposes are accomplished despite them.

1. Correcting defection. Hymenaeus and Alexander were "delivered over to Satan, so that they may be taught not to blaspheme" (1 Ti 1:19-20, NASB). The incestuous Corinthian was delivered "to Satan for the destruction of his flesh, that his spirit may be saved in the day of the Lord Jesus" (1 Co 5:5, NASB, cf. vv. 1-5).

2. Creating discernment. Job had to learn of the greatness and goodness of God through suffering induced by Satan. He did not understand that God works in the believer's life by grace and that suffering is not always recompense for evil. He learned that trusting God through all trials was true wisdom (Job 40:1-3; 42:1-6). He also later learned of the great invisible battle between God and Satan and his armies, in which Job was the prime human contributor to God's glory.

3. Cultivating dependence. Paul prayed that his "thorn in the flesh," "a messenger from Satan," might be removed (2 Co 12:7). Receiving adequate answer in three attempts, he submitted to God's purpose. It was to prevent his boasting of privilege and to cultivate further dependence upon God's strength instead of relying upon his own (vv. 9-10).

B. IN DEFEATING THE UNGODLY

In pouring out His punishment on Egypt, God seems to have

used demons. Psalm 78:49 says He sent "a band of destroying angels" ("Lit., *A deputation of angels of evil,*" NASB margin).

God led wicked Ahab to death through the mouth of a lying prophet energized by a lying spirit (1 Ki 22:20-23, 37-38). However, God warned Ahab of the lying prophet through a true prophet (vv. 24-28).

Demons will lead rebellious armies of men against God in the war of Har-Magedon (Armageddon), where great slaughter awaits them (Rev 16:13-16).

C. In Displaying God's Righteousness

God's righteous Son demonstrated His power over all wicked forces as He cast out demons Himself and through His disciples (Lk 10:17-19). He is the strong man who overpowers Satan and his forces (Mt 12:28-29). His teaching was backed by His authoritative miracles when demons obeyed Him (Mk 1:27).

God's righteous judgment will be displayed in the final defeat of Satan and demons when they are consigned to the lake of fire prepared for them (Mt 25:41; Rev 20:10). The cross of Christ and the lake of fire vindicate God's permitting their existence and activity. Through their punishment, God will demonstrate the futility of evil, its exceeding wretchedness, and its ultimate defeat.

Summary

Demons' activities range widely. Basically they promote Satan's program of the lie, extending his power and promoting his philosophy. As does Satan, they oppose God and His program by promoting rebellion, positing slander, promoting idolatry, rejecting grace, and fostering false religions and cults. In their wickedness and cruelty they oppress mankind, distressing through natural phenomena, degrading man's nature, distracting from truth, afflicting the body, causing mental problems, driving men to injury, destroying life, and dominating through possession.

They oppose believers by waging spiritual warfare on all

fronts. They seek defeat of individuals through attacking confidence, tempting to sin, and inflicting maladies. They seek the defeat of the Church through creating divisions, counteracting the gospel ministry, and causing persecution. In all these activities, God's sovereignty and grace overrules, using them to discipline the believer, defeating the ungodly, and displaying God's righteousness.

20

DOMINATION BY DEMONS

THE REALITY of demon possession is clearly stated and described in the New Testament. The synoptic gospels and the preaching of the apostles recorded in the book of Acts make Christ's casting out of demons from the possessed an evidence of His deity and Messiahship (Mt 12:22-23, 28-29; Ac 2:22; 10:38). The apostles and evangelists substantiated the truth of the Gospel by miracles, which included casting out demons (Ac 5:16; 8:7; 16:16-18; 19:12). The enlightened Christian should doubt neither the historicity nor the present possibility of demon possession.

I. THE CHARACTER OF DEMON POSSESSON

We must define the term from an analysis of biblical evidence.

A. CONTROL OF THE PERSON BY A DEMON

1. Suggested definition. "Demon possession is a condition in which one or more evil spirits or demons inhabit the body of a human being and can take complete control of their victim at will."[1] This seems to fit the biblical data.

2. Scriptural designations. "Demon possessed" is a translation that gives the sense of a participle *daimonizomenos,* used twelve times in the Greek New Testament. The verb, *daimonizomai,* means "to be demon possessed" or simply "to be demonized,"* and is found in Matthew 15:22.

Other expressions describing the same phenomenon are "a man with an unclean spirit" (Mk 1:23), "a dumb [mute] spirit"

*See pp. 152-53.

(Mk 9:17), "many who had unclean spirits" (Ac 8:7, NASB), "a spirit of divination" (Ac 16:16). In the context of these and many other cases, the spirit or demon was "cast out" or "came out" of the person possessed.

3. Saviour's delineation. Christ's own words vividly describe the case of demon possession. When they brought to Him "a demon-possessed man who was blind and dumb" (Mt 12:22, NASB), He healed him so that he spoke and saw. He described the healing as casting out demons (vv. 27-28), and on this type of miracle He built His claim to be Messiah (v. 28).

Christ further describes the phenomenon and attendant activity (vv. 43-45): "When the unclean spirit goes out of a man ... Then it says, 'I will return to my house from which I came'; and when it comes, it finds it unoccupied. . . . Then it goes, and takes along with it seven other spirits more wicked than itself, and they go in and live there" (NASB). Note that He regards the demon as residing in the man as its home, a place where it lives by choice. Note also that more than one demon may possess a man.

B. CHANGE OF PERSONALITY IN THE POSSESSED

Demon influence in its many manifestations may be mild or severe.† It may vary from mild harassment to severe subjection. However, says Unger, "Demon influence, even in its most severe forms, does not manifest the same abject domination by evil spirits that so saliently characterizes actual possession. There is no blacking out of consciousness, no demonized state, no usurpation of the body as a mere tool of the inhabiting demon, no speaking with another voice and the projection of another personality through the victim."[2]

Demon possession is not merely a word for schizophrenic illness, for that is merely one person projecting a different aspect of his own mind. But in possession the personality of the demon eclipses the personality of the possessed and the demon displays his personality through the means of the victim's body. Note the case of the demoniac of the Gerasenes, where one

†See chap. 19.

voice spoke for the many demons, "My name is Legion: for we are many. . . . Send us into the swine, that we may enter into them" (Mk 5:9, 12).

C. CULPABILITY OF PERSONS POSSESSED

1. Cause for possession. Causes for initiating the condition vary and are often complex. Probably "in the great majority of cases possession is doubtless to be traced to yielding voluntarily to temptation and to sin, initially weakening the human will, so that it is rendered susceptible to complete or partial eclipse and subjugation by the possessing spirit."[3] In other cases, moral responsibility may be less, as in the case of the boy who suffered possession from childhood (Mk 9:21). It may be in such cases that the occult sins of the parents back to the third or fourth generation preceding have rendered children susceptible. The second commandment, forbidding idolatry, warns that God will recompense this iniquity of the fathers on the third and fourth generations of those who hate Him (Ex 20:4-5). Demons are the dynamic behind idolatry,‡ and they may be allowed to lay claim to their devotees.

2. Continuation of possession. Moral responsibility for continuing in the state of possession and for acts committed while in that state stands as a clouded issue. When the demons control the victim, the possessed person is not capable of controlling his mental and moral actions. At that time, the victim is not responsible. When the demons are not actually controlling and the person has charge of his faculties, he may be responsible for seeking help. However, in some cases, blackouts of consciousness during attacks may prevent the person from realizing his plight and seeking help. It is difficult to determine whether thoughts or actions are due to the victim or the demon. In any case, an analyst should not lay unnecessary guilt upon the sufferer.

II. CHARACTERISTICS OF DEMON POSSESSION

What are the marks of demon possession? "The chief char-

‡See pp. 171-72.

acteristic of demon possession . . . is the automatic projection of a new personality in the victim."[4] This we treated above. In addition, certain marks give substantial evidence.

A. MARKS SUGGESTED BY SCRIPTURE

Koch analyzes the story of the Gadarene (Gerasene) demoniac in Mark 5. He suggests eight distinct symptoms of possession:

1. Indwelling of an unclean spirit (v. 2). This is the cause of the symptoms. It means he was possessed.

2. Unusual physical strength (v. 3).

3. Paroxysms or fits of rage (v. 4). He broke chains and fetters.

4. Disintegration or splitting of the personality (vv. 6-7). The demoniac ran to Jesus for help, yet cried out in fear.

5. Resistance to spiritual things (v. 7). He asked Jesus to leave him alone.

6. Hyperaesthesia or excessive sensibility, such as clairvoyant powers (v. 7). He knew immediately, without former contact, the true identity of Jesus.

7. Alteration of voice (v. 9). A legion of demons spoke through his vocal facilities.

8. Occult transference (v. 13). The demons left the man and entered into the swine.[5]

The last four characteristics fail as psychiatric illnesses. "For example clairvoyance itself is never a sign of mental illness, and a mental patient will never be able to speak in a voice or a language he has previously not learned. Yet this is exactly what has happened and still does happen in some cases of possession."[6]

Strictly speaking, transference cannot be classified as a characteristic of the possessed. It is a result of the casting out of demons. At that time they may turn their attention to other objects.

B. MARKS SUGGESTED BY COUNSELORS

Counselors of the possessed note several symptoms not unlike the list above. The agreement of many counselors stands as significant.

Unger lists several: projection of a new personality, supernatural knowledge (including ability to speak in unlearned languages), supernatural physical strength, moral depravity; in addition there may be deep melancholy or seeming idiocy, ecstatic or extremely malevolent or ferocious behavior, spells of unconsciousness, and foaming at the mouth.[7] (Note some of these in Lk 9:39, 42.)

From his counseling, Koch lists these: resistance to prayer or Bible reading, falling into a trance during prayer, reaction to the name of Jesus, exhibition of clairvoyant abilities, and speaking in unlearned languages. He warns those who put so much stress on speaking in tongues that Satan has his counterfeits.[8]

Lechler lists the following: passion for lying and impure thoughts, restlessness and depression and fear, compulsion to rebel against God or blaspheme, violence and cursing, excessive sexual or sensual cravings, resistance and hatred of spiritual things, inability to pronounce or write the name of Jesus, appearance of mediumistic or clairvoyant abilities, inability to act on Christian counsel, resistance to a Christian counselor, inability to renounce the works of the devil, seizures or spells of unconsciousness, speaking in unlearned languages, extraordinary physical strength, molestation with pain unrelated to illnesses or injuries. He advises that some of these marks may stem from mere subjection or affliction rather than actual possession, since their marks have much in common.[9]

From the above symptoms listed by counselors of present-day demon-possessed persons, we can see the similarities to biblical examples.

III. Continuation of Demon Possession

The biblical phenomenon of demon possession continued through the days of the early Church, was cited at various points in Church history, and continues today in many regions.

A. IN THE DAYS OF CHRIST

During Christ's public ministry there broke out an unusual display of demonism. The synoptic gospels recount many stories of Christ delivering men, women, and children from possession by unclean spirits. The Gospel of Mark, for instance, frequently shows His power as the Servant of God over these evil forces (1:23-27, 32-34, 39; 3:11-12; 5:1-20; 7:25-30; 9:17-29, 38). Christ also delegated power over demons to the twelve (Mt 10:1; Mk 3:14-15) and to the seventy (Lk 10:1, 17).

B. IN THE DAYS OF THE APOSTLES AND EARLY CHURCH

Cases of demon possession and expulsion continued through the apostles and evangelists in the narrative of Acts (5:16; 8:7; 16:16-18; 19:13-19). Casting out demons in Jesus' name became a sign of apostolic authority and of the genuineness of the Gospel they preached.

C. IN THE ANNALS OF CHURCH HISTORY

References to demon possession can be found in some of the early Church Fathers and writings. "The Shepherd of Hermas" treats demon possession. Justin Martyr and Tertullian show acquaintance with the phenomenon.[10] Oesterreich believes that much of so-called demon possession can be explained in terms of psychology and sociology, something like a social hysterical neurosis, yet his work testifies to genuine examples of demon possession with examples taken from all ages and many countries.[11] His findings support the fact that the symptoms of possession follow from Christ's time to the present.

D. IN THE PRESENT DAY

Nevius, missionary to China in the last half of the nineteenth century, was forced to recognize the reality of demon possession in modern pagan China. The cases he presents bear many parallels with what we have seen of demon possession in the New Testament.[12] Unger cites several sources documenting the continuance of demon possession at the present time.[13] He claims that it manifests itself more noticeably where Christianity has not so much penetrated and affected society.

Koch, a leading authority on demonism and the occult, presents many cases of demon possession from his cases of counseling for over more than forty years in Germany and all parts of the world.[14] Lechler agrees that demons may possess men today, but cautions against too readily accepting that diagnosis in particular cases.[15] He warns that we must distinguish between the demonic and disease, as does the New Testament.[16]

IV. CONSIDERATION OF POSSESSION OF CHRISTIANS

Can a genuine Christian be demon possessed? Good men differ on this question—sometimes very emotionally. We must consider the biblical and clinical evidence.

A. BIBLICAL CONSIDERATIONS

The biblical evidence is not conclusive. There is no direct statement on the matter, and interpretations of relevant data vary. There seem to be two main considerations.

1. Personal indwelling of the Holy Spirit. Unger previously said, "To demon possession, only unbelievers are exposed."[17] In this he argued from the assumption that an evil spirit could not indwell the redeemed body together with the Holy Spirit. Later, on the basis of the claims of many missionaries all over the world, he modified his opinion to allow that in certain cases a true believer may become possessed or repossessed, particularly in idolatrous cultures.[18]

How shall we evaluate the argument against possession from the indwelling of the Spirit? It is true that every genuine Christian is indwelt with the Spirit (Ro 8:9; 1 Co 6:19-20). But to say that His presence excludes the presence of any evil within the believer is to forget that the sin nature, entrenchantly evil, remains in the believer (Ro 7:15-24) and the Spirit's presence is required to control it (Gal 5:16-17). If one argues that the sin nature has been judged (Ro 6:6), he must remember that Satan and demons were also judged by the same instrument, the cross of Christ (Jn 12:31; Col 2:15). Victory over the influence of the sin nature results not from the mere presence of the Spirit, but from His *control* in filling (Ro 8:4; Gal 5:16-17; Eph 5:18). This involves a willful *yielding* on the believer's part (Ro 6:11-14; Gal 5:16, 25).

Some modify the argument to say that there is not room for both the Spirit and a demon, appealing to spatial limitation. Spatial considerations do not affect the matter. The omnipresent Spirit can in His total person indwell each believer despite our limited bodies. Furthermore, a legion of demons may dwell in one person (Mk 5:9). Space would not crowd out the possibility of the Holy Spirit and a demon residing in the same body.

2. *Personal identity with Christ.* Some argue that one who is "in Christ" eternally and unforfeitably and who is Christ's own possession cannot fall to demon possession. We agree that genuine children of God stand forever secure in their salvation. They will without a single failure arrive in glory (Ro 5:1-10; Eph 1:4, 13-14; 4:30). No demonic force, no creature is able to separate such a one from the love of God and the life of the Saviour (Ro 8:38-39). To this end the Saviour prayed and was heard (Jn 17:15, 24). However, the question is, Can demons temporarily inhabit and control the believer?

If sin can control and dominate the believer's practice so as to cause carnality, defection, and chastisement unto death (1 Co 3:1-4; 5:1-5; 1 Ti 1:19-20), then position in Christ does not guarantee spiritual living. Again it is a matter of the control to whom the believer yields—to sin or to the Saviour (Ro 6:16). It is possible for a weak or ignorant believer to trifle in the occult or to return to pagan practices associated with Satan.

The arguments from the Spirit's presence or the Saviour's property do not shut out the possibility of a genuine believer being possessed.

B. EXPERIENTIAL CONSIDERATIONS

We do not base doctrine on experience. For this, Scripture is sufficient (2 Ti 3:16-17). But where Scripture is not decisive, we may gain insight from experience, keeping aware of possibilities of misinformation, lack of information, and misinterpretation of evidence.

With this in mind, we yet recognize that evidence from mission fields and clinical counseling seem to say that a genuine Christian may under unusual circumstances become possessed or repossessed. Koch cites several examples, including the case of a missionary who was himself possessed and changed his concept on the matter. He also cites the opinions of Dr. Edman, the late chancellor of Wheaton College, and of Dr. Evans of Wales that Christians might be possessed.[19] Koch is inclined to agree that it is possible, but suggests points of consideration: (1) perhaps the person was not a genuine believer, (2) perhaps obsession or influence is confused with possession, (3) possibly God allows temporary possession for chastisement regarding a stubborn sin. Further, he holds that believers are only temporarily possessed, whereas unbelievers can remain possessed.[20]

Koch suggests an example of what type of unusual circumstances must pertain for a Christian to be possessed. In the Philippines, a boy had been a Christian for about one year. As Dr. Koch prayed with him, "a rough voice called out of him, 'He belongs to us. His whole family has belonged to us for more than 300 years. . . . His ancestors have subscribed themselves to us. He is ours by right.' The conversation revealed that the ancestors of this unhappy student had not only practised sorcery, but some of them had even subscribed themselves to the devil with their own blood. This was the reason why, in spite of his conversion, the student had become possessed."[21]

The popular author Hal Lindsey holds that a Christian rarely has the same degree of complete subjugation as a nonbeliever. He adds, "However, I've talked to many missionaries who have had to deal with these things personally, and I must say that it seems to be possible for a Christian to have a certain degree of demon possession."[22] He refers also to an example of demon possession of an unquestionable believer. Dick Hillis of Overseas Crusades reported that a Chinese man, an elder in the church, became so possessed that his personality changed, his language became vile, his strength greatly increased, and he spoke in a strange voice with which Hillis conversed as with a demon.[23]

From my own study and interviews with those who have carefully and biblically treated the demon possessed, I must conclude that under the unusual circumstances a genuine Christian may become possessed at least to some degree, even to the point where they speak with strange voices or in foreign languages.

However, we must make it clear that no Christian who is walking in fellowship with God and obeying God's Word can become demon possessed. We have no fear of this, for if we walk in the Holy Spirit's control, neither the flesh nor demons can possess us or control us. Where Christians have been possessed, they have been involved in occult or demonic things. If a person was possessed before conversion, and the demons linger on to claim the person, then renunciation of the devil and all his works, specific confession of known sins, and commitment to Christ as Lord can solve the problem. If such occurs after conversion, it is the result of persistence in rebellious and wicked works, such as pursuing occult practices or continuing in gross and vile lusts. Possession does not usually come in just one moment, but results from a course of pursuing sin and not responding to God's clear warnings through the Word, Christian counselors, or the Holy Spirit working in the conscience.

In any case, a Christian does not need to continue under demon influence or control. He can be helped, and he can help himself by turning from sin to Christ. Never does he become separated from God's family or the love in Christ, not even by his own life or demonic forces (Jn 17:15, 24; Ro 8:38-39).

A word of warning is due here. Some Christian counselors see demon influence or possession as the cause or possible cause behind every sin or sickness, physical or mental. They actively seek out "demons" in Christians, pursuing their "deliverance ministry." Remember, first, that the Bible distinguishes between the demonic and disease. Second, Satan would have us to overestimate his power and activity and to become occupied with his power and influence, thus causing fear and imbalance in our thinking. Third, sensitive souls cannot handle the uncertainty and fear created by such overemphasis. Fourth, Satan would love to divide churches over this issue, and overemphasis and radicalism contribute to this. Fifth, Satan would encourage pride in those who cast out demons. Jesus said not to rejoice in our power over demons, but in our relationship to Him (Lk 10:20). This relationship should be our joy and the main emphasis of our preaching. We must preach the whole Word in balanced fashion (Ac 20:20, 27; 2 Ti 4:1-2).

V. CONQUEST OF DEMON POSSESSION

There is a cure for demon possession. No one, especially a Christian, need remain in that condition. There is help in Christ and in Christian counselors.

A. CONQUEST BY CHRIST

1. In His career. Christ released those possessed by casting out the demons in His own power, a public display of His authority over the spirit world (Mt 8:16, 32; 9:33; and particularly Mt 12:28; Mk 1:27). The cure was instantaneous and lasting (Mk 5:15).

2. In His commission. Christ gave to His disciples authority over demons (Mt 10:1; Mk 3:14-15). When the seventy returned with reports that even the demons were subject to them in Christ's name, the Lord connected this to the defeat of Satan, the enemy (Lk 10:17-20).

3. In His cross. Christ judged Satan and demonic forces in the judgment of the cross (Jn 12:31-33; 16:11). His death for man's sin delivered men who were once bondslaves to Satan and his demons (Heb 2:14-15). By the cross, Christ disarmed or stripped them of their spoil, making a public display of them (Col 2:14-15). The resurrected Saviour stands exalted over them (1 Pe 3:22), and they are subject to His name (Phil 2:9-11).

Christ stands victor over Satan and demons and is the deliverer of those who trust Him. Only by coming to Christ are men freed.

B. CONQUEST BY CHRISTIANS

Christ promised that the authorities of the unseen world would not be able to resist those who follow Him (Mt 16:18). Christians who are qualified may help others find release from demon powers.

1. By Christ's power. Just as the Lord granted power to His own to cast out demons in His day on earth, so today genuine followers may do the same (Mt 10:1). The apostles and their followers cast out demons in their day (Ac 5:16; 16:16-18), and Paul states that Christians have all they need to wage warfare against Satan (Eph 6:10-18). Though we have no resources of our own, we have all we need in Christ by virtue of our union with Him (Col 2:9-15).§ It should be carefully noted that casting out of demons is not a spiritual gift nor the peculiar ability of a few Spirit-filled believers."[24] We need not live in terror of Satan or demonic power as if Christ had not defeated them and as if they were not subject to Him and to us as we abide in Him. Where there is need for deliverance, the Church of Christ Jesus the Lord must appropriate His promise and do His works (Mt 16:18).

2. By biblical principles. First there must be *diagnosis*. Not every suspected case is in reality demon possession. Extreme caution must be used here, because the suggestion of demon power can further complicate the plight of one mentally or emotionally disturbed . But, "if it becomes transparently clear that the demonic is present, then the person concerned must be told quite definitely, but in love, that Satan has bound him to himself. . . . Any resulting shock will only have a wholesome effect in the end. The patient must be made to realize who the enemy of his soul really is."[25] This seems to agree with the biblical example of Peter dealing with Simon, the magician, who con-

§Some Bible students appeal to Mk 16:15-20 for support in casting out demons and in supernatural signs. However, the textual evidence of some better Greek manuscripts makes these verses of doubtful support, since they may have never been part of the inspired originals.

tinued under some satanic delusion (Ac 8:9-24). It also fits Paul's treatment of the slave girl in Philippi (Ac 16:16-18). The Christian should pray for similar discernment.

Following proper diagnosis, there is *deliverance*. The believer must be armed with prayer, not just at the moment, but as a habit of life. However, there usually must be specific prayer. Jesus prescribed prayer for deliverance (Mk 9:29). Lack of prayer may exhibit lack of faith (Mt 17:18-20). The prayer may best be corporate to enter into the special promise of Christ about two or more agreeing in prayer (Mt 18:19-20).

Many times deliverance demands a *direct command* to the demon resident in the possessed. The Lord Jesus and the apostle Paul both spoke to demons directly (Mt 8:32; Mk 5:8; Ac 16:18). They commanded them to depart, and the demons had to obey the authority of Christ. It might be necessary to order the demon to name himself or to discover if there are more than one present (Mk 5:9). In all of this there must be a firm stand in the power of Christ (Eph 6:10-12).

C. QUALIFICATIONS FOR THE COUNSELOR

Though exorcism is not a special spiritual gift, nevertheless there are certain qualifications that are preferable if not necessary.

1. Spiritual. The counselor must be born of the Spirit by trusting Christ, having the assurance of his right standing before God (Jn 1:12-13; 1 Jn 5:4-5 ,18). He must have dedicated his life to God so that he does not participate in Satan's sin of independence (Ro 12:1-2). Only in this way can he resist the devil (Ja 4:6-8). He must allow the Holy Spirit of God to control his life (Gal 5:16-18, 25; Eph 5:18). Only in this way can he know God's power operating in his life to live for Christ and to help others.

2. Scriptural. The counselor must know God's Word. He must know what it says about the enemy, Satan and the demons, their power and methods (2 Co 2:11; 11:14). He must know God's armor and how to use it (Eph 6:10-18). He must know of Christ's victory over Satan and be convinced of his position of power in Christ (Col 2:15). He should be acquainted with the biblical accounts of Christ and the apostles in their dealings with demons.

3. Special. If possible, the counselor should have some medical qualifications and psychiatric training. Correct diagnosis is highly important and distinction between disease and demonic must be made. A mature Christian with experience in dealing with the demonic is preferred. There are definite symptoms of demon possession, but discernment is essential. The wise counselor will seek advice and confer with other counselors for the oppressed when in doubt.

SUMMARY

The Bible certifies demon possession as a reality, not just superstitious misconception.[26] The Scriptures' terms, the Saviour's own description, the testimony of the apostles and Christian workers support this. Possession is marked by a drastic change of personality and certain other well-defined characteristics—a demonic syndrome, obvious in Scripture and in case studies today.

Christians disagree on whether believers can be possessed, and biblical evidence is inconclusive. Certain case studies seem to indicate that they can, under unusual circumstances, become or remain possessed after conversion. But there is a sure cure found in the deliverance that only Christ gives. Those in fellowship with Christ should not fear becoming possessed. The New Testament dispels the fear of demons from Christians while keeping them aware of the reality and power of demons.||

Christ defeated Satan through His death and resurrection, and He grants to believers power and wisdom to continue His work of destroying the works of the devil (Ro 16:20; 1 Jn 3:8; Rev 12:11).

||"The healing of the demon-possessed is an essential part of the record in the Synopt. and Acts. The crucial thing is that demons are expelled by a word of command issued in the power of God and not by the invocation of a superior but essentially similar spirit, nor by the use of material media. . . . The NT view of demons is consistently opposed to the Gk. divinisation of the demonic. It also dispels the constant fear of evil spirits. Yet it confirms the popular sense of something horrible and sinister in such spirits, bringing out the demonic nature of their activity as an attack on the spiritual and physical life of man in fulfillment of the will of Satan" (*Theological Dictionary of the New Testament,* 2:19).

21

DISTRACTIONS BY DEMONS— THE OCCULT

WITHOUT DOUBT, one of the outstanding marks of this age is a great and increasing attraction to the occult practices. We do not aim in this chapter to treat the subject thoroughly, describing the details and answering point by point from the Bible. Instead we would give general definitions and characteristics, point out the source and effects of occultism, and set forth a plan of deliverance for those in bondage.

I. DEFINITION OF THE OCCULT

A. DESIGNATION

The term *occult* derives from the Latin *occultus,* a form of the verb *occulere,* to cover up, hide. It means hidden, secret, dark, mysterious, concealed. It is used to describe phenomena which transcend or seem to transcend man's senses or realm of natural experience. It is applied to the occult arts or sciences.

B. DESCRIPTION

Occultism as a part of folklore has been practiced for thousands of years. Two main features have remained the same throughout its history: the practices and the principles.[1]

Scholars divide the occult into three main categories: divination, magic, and spiritism.

1. Divination. From Latin, *divinare,* to foresee, divination refers to foretelling the future, or fortune telling. It includes two divisions: (1) artificial or augural divination, interpreting signs or omens under indirect demonic control, and (2) inspirational divination, using a demon-controlled medium to forecast what he sees.[2]

In its various forms, divination includes astrology, rod and pendulum, palmistry, card laying, psychometry, dreams and visions, Ouija boards, crystal balls, and water dowsing.[3]

Astrology is an ancient art or pseudoscience which claims to foretell events on earth by interpretation of the relative positions of the sun, moon, planets, and constellations. It claims to predict human character and fate. Actually, it "invites the intervention of demons because it originated in star worship and seeks secret knowledge in opposition to God's will and God's Word."[4] Scripture specifically forbids such and prescribes the death penalty for one guilty of such evil (Deu 17:1-7; Is 47:13-14; Jer 10:2).

Cartomancy is the art of forecasting by the laying of cards whose faces and relationships have certain meanings. Tarot cards would fall in this category. Seeress Jeane Dixon sometimes uses a deck of cards and a crystal ball which she received from a gypsy.[5] The same condemnation applies to this as to astrology.

Palmistry seeks to tell the future through interpreting the lines, elevations, and depressions in a person's palm. It is somewhat related to astrology.

The *divining rod and pendulum* are used on location or on a chart or map to locate unseen objects, such as deposits of oil or water. They may also be used to diagnose illness in the human body.

Psychometry is a type of clairvoyance that can identify something about a person through some object he wore or used. The clairvoyant claims he can detect such things as character or location by sensing impressions emanating from the person.

Dreams and visions, though used in biblical times (note Gen 28:12-15; Is 6:1-11; Dan 7-12, Zec 1-6), are part of the occult experience. Prognostication in any form is highly suspect.

The Bible prohibits divination in any form. Fortune tellers were to be put to death in Israel. God warned, "For thus says the LORD of hosts, the God of Israel, 'Do not let your prophets who are in your midst and your diviners deceive you, and do not listen to the dreams which they dream. For they prophesy falsely to you in My name' " (Jer 29:8-9, NASB). "Any one who used 'divination' or was 'an observer of times, or an enchanter, or a witch (fortune-teller), or a (magic) charmer, or a consulter with familiar spirits (a medium), or a wizard (clairvoyant), or a necromancer (one who communicated with the spirit-world)' was outlawed from the community of the Lord's people (Deut. 18:10, 11)."[6] The Bible sees divination as open to demon influence and producing spiritual degradation. So the Bible consistently condemns it (Lev 19:31; 20:6, 27; Is 44:24-25; Eze 21:21; Ho 4:12; Amos 5:25-26; Zec 10:2; Ac 7:41-43; 16:16-18; Gal 5:20).

2. *Magic.* This refers to the ancient "art of sorcery and magic mentioned in the Bible, the actual cult of demons performed in collaboration with the powers of darkness."[7] Magic seeks accomplishment of results beyond human power by recourse to superhuman spirit agencies, such as Satan and demons.[8] Divination taps secret knowledge, whereas magic taps secret power.

Magic may be impersonal or personal. Impersonal magic seeks superstitiously to control natural law or events by such means as incantations, spells, amulets, and charms, apart from demonic intervention. Personal magic calls upon real personal agents in the spirit world to accomplish the supernatural effect desired.[9] Whether black, white, or neutral magic, it is demonic in character.

Magic includes the healing and inflicting of diseases, love and hate magic, curses, fertility charms, persecution and defense magic, banning and loosing, and death magic.[10]

The Bible recognizes the reality of magic and attributes it to satanic and demonic forces. Pharoah's magicians performed supernatural feats (2 Ti 3:8) in opposing Moses' miracles (Ex 7-11). Their power was limited by God, however. The magicians of Daniel's day had obvious occult powers (Dan 1:20; 2:2, 27; 4:7), but Daniel's God-given wisdom surpassed them (Dan 1:20; 4:9; 5:11). Jesus acknowledged that miraculous works might be done by those whom He never knew as His own (Mt 7:22-23). The Antichrist who precedes Christ's coming will do lying miracles (2 Th 2:9) and so will his religious supporter (Rev 13:11-15). In fact, many may have the ability to show great signs and wonders (Mt 24:24). All magic of supernatural origin is anti-Christ and demonic, even the practices that call on the name of Christ and the Trinity.

3. Spiritism. Some are persuaded that certain mediums can make contact with the spirits of deceased humans. From this they receive comfort and revelation. It results in pride, deception, and bondage to occult powers.

Consulting with those who had familiar spirits or with wizards was banned in Israel (Lev 19:31; Deu 18:10-11). Corrupt religions about them practiced such things, but Israel would commit apostasy in turning to them. Severe penalties were attached to guilty persons (Lev 20:6, 27). King Saul, even though he had put away familiar spirits and wizards from the land (1 Sa 28:3, 9), sought to contact Samuel through the witch of Endor. For this sin, along with other rebellion, he died (1 Ch 10:13-14). The Bible elsewhere condemns this sin (2 Ki 21:6; 23:24; 2 Ch 33:6; Is 8:19).

The unusual case of Samuel returning to speak judgment to Saul stands as God's exposé of spiritism as a fraud and as a sign of His "unequivocal condemnation of all traffic in occultism and His sure punishment of all who break his divinely ordained laws in having recourse to it."[11] We may explain the incident of Samuel's appearance as the intervention of God allowing Samuel to appear to pronounce judgment on Saul. The medium was terrified in surprise when Samuel actually appeared, not in body, but in spirit representation by God's special power and permission. The rebuke to Saul and his death as predicted by Samuel were evidences of God's intervention.[12]

At this point it is impractical to define or treat in detail all the phenomena associated with spiritism. Unger's summary will suffice.

> Spiritistic phenomena may be conveniently divided into the following categories: 1. *physical phenomena* (levitations, ap-

ports, and telekinesis); 2. *psychic phenomena* (spiritistic visions, automatic writing, speaking in a trance, materializations, table lifting, tumbler moving, excursions of the psyche); 3. *metaphysical phenomena* (apparitions, ghosts); 4. *magic phenomena* (magic persecution, magic defense); 5. *cultic phenomena* (spiritistic cults, spiritism among Christians).[13]

The dynamic behind these phenomena is demonic. Demons with their great power and intelligence accomplish many sense-defying effects. Behind the supposed communication with the dead are deceiving spirits who through the mediums under their control impersonate the dead. Through their large number and pooling of their great intelligence they may supply much information, even detailed personal matters; for they have long been observers of the human scene.[14]

Spiritism and biblical Christianity are diametrically opposed. One is error and darkness; the other, truth and light. Christians who attend seances or experiment with spiritism expose themselves to demonic oppression and become disinterested or opposed to God's Word and work . Christians should recognize that departed spirits do not rise and praise God (Ps 88:10, NASB). Jesus said the Scriptures are to be trusted and would not allow the dead to return, for there is a great gulf fixed that precludes the dead returning (Lk 16:22-31, particularly vv. 26, 29, 31).

II. DISPLAY OF THE OCCULT

A. ITS POPULARITY

The occult has enjoyed a history of popularity among pagans for centuries. But recently a boom of interest has descended on us. The new witchcraft, the romanticizing of Satan, the rise of astrology to new heights in the use of the computer, the television and movies in their programming, all witness to the rise of occultism.[15] Unbelievers have little discernment, if any; and Christians are often caught up in deception by Satan due to their ignorance. The "age of Aquarius" has struck with force.

B. Its Promotion

Why the popularity? Why do several million West Germans subscribe to some form of the occult? Why do some reports estimate as many as two hundred thousand witches in the USA?

There are several reasons: (1) man's sense of personal inadequacy—he needs outside help in this complex and confusing world; (2) the impersonalization of society that treats man as a number on a list to be used and discarded; (3) the inadequacy of science to contribute to the real meaning and purpose of life with personal dimensions; (4) the bankruptcy of religion that has no answer, no absolutes, no dynamic. So men have turned to the mystical to peer into the depths of their personality in self-contemplation. They have taken the "leap upstairs" to fill the God-dimension with the supernatural and the occult. The craze for the occult may be analyzed as a retreat to nature or the rise of a counterreligion. Man wants not to be isolated from meaning and power, but to be at one with the universe about him, tapping its sources for the meaning and power he needs for self-assertion and gratification.

III. Derivation of the Occult

A. Pagan

Occultism is not new. Archaeological discoveries from Sumeria and Babylon, the earliest of civilizations, display the occult practices of that day. Egyptian, Chaldean, Greek, and Roman antiquity are rich in demonic phenomena. The great ethnic religions of India, China, and Japan, as well as the animism of Africa, South America, and many islands abound with occultism and demonism. History pictures demon-controlled religions clashing with the Hebrew faith and later with Christianity. Degenerating from monotheism, men took to idolatry and attendant occult practices (Ro 1:21-32). By Abraham's time, men had sunk to crass polytheism influenced by evil spirits.[16]

B. Satanic

The original source of all false religions is Satan. He sought to replace God (Is 14:12-17; Eze 28:12-20).* He is a liar from the beginning and is the father of lies (Jn 8:44). He and his demon-angels actively promote occultism, promoting interest in the supernatural and providing its dynamic that enslaves men (1 Ti 4:1-2; 1 Jn 4:1-4; Rev 13:11-18).

Satan promoted occult type interest in Adam and Eve, tempting them with knowledge and power beyond what God had provided and revealed (Gen 3:1-5). He cast doubt on God's Word, denied God's Word, questioned God's goodness and restrictions, and promoted looking into forbidden things. When man succumbed to Satan, he was immediately brought into the bondage of sin and darkness (Gen 3:6-7). Man was estranged from God and cursed because of rebellion (Gen 3:8-19).

Today Satan's lie system promotes Satan in place of God (Is 14:14). His demons would replace God's angels (Rev 12:7). He rules over a kingdom of men and angels (Eph 2:1-2; 6:10-12). Satan preaches a message of "deliverance" through false prophets (1 Jn 4:1-4). His workers perform lying miracles (Ex 7:11; 2 Th 2:9). They speak in tongues, heal, and predict the future. Antichrist would replace Christ, and Satan receives worship directed to him (2 Th 2:3-10). Satan's counterfeit system is at work.[17]

Not all occultism is genuinely satanic. Human greed and self-seeking account for much of it. Perhaps as much as ninety percent of all fortune telling is faked by frauds and swindlers.[18] Yet Satan stands ready to pounce upon his victims who exhibit interest in the occult, for it is his domain. A Christian neurologist once said that sixty percent of the inmates of his psychiatric clinic were not so much suffering from mental illness as from occult subjection or even demonization.[19]

IV. DOMINATION BY THE OCCULT

The forms of bondage introduced by following the occult vary in extent and effect. Slavery must follow sin (Jn 8:34; Ro 6:16).

*See chap. 13.

A. EXTENT

Occult oppression can be divided into four stages: (1) simple subjection, which can often pass unnoticed by the subject; (2) demonization, which affects a person unknowingly; (3) obsession, in which the subject is almost continually harassed by demons; and (4) actual demon possession by an indwelling demon or demons.[20]

B. EFFECT

There are sinister results from practicing the occult, whether in seriousness or in fun. (1) Christian faith and growth is prevented; some find it difficult to trust Christ. (2) Subjects change in character, becoming ill-tempered, moody, hard-hearted, extreme. (3) Mental and emotional disturbances such as depressions, neuroses, oppression, suicidal thoughts occur. (4) Tendencies toward mental or emotional illness are frequent. (5) Mediumistic abilities opposed to the Holy Spirit develop.[21]

We must not assume that the first four effects are immediately to be identified as stemming from demonic influences. They may be purely natural illnesses or human faults.[22] Koch says that there are four basic categories of depression, for instance, only one of which stems from the occult.[23]

God speaks clearly to the judgment and continuing effects of trafficking in the occult, particularly idolatry (its basic root and form) in the Second Commandment (Ex 20:4-6).

C. CAUSE

How are men brought under domination by the occult? Bondage may result from any of three sources.

1. Inheritance. Bondage or mediumistic abilities are not genetically transferred. Certain natural weaknesses of disposition may contribute toward a person's seeking the occult, but the bondage is not inborn. However, if the parents back to the third or fourth generation were involved in the occult or had mediumistic abilities, subjection to demonic influence may result as a judgment from God, according to the Second Commandment, as He visits the iniquity of the fathers upon the third and fourth generations. The connection of demons to the idolatry forbidden in the commandment makes this a likely cause of much occult bondage.

2. *Experimentation.* Personal dabbling with occult practices, such as experimenting with rod and pendulum, water dowsing, Ouija board, magic spells, card laying, may lead to becoming mediumistic. Submitting to occult healings may also lead to bondage or oppression. This type of activity provides an open avenue for demonic powers to influence and invade the life of the one who rebels against the clear command of God to avoid occultism. God warns even believers, lest we provoke the Lord to jealousy in sharing with demons and He chasten us. As wise men, we are to flee idolatry (1 Co 10:14-22).

3. *Transference.* Close contact with a person with occult or mediumistic powers may transfer those powers to the other person. The laying on of hands, the holding of hands, or the treatment by a mediumistic person of a seeker or a patient may be enough to bring him into bondage and delusion. The so-called gift of tongues or the gift of healing may be transferred by occult means. Supernatural abilities and personal joy may result, but so do deception, bondage, and psychological disturbance. It is a tragedy when a Christian who has acquired mediumistic abilities through one of these three means assumes that they are gifts of the Holy Spirit. Satan is the great counterfeiter (2 Co 11:13-15).[24]

V. Deliverance from the Occult

Since the occult deals with error and darkness, the remedy to its oppression and bondage lies in the truth and light in Christ. Whether human ignorance and superstition or actual demonic influence and power, relief from slavery comes from the person of God's Son and through the principles of God's Scriptures.

A. Responsibility of the Church

The Church of Christ has weapons of warfare that are divinely powerful for the destruction of fortresses (2 Co 10:3-5). She has the whole armor of God for defense against evil powers (Eph 6:10-20). She possesses the promise of her Head that the authorities of the unseen world will not prevail against her (Mt 16:18). She must, then, actively oppose Satan and the occult.

1. To expose the demonic. Christians must not dismiss the demonic as superstition, but recognize the reality and activity of Satan and his hosts in opposing God, the Church, and the Gospel. Pastors must preach the whole counsel of God in face of apostasy (2 Ti 4:1-4). They must point out the error of the occult as a doctrine of demons if they would be good servants of Christ (1 Ti 4:1-6). Christians are not to participate in the unfruitful deeds of darkness, nor remain neutral, but rather expose them (Eph 5:11, NASB). Furthermore, the Church must preach Christ as the Deliverer from darkness and bondage to Satan (Lk 4:18-19; Col 2:15; Heb 2:14-15) and exhort and warn men to turn to Him in faith and submission (Jn 16:7-11).

2. To exercise the ministry. The Church is, through the authority of Christ, an instrument of deliverance to turn men from darkness to light and from the power of Satan to the Kingdom of Christ (Ac 26:18).

We are to *test the spirits* and their teaching, whether they are of God (1 Jn 4:1-3). The basis for testing is God's Word (Is 8:20). Christians should pray for discernment in recognizing error and in applying scriptural truth.

We are to *teach the saints* in the full-orbed life of the Spirit in Christ so that they may know fulfillment and satisfaction and not seek after illegitimate spiritual experiences. Teaching involves warning against error and rebellion in the occult, and it involves positive answers in doctrine and in a method of deliverance.

We are to *train the specialists* who can exercise their spiritual gifts of pastoring and teaching in counseling those oppressed by Satan and the occult. Freeing men from occult bondage and delivering from demon possession are not special spiritual gifts, but trained persons acquainted with scriptural principles and psychological practices may be more effective. Here we need mature and balanced men.

We are to *treat the slaves* in occultism. We cannot shun them, but we must minister to them in Christian love and spiritual power. We must let the oppressed go free. There is no place for fear or unbelieving hesitation. We must—with intelligent caution, loving consideration, and genuine dedication to God— fulfill our calling. Our personnel and our program must be adjusted to include ministering to this ever-increasing malady in our society.

B. Responsibility of the Chained

What must the person occultly oppressed do to receive deliverance?

Koch and Unger agree basically in the elements necessary for experiencing deliverance from demonic oppression.[25] They essentially include the following:

1. Receiving Christ. This must be the first step, because only in Christ is there the position and power for deliverance. There can be no cooperation with God against the evil forces unless there is a new capacity to cooperate through the new birth. This new position and new capacity comes from God when a person trusts Christ to save him from sin's guilt and power (Jn 3:3-7; Eph 1:18-21; Col 1:13; 2:15; 1 Jn 5:4-5, 18).

2. Confessing sins. Any personal involvement in the occult practices must be judged as rebellion against God and as a wretched sin of siding with Satan (1 Co 11:31; 1 Jn 1:9). The sinfulness of family involvement, even back to great grandparents, must be confessed (Ex 20:3-5). This is siding with God against Satan.

3. Renouncing the devil and his works. An official repudiation of Satan and his claims on the oppressed may be necessary, especially if there was a pact or agreement made with the devil. This may involve a command to Satan and the demons that they depart. This must be done in Christ's name and in dependence upon His power, just as did Christ and the apostles

(Mt 8:16, 32; Ac 16:16-18). Renunciation at the time of baptism seemed to be a practice in the early Church when many were involved in the occult. Satan may claim the right to continue his influence in a life once voluntarily given to him unless there is specific separation and command.

4. *Removing occult objects and connections.* For this step we have the biblical example of godly kings destroying idols and their groves of worship (2 Ch 14:2-5; 23:16-17). Converts to Christ among those who practiced magic destroyed their occult books and idol makers were losing business in Ephesus (Ac 19:17-20). Many objects of idolatrous worship or books of magic carry with them a secret ban or curse invoked in demonic power. The possession of such objects is an invitation for demonic powers to concentrate their efforts on the owners of the objects. Refusal to destroy them becomes a willful rebellion against God and opens the door for Satan's influence.[26]

Mediumistic contacts and friendships should also be broken. One cannot continue to have fellowship with those who traffic with demons and expect to have fellowship with Christ and know His deliverance (1 Co 10:20-22; 2 Co 6:14-18; Eph 5:11).

5. *Resting in Christ and resisting the devil.* Christ promises forgiveness and deliverance to those who trust Him and call upon His name for deliverance in the occult. Confidence in our position and authority in Christ and in Christ's own concern and victory is essential. We must rest in His victory and His forgiveness (Col 1:13; 2:9-15; Heb 2:14-18). We are to take our stand against the devil in the will and power of God, and he will flee from us (1 Pe 5:8-9; Ja 4:7).

6. *Submitting to Christ and cultivating spiritual life.* The mercies of Christ's deliverance from sin's condemnation and control encourage us to yield our total life to Him and follow His will in total (Ro 12:1-2). Submission to God is a prerequisite to victory over the devil (Ja 4:6-7). The new life in the Spirit demands a new walk in the Spirit (Gal 5:25).

In our new life there are provisions for continued victory.

Through the *baptizing work* of the Spirit in His placing us into Christ upon faith in Christ, we are separated from the control of evil within and without (Ro 6:1-10). Knowing this, we are to continually reckon ourselves dead to sin and Satan and alive to God (Ro 6:11). We must also present our lives and members to God for His control (Ro 6:12-14).

The *filling work of* the Spirit controls us and causes us to live pleasingly to Christ, reflecting His character (Eph 5:18-33). We are filled when we meet the conditions. (1) "Quench not the Spirit" (1 Th 5:19). This means we do not resist His control and leading, but yield and follow. (2) "Grieve not the Holy Spirit" (Eph 4:30). Unconfessed sin against God or men grieves the Holy Spirit in us. Confession and rededication relieves this condition (1 John 1:9). (3) "Walk in the Spirit" (Gal 5:16, 25). We are to depend upon His power to give us victory over sin and to follow His direction in all aspects of our lives.

The Holy Spirit cultivates the new life in Christ within us by several provisions of grace. First, the Word of God causes growth and provides defense against the devil (Mt 4:4, 7, 10; 1 Pe 2:1-2; 5:9). Second, prayer affords communication with God and accomplishes His purposes as we ask and receive. In this we must not forget the privilege of praise and thanks to God that results in honoring Him as He deserves and in strengthening us in devotion and assurance (Ps 91:14-16; Jn 4:23-24; 15:7, 16). Third, Christian fellowship and sharing in worship, praise, prayer, breaking of bread, and the exercise of spiritual gifts in mutual edification provides corporate encouragement and growth with stability (Ac 2:42; 1 Co 12:12-27; Eph 4:11-16; Heb 10:23-25). Fourth, sharing the gospel with the unsaved will not only stimulate one's faith and study of the Word, but will be an active war against Satan who would keep men in the bondage of sin. Unselfish dedication to the work of Christ will contribute to Satan's defeat (Rev 12:11). Fifth, we must put on the whole armor of God described in Ephesians 6:10-18. Some of the pieces have been mentioned in the above provisions. With these great defenses and the offensive weapons of the Word of God and prayer, we will be able to resist Satan and all his armies in the power of God and to take his strongholds (2 Co 10:3-4; Eph 6:10-11).

SUMMARY

The occult is Satan's realm. When men seek secret power and knowledge through supernatural means, they open the door for demonic influence and control. Divination, magic, and spiritism are its three main divisions. The Bible clearly condemns any occult art or practice. It is a form of idolatry and apostasy. The extent of bondage it incurs varies, but the effect is always damaging to spiritual life, because it is anti-Christ. Men may enter its bondage by family involvement, personal experimentation, or transference. Deliverance is solely and surely found in Christ and His power and His provisions.

22

DEFEAT AND DESTINY OF SATAN
AND DEMONS

THOUGH THEY ARE FORMIDABLE and cunning, Christ has defeated Satan and his hosts; and their doom is certain.

I. THEIR DEFEAT

The Lord Jesus, the Creator and Sovereign, will judge all creatures, including evil angels (Jn 5:22). He defeated Satan and his demons during His career by invading Satan's territory and casting out demons from those possessed (Mt 12:28-29). He anticipated the final defeat of Satan when His disciples returned with reports of demons being subject to them through Christ's power (Mt 10:1, 17-20). But the cause of their defeat obviously centers in the death of the God-man. Why is this the case?

A. THE CROSS REALIZED THE PURPOSE OF GOD

God's great purpose is to glorify Himself. This is only right and necessary. God's grace and love are magnified in the gift of His Son as a sacrifice for human sin. Christ became human to offer Himself as a representative and substitutionary sacrifice for sin (Gal 4:4-5; Heb 2:9-10; 10:4-7). All along the line, Satan opposed God's purpose in His program of self-glorification and salvation of sinners. But the cross finished the work for which Christ was sent (Jn 6:38; 12:23-27; 17:4-5; 19:30). In the accomplishment of the death of the Son of God, Satan was defeated. Perhaps this is what Jesus meant when in referring to His coming death He said, "Now the ruler of this world shall be cast out" (Jn 12:31, NASB). Satan had desired to ascend to heaven and to be like God. Now by the cross he is cast out and his purpose defeated.

B. THE CROSS RELEASED THE PRISONERS OF SATAN

"The Son of God appeared for this purpose, that He might destroy the works of the devil" (1 Jn 3:8, NASB). Satan's work was to involve man in sin so as to captivate him in sin (Jn 8:34, 41, 44; Eph 2:1-3; 1 Jn 3:10). Christ came to release Satan's prisoners (Lk 4:18-19). By His death Christ paid the price a righteous God required for releasing men from sin and Satan and so broke Satan's power that operates in the realm of death (Heb 2:14). He delivers those who trust Him from the fear of death and from slavery (Heb 2:15). By His incarnation and death as genuine man, the God-man led those once captive to Satan now captive to Himself (Eph 4:8-10), translated them from the dominion of darkness to the kingdom of light in God's Son (Ac 26:18; Col 1:13), and will one day lead them to glory as the Captain of our salvation (Heb 2:10).

C. THE CROSS ROUTED THE POWERS OF EVIL

Colossians warns against legalism and mysticism in which there was a worship of angels (Col 2:8, 16-23). The error probably was incipient gnosticism. Paul reminds believers that they are complete in Christ who is completely God as well as man (Col 2:9-10). He is the Head of all angelic rule and authority. He not only delivered believers from spiritual death and condemnation from the law (Col 2:11-14), but He "disarmed the rulers and authorities" (Col 2:15, NASB). This probably refers to a judgment that disarms the enemy of position and power. The cross of Christ disarmed the flesh's control of the body (Ro 6:1-10; Col 2:11-12). The cross also disarmed demonic control of the believer in Christ. When Christ had stripped evil forces of their power, "He made a public display of them, having triumphed over them" (Col 2:15, NASB). Not only does the cross cancel man's debt to God, but through it the powers that held men captive are themselves openly defeated and led in His triumphal march. Christ thoroughly routed and publicly embarrassed Satan and demons so that men would never have to fear or follow them again.

D. THE CROSS RATIFIED THE PUNISHMENT OF SATAN

Through His death and resurrection, Christ sealed the final judgment of Satan and demons. The cross reveals God's hatred and judgment of all sin. The just One had to die if the unjust ones were to be forgiven (1 Pe 3:18). He became legally identified with sin that we might be legally identified with God's righteousness (2 Co 5:21). If God did not spare His own Son, but delivered Him up for sinners, not only will He preserve those who own His Son, but He must judge those who disavow His Son (Jn 3:36; 5:22-23; Ro 1:18; 3:25; 8:32, 38-39). The cross, then, was a judgment of all sin and therefore a judgment on the originator of sin, Satan, and all among men or angels who follow him. There will be a final judgment of Satan and his kingdom, the world of sinners, because judgment was passed on him at the cross (Jn 16:11), He is a condemned criminal awaiting final judgment. The resurrected and exalted God-man will be the judge of Satan and his angels (Jn 5:22; Eph 1:21-22; Phil 2:10-11; Col 2:10; 1 Pe 3:18-19, 22).

II. THEIR DESTINY

The future course of activity and the final condemnation of demons have much in common with the outcome of Satan. Yet at certain points there are some distinctions.

A. THEIR CAREER

1. Expanding activity in the Church age. The Spirit of God has warned of increasing activity of deceitful spirits promoting doctrines of demons (1 Ti 4:1-3). The lifestyle found in the last days reflects demonic influence (2 Ti 3:1-9). False teachers of religion, empowered by Satan and demons, will continue to creep in and entrench themselves in the church (2 Pe 2:1-3; 1 Jn 4:1-3; Jude 4). They will twist the character of God

(2 Ti 3:3-4; Jude 4), deny the deity and redemption of Christ (2 Pe 2:1), and scoff at the second coming of Christ (2 Pe 3:3-4). Present-day apostasy will grow worse (2 Ti 3:13), and interest in the occult will escalate (1 Ti 4:1).

2. *Empowering Antichrist in the Tribulation.* Satan seems himself to energize the man of lawlessness (2 Th 2:8-9). Deception shall run wild when the restraining influence of the Holy Spirit is removed (2 Th 2:6-7, 9-10). Miraculous acts will cause awe and respect so that many will follow this world leader who is a proud rebel against God (2 Th 2:9; Rev 13:4-6, 11-15). Just as Satan, Antichrist will promise men much, but will bring them into bondage (Rev 13:7, 16-17). The outward manifestation of satanic and demonic power will reach a high point during the reign of Antichrist.

3. *Engaging angels and saints in warfare.* Satan and his demons will persecute the saints and cause many to die (Rev 13:7). Special persecution will come to the remnant of Israel (Rev 12:3-6). At this time, Michael, the archangel, will lead God's holy angels into a great battle with Satan and his angels (Dan 12:1; Rev 12:7). Satan and his angels will then be cast out of heaven and down to earth (Rev 12:8-9). Yet in rebellious madness they will continue opposing God and the saints (Rev 12:12-13).

4. *Enduring arrest during the Millennium.* When Christ returns, He will defeat Antichrist and his followers, casting them into the lake of fire (Rev 19:11-15, 19-21). Then Christ will bind Satan for one thousand years, eliminating his activity from the world scene. Having wrested the kingdoms of this world from Satan's power, the true King of kings and Lord of lords will reign on earth, the scene of conflict between God and Satan (Rev 19:16; 20:4). It would seem that not only Satan but all his angels will be cast into the abyss for this Kingdom age. It is unthinkable that Satan would be bound and his angels free, for the picture of the millennial Kingdom is one free from satanic influence (Is 24:21-23).

5. *Energizing anarchy after the Millennium.* Satan will be released after the thousand years (Rev 20:3, 7). Again be-

cause of his limitations as a creature and because of the magnitude of the worldwide work and the shortness of time it takes (Rev 20:3, 7-8), it seems that the demons bound in the abyss must be released to aid Satan in leading the final rebellion against God and Christ. (Is 24:21-23 supports the idea that demons are bound during the millennial Kingdom and are afterward released.) They promote anarchy and march all unregenerate men against Jerusalem. But fire from God destroys all human participants, and Satan himself is judged (Rev 20:9-10).

B. THEIR CONFINEMENT

1. Temporary confinement. Some demons are now confined in *the abyss* (Gr., *abyssos*). This seems to be a place of torment to which Christ sent some of the demons which He cast out of men (Lk 8:28-31). At least some of these demons are released for a short period during the Great Tribulation (Rev 9:1-11).

Some demons are bound in the *River Euphrates.* Four demons will be allowed upon their release to kill a third of mankind. They are probably leaders of a great army of free demons who aid them in the great slaughter (Rev 9:14-19).

Certain demons are bound in *tartarus* (2 Pe 2:4). We understand this to be a different place than the abyss, since these sinner angels are "kept in eternal bonds under darkness for the judgment of the great day" (Jude 6, NASB). On the other hand, these angels who were involved in such a peculiar type sin may have a special place of solitary confinement within the abyss. These are not released but are cast from tartarus into the final judgment.

2. Permanent confinement. Satan and his rebellious angels will come to their final judgment when they are cast into *the lake of fire* (Rev 20:10). This is the place for which he was destined after his fall, and the demons following him must follow him there (Mt 25:41). From this point on, there is never again the possibility of release for either Satan or demons. Just as with men, the smoke of their torment ascends throughout eternal ages (Mt 25:46; Rev 12:10; 14:9-11).

SUMMARY

Satan and the demons are no match for Christ, the God-man. In face of satanic opposition, the cross accomplished God's self-glorification, released the devil's prisoners, publicly routed evil spirits, and sealed their judgment. Though judged, Satan and his angels are actively promoting apostasy and occultism. Their increasing activity will reach a high point during the Tribulation, when God's restraining is removed so that the human Antichrist may become a world ruler and demons will, under Satan, persecute and kill men and battle with God's angels. Righteousness will characterize the Kingdom when Satan and demons are bound, but upon their release they find rebels ready to join them in one final rebellion against God. Some demons are bound now in the abyss, some in the River Euphrates, and some in tartarus, but all will be bound forever in the lake of fire.

23

DEFENSE OF BELIEVERS AGAINST SATAN AND DEMONS

WE MUST FACE the facts as they are. Satan is real. Demons are real. Our battle is real. We can expect their evil influences to increase in the world and in the Church. What defense does the Christian have, and what direction should he take? Three words, properly understood, summarize our responsibility: recall, resist, rely.

I. RECALL

We must keep certain facts in mind to govern our attitude in the battle if we are to be victorious.

A. POWER OF SATAN

1. He should be respected. There is a difference between fear that causes cringing and respect that calls for caution. Satan is never to be regarded lightly or contemptuously (Jude 8-9). He yet retains great dignity and power. Puny man is no match for him.

2. He sovereignly is restricted. Satan is a mere creature, and as such is limited by God in his power and activity. He can do only what God permits him to do as God carries him down to defeat (Job 1:12; 2:6; 1 Jn 4:4). He cannot touch our salvation, nor separate us from the love of God (Ro 8:38-39).

B. PRACTICE OF SATAN

We cannot remain ignorant of his devices. We should be aware of his schemes and purposes, just as soldiers must be

aware of the strategy of the enemy (2 Co 2:11; Eph 6:11).
He accuses, deceives, plants doubt, tempts to pride and fleshly
satisfaction, divides brethren, discourages, distracts—all this to
oppose God's purpose.*

C. PRINCE OF VICTORY

1. Christ purchased victory. He defeated and judged Satan
by His redemptive death and resurrection. Our Saviour is
exalted above all powers. They are subject to Him and to His
final judgment (1 Co 15:28; Eph 1:21-22; Col 2:15; 1 Pe
3:22). We are in His care, and He is our defense (Ro 8:31-
39).

2. Christ prays for victory. He prayed we might be kept from
the evil one (Jn 17:15). He prayed for Peter's faith and
service (Lk 22:31-32). Even so He intercedes for us and is our
defense against Satan (Heb 7:25; 1 Jn 2:1-2; compare Zec
3:1-2). The prayer of Christ is always answered (Jn 11:42).

D. POSITION OF VICTORY

Our position "in Christ" means we stand before God in
Christ's righteousness (Ro 8:1; Eph 1:6). We also share His
victory over the powers of evil (Col 2:9-10, 15). He leads us
in the train of His triumph (2 Co 2:14), and we are delivered
from the realm of Satan's dominion (Heb 2:14-15). We are
seated with Christ far above all principality and power (Eph 1:
21-22; 2:6). We operate against Satan out of a position of
victory.

E. PURPOSE OF GOD

1. God uses Satan. As with Job and Paul, God may use
Satan to accomplish His good purposes (Job 1-2; 2 Co 12:7-
10). Time spent in battle is not wasted when God is glorified,
the believer edified, and Satan defeated.

2. God keeps saints. His purpose is to see us through. He
keeps us through temptation (1 Co 10:13), delivers us from
evil (Mt 6:13; 2 Th 3:3), and sees us through to glory (Ro

*See chap. 15.

8:28-30, 38-39). Satan cannot thwart the purpose of the Almighty.

II. RESIST

Victory demands more than a recalling to fix our attitude; it calls for activity in resisting the powers of evil. We resist in the following ways.

A. IN ALLEGIANCE TO GOD

Victory demands submission to our Captain and obedience to His commands. We cannot love the world and God at the same time (Ja 4:4; 1 Jn 2:15). God resists those who side with Satan in pride (Ja 4:5-6). We are to humble ourselves and submit to God. Then we can resist the devil and he will flee from us (Ja 4:7). The sharp cracks of the commands in James 4:7-10 (Gr. aorists) say to take your stand with God and resist the devil. Our lives must be His.

B. IN ARMOR FROM GOD

We can stand against Satan and demons only in the armor provided by God. Each item mentioned by Paul in Ephesians 6:10-18 has its proper and necessary function. The whole armor (panoply) speaks of what we have in Christ as His provision for battle.† There are defensive garments, useful garments, and offensive weapons included. Our victorious Cap-

†Interpreters vary somewhat on the meaning of each piece of equipment. The major question is perhaps this: do certain pieces represent Christian position or practice? In all discussion we must remember they are perfect protection that enables a successful stand against Satan and demons. Their source is God, but they must be "put on," or used. For instance, the "breastplate of righteousness" is taken by some to mean practical righteousness in our living. It is better taken, I believe, to mean God's gift of right standing in Christ. The meaning of Old Testament sources for these expressions seems to favor this (Is 54:14-17; 59:16-20). Further, our practical righteousness depends upon our obedience to God's standards for Christian living. This is far from perfect and, indeed, the very object of Satan's attack through accusation. Our answer is that we stand in Christ's own righteousness, not our own, and that we are developing by God's grace in practical righteousness. (Zec 3:1-2 and Rev 12:11 also refer to our righteous standing in the blood of Christ.) Likewise, "truth" which is pictured as a belt about the waist provides readiness to answer "the lie" of Satan. We must know the truth as contained in God's Word and hang our offensive weapons on it. The useful sandals of "the gospel of peace" speaks of the readiness to share the peace with God with others—dedication to evangelism. The "shield of faith" speaks of a large sized defense against Satan's attempts to break up our composure and cooperative advance. "The helmet of salvation" may refer to the protective attitude that we

tain has supplied us with all we need to successfully resist and defeat the devil. We must appropriate ("put on") these provisions to attain victory in our lives.

C. IN ACTION OF GODLINESS

Some of the armor described above clearly involves action on our part. There are some positive things we must do and some things we must avoid doing. We can pray for deliverance from testings that are too much for us (Mt 6:13; 26:41). We can pray for protection of God's servants (2 Th 3:1-2) and for the advance of the gospel (Eph 6:18-19). We can be alert, watching in soberness (Mt 26:41; 1 Th 5:6-8; 1 Pe 5:8). We are to guard our attitudes and actions to avoid leaving an opening for Satan's fiery darts or temptations (1 Jn 5:18; Mt 16:23). Forgiving removes an occasion for Satan to cause division or discouragement among the brethren (2 Co 2:10-11). Putting away attitudes or actions of vengeance and doing good instead overcomes evil with good (Ro 12:17-21). We are to make no provision for the flesh (Ro 13:14). Anger must be controlled, lest bitterness develop and the devil take advantage of the opportunity (Eph 4:26-27).

In general, dedication to the cause of Christ, obedience to the commands of Christ, and cultivation of the life of Christ serves as a practical bulwark against Satan (Ja 4:4-8; 1 Pe 5:7-9).

III. RELY

Victory is found ultimately in relying upon God, trusting Him for our welfare and in our warfare. We can rely on these supports:

are on the winning side and final victory in the Lord who will return to bring us final deliverance (salvation) and to take vengeance on all His enemies, including Satan (2 Th 1:6-10; Rev 19:11—20:1-3, 7-10). The "sword of the Spirit, which is the word of God" is the basic offensive weapon. The Holy Spirit uses the word, for He is its author. The term here is not *logos,* as a reference to the whole Bible, but *hrēma,* which refers to the utterances or sayings of the Scripture. We are to use the particulars and principles of God's word to counter the enemy, fitting them to the occasion as our Lord did with Satan in His temptations (cf. Mt 4:1-11). Some include prayer as an offensive weapon, as it well might be. Communication with our Captain in specific requests will bring answers that defeat the enemy; and by it we are kept watchful and dependent upon the person and power of Christ.

A. THE POWER OF CHRIST

There is no higher authority or power. God has given Christ all authority in heaven and on earth (Mt 28:18; Eph 1:20-23; Phil 2:9-10). The Christian stands in the authority of Christ as His official representative (2 Co 5:20). With such backing, we have nothing to fear. In that name we can resist and command evil powers, and they must obey. And yet in all this we must not glory in delegated power, but in our relationship to the Saviour (Lk 10:17-20).

However, we ourselves must be subject to Christ's authority (Ro 12:1-2). We must first submit to God, then we can resist the devil in the authority of Christ (Ja 4:7).

B. THE PROVIDENCE OF GOD

God cares for the believer and guards him as the apple of His eye (Deu 32:10). We are not to be fearful of men or angels (Heb 13:5), nor of events in this life or even death itself (Ro 8:38-39; Rev 12:11). God is for us, and no one can prevail against us (Ro 8:31-32). He will provide all we or our loved ones need, and we are not to be overcome with anxiety (1 Pe 5:7-9; Phil 4:6). He is our refuge and will defeat our enemy (Deu 33:27).

God rules over all, controls all, and uses all for His glory and our good. With such a God who providentially controls all things and cares for us, we have nothing to fear.

C. THE PROMISE OF GOD

When we have done all to stand, we shall stand; for God is able to make us stand (Eph 6:10-11, 13). His promise is clear: "Submit to God. Resist the devil and he will flee from you" (Ja 4:7, NASB). When we have resisted him in the faith, standing firm in Christ, he must flee. It is the promise of God.

SUMMARY

If we are to have the victory that is rightfully and certainly ours in Christ, we must remember Satan's power and schemes.

We must recall that Christ is our Victor and that we are victors in Him. God may allow Satan some action, but He guards His own. We must resist the devil in allegiance to God, in the armor He provides, and in actions that leave no opportunity for his success. In the final analysis, we can and must rely upon God's authority, control, and promise of victory.

Appendix

DIFFICULTIES IN ANGELOLOGY

IT WOULD HARDLY be appropriate to present a study of angels without treating at least two prominent problems of interpretation. Though some mention may have been made in the main body of the study, yet these problems were not discussed because they did not bear significantly upon the main issues. We will treat these problems briefly at this point. Who are "the sons of God" (Gen 6), and who are "the spirits in prison" (1 Pe 3).

I. IDENTITY OF "THE SONS OF GOD"

A. THE CONCEPTS OF THEIR IDENTITY

The question is, Were "the sons of God" of Genesis 6:4 men or angels? They are pictured as cohabiting with "the daughters of men" and producing unusual offspring. One view holds that they were pious descendants of Seth and the women were ungodly descendants of Cain.

The second view holds that they were angels (usually understood as fallen) who took human forms temporarily and lived with women.

There is no easy solution. Either view has its problems, and good men are divided on the question.[1]

B. THE CONSIDERATIONS TOWARD THEIR IDENTITY

In support of their identification as men, there are several main considerations. (1) The idea of a union between angels and humans is unreasonable, abnormal, and grotesque, partaking of the mythological and magical. (2) Angels are sexless and do not marry (Mt 22:30). (3) The term "sons of God"

222

could easily refer to men, since it is used elsewhere of godly men (Deu 14:1; Is 43:6; Ho 1:10; 11:1). (4) The context preceding Genesis 6 contrasts the lines of godly Sethites and the ungodly Cainites (Gen 4:16-24 and 4:25—5:32).

Supporting the view that they are angelic beings, we suggest these considerations. (1) It is true that outside of Genesis 6 the exact term "the sons of God" (*bene elohim*) is used only of angels (Job 1:6; 2:1; 38:7). The references cited to support the other view do not use *bene elohim*. Angels are termed *elohim, bene elohim,* or *bene elim* because they belong to a class of mighty beings.* Most likely, then, the term should be understood as in other biblical usage as of angels.

(2) The context presents the cohabitation as unusual, probably one of the causes for the flood. (Probably 6:1-4 presents the angelic cause and 6:5-6 the human cause). So, then, unusual relationships might be involved. We do not know the total powers of fallen angels. Matthew 22:30 does not exclude such cohabitation, but its point is that angels do not procreate among themselves. Furthermore, angels have taken human form and performed other human functions, such as eating, walking, talking, and sitting. Some angels were mistaken for men and were sought for homosexual use by the men of Sodom (Gen 18:1—19:5).

(3) What justification would we have for confining "daughters of men" to ungodly women? The term could be a class designation for "womankind," in contradistinction to the class of sons of God or angelic beings. Further, it would seem strange to confine the supposed human marriages to those of godly men with ungodly women. Intermarriage between two strains of humanity would most likely include godly women with ungodly men (sons of men with daughters of God). But the text does limit the relationship.

(4) Why are the unusual and famous offsprings of this union designated *nephilim,* translated by the Greek Septuagint as *gigantes,* rendered "giants" in the King James Version? The basic idea of the Greek term, however, is not monstrous size,

*See pp. 59-60.

but "earth-born" (*gegenes*) and was used of Titans, who were partly of celestial and partly of terrestrial origin.[2] The Hebrew term *nephilim* means "fallen ones" and designates the unusual offspring of the unholy union. The same term is used in Numbers 13:33 of the sons of Anak in Canaan who seemed of great size, but the Genesis reference seems to be of monsters of mixed natures.[3]

(5) Without Genesis 6 referring to angelic beings, it is impossible to find the supposed well-known judgment of God upon angels who sinned peculiarly and are especially bound (2 Pe 2:4-5; Jude 6-7). Several factors must be noted here. First, their peculiar sin is compared in Peter and in Jude with sexual perversions as in Sodom and Gomorrah. Second, the time and sequence of mention connects this angelic sin closely with the flood. Third, if the sin were the original fall of angels with Satan, all evil angels, not just some, would be bound. Further, there would be no biblical explanation for Satan's angels now being loose (as demons), and Satan himself would be expected to be bound since the fall.

(6) The language of both 2 Peter and Jude seems to describe the very type of unusual sexual sin that would have been involved. In 2 Peter the author sets forth the sure destruction of false teachers whose chief characteristics involve a denial of Christ's redemption and right to rule and a devotedness to sensual satisfaction (2:1-3, 12-15, 18). As mentioned, it is significant that here as well as in Jude the angelic sin is compared with sex perversion, as in Sodom and Gomorrah.

The language in Jude is pointed. The phrase "since they in the same way as these indulged in gross immorality and went after strange flesh" (v. 7, NASB) should most likely be understood as a description of the angels' activity which is compared with Sodom and Gomorrah. The angelic sin would be "gross immorality" further defined as going after "strange flesh," understood as a flesh they did not have. These same angels are described in Jude 6: they "did not keep their own domain [*archēn*, place of assigned authority and activity], but abandoned their proper abode [*idiov oiketerion*, peculiar place of residence]" (NASB). Instead of remaining in their usual state and residence, they invaded a new state and residence to commit gross immorality with alien flesh. No other angelic sin or human sin can begin to be described in this amazing and unparalleled fashion.† Genesis 6 offers the only biblical solution when we take "the sons of God" as fallen angels or demons.

Those angels involved in the extraordinary sin were confined permanently in tartarus awaiting the great judgment of the lake of fire with Satan their leader (Mt 25:41; 2 Pe 2:4; Jude 6; Rev 20:10).

If we would postulate on the satanic purpose in such a crime, we might say that he designed to corrupt the line of the Redeemer (Gen 3:15) to keep Him from becoming truly human to represent us on the cross. If the whole race were to eventually become hybrid angelic-human, then Christ could not have become a genuine and complete representative. God's judgment in the flood punished human folly and destroyed the monstrous offspring of the ungodly union.

II. IDENTITY OF "THE SPIRITS IN PRISON"

Who are the spirits to whom Christ preached as mentioned in 1 Peter 3:19?

A. THE CONCEPTS OF THEIR IDENTITY

There are several leading views. Some hold that they are men, the lost of all ages, to whom Christ preached the gospel in a descent to hades, so that they might have a second chance to be saved.

A second view holds that they are the spirits of men of Noah's day (mentioned in context, v. 20) to whom Christ preached either in person or through the Holy Spirit. If in person, Christ preached as the preincarnate Logos (Jn 1:1-2) operating in the person of Noah.

---

†"We cannot . . . avoid the conclusion, that St. Jude . . . has drawn a comparison between the sin of Sodom, and the sin of the angels—in each case, a going after strange flesh. . . . The Sodomites resembled the angels, in that, like the latter, they departed from the appointed course of nature, and sought the gratification of lawless and unnatural desires" (John Fleming, *The Fallen Angels and the Heroes of Mythology* [Dublin: Hodges, Foster, & Figgis, 1879], pp. 175-76).

A third view believes that Christ, between His death and resurrection, while dead in the flesh but acting in His spiritual nature (Logos and human spirit united), went to the place of confined angels. There He announced judgment for them, which He had just accomplished and sealed at the cross.‡ Then He arose from the grave and was exalted over angels.

B. THE CONSIDERATIONS TOWARD THEIR IDENTITY

The first view, that they are the lost men of all ages, is usually supported by referring to 1 Peter 4:6. However, this verse does not specifically teach a second chance. It seems best to take it as referring to those who heard and believed the gospel while they were living but who were put to death for their faith. So, though they were judged according to men who opposed them, they live according to God who gave them real life. Furthermore, any attempt to allow men a second chance after death stands in direct contradiction to Hebrews 9:27 and John 8:24.

The second view above recognizes that the sinning ones to whom the preaching came lived in Noah's day, thus accounting for verse 20. It also finds support in 1 Peter 1:11, which presents a possible analogy of the Holy Spirit speaking through prophets to the ancients (see also Heb 1:1-2). However, our text seems to state that Christ Himself did the preaching, not the Holy Spirit. But the most serious objection to this view is that it interrupts a natural historical sequence of acts performed by Christ between death and resurrection by inserting a reference to one of Christ's preincarnate activities.

The third view above seems best supported. The spirits in prison are angels to whom Christ announced their judgment. We support this view for several reasons. (1) The term *spirits,* when used in the New Testament without further definition or modifying adjectives, refers to angels or demons. (2) Verse 18 is best understood as a contrast of the two elements of Christ. "Put to death in the flesh" refers to His human body. "Made alive in the spirit" refers to His spiritual essence (Logos

‡For Christ's judgment on demons, see chapter 22.

and human spirit united as the God-man). Both phrases lack the article in the Greek and stand as "in flesh" and "in spirit," and seem to refer to the kind of sphere in which the action took place. His flesh and His spirit are contrasted here in similar fashion as in Romans 1:3-4; 9:5.

(3) The expression "in which" or "in whom" in verse 19 may be taken as "in which state" (*en hō*). The sense could be either "in which spirit of his" or "in which state" as without His body but in spirit. (4) Peter would know of angels in prison, either in the abyss or in tartarus who would be awaiting judgment (2 Pe 2:4). (5) The verb "preached" is not "to preach the good news" (*euangelizō*), but "to announce or proclaim" (*kērussō*), a word that fits judgment better than redemption (see 1 Pe 1:25 where *euangelizō* is used).

(6) This view keeps the sequence of Christ's actions in order as the series of aorist tenses would prefer. The order of events is "put to death," "made alive in spirit," "went," "preached," and then the resurrection and exaltation to God's right hand is mentioned with "having gone into heaven." (7) Finally, angels seem to have been in view all through the context, because the outcome of the whole story is that "angels and authorities and powers" are now subjected to Him (1 Pe 3:22).[4]

In the context and purpose of Peter, it relates effectively that the order of events in God's purpose for the believer as well as for Christ is "the sufferings . . . and the glories to follow" (1 Pe 1:11, NASB). The point in 1 Peter 3:18-22 is that we are to follow Christ's example, for He suffered, the just One for the unjust ones, that He might bring us to God. In this He even suffered at the hands of Satan and demons as Satan bruised His heel in death. But that death caused the destruction of Satan in the bruising of his head (Gen 3:15). Now after the sufferings Christ is glorified as the divine-human redeemer, exalted over all angels.

NOTES

Introduction

1. Arthur Lyons, *The Second Coming: Satanism in America*, p. 13.
2. "The Occult: A Substitute Faith," *Time*, June 19, 1972, p. 62.
3. *The 1974 World Almanac*, p. 342.
4. See James A. Pike, *The Other Side;* and Merrill F. Unger, *The Mystery of Bishop Pike.*
5. Roger C. Palms, *The Christian and the Occult*, pp. 12-13.
6. "Boom Times on the Psychic Frontier," *Time*, March 4, 1974, pp. 65-72.
7. "The Occult: A Substitute Faith," p. 66.
8. John P. Newport, *Demons, Demons, Demons*, pp. 17-18.
9. "Boom Times on the Psychic Frontier," p. 69.
10. Palms, p. 15.
11. Ibid., pp. 9, 17.

Chapter Three

1. L. Berkhof, *Systematic Theology*, p. 145.
2. Charles Hodge, *Systematic Theology*, 1:638.
3. Ibid.

Chapter Four

1. Franz Delitzsch, *Biblical Commentary on the Psalms*, 1:154.
2. Ibid.
3. Ibid.

Chapter Five

1. A. B. Davidson, *The Theology of the Old Testament*, p. 293.
2. Ibid.
3. J. Barton Payne, *The Theology of the Older Testament*, p. 285.
4. Merrill F. Unger, *Biblical Demonology*, pp. 45-52.
5. Davidson, p. 293.
6. Payne, p. 285.
7. Ibid.
8. Unger, pp. 123, 133-39.
9. Ibid., p. 136.
10. Payne, p. 286.
11. Gustave Friedrich Oehler, *Theology of the Old Testament*, p. 258.
12. Payne, p. 286.
13. Oehler, p. 259.
14. Ibid.
15. Ibid, pp. 259-60.
16. Ibid., p. 260.
17. Oehler, p. 444.
18. Ibid.

19. Payne, p. 286.
20. Oehler, p. 446, referring to Hengstenberg.
21. Oehler, p. 446.
22. Ibid.
23. C. I. Scofield, *New Scofield Reference Bible,* p. 1356; and John F. Walvoord, *The Revelation of Jesus Christ,* pp. 105-7.
24. W. R. Newell, *The Book of Revelation,* pp. 373-74.
25. Charles Caldwell Ryrie, *Revelation,* pp. 60-61.
26. For a list of seven archangels and many fallen angels that men suppose exist, see Gustave Davidson, *A Dictionary of Angels,* particularly pp. 338-39, 352.

CHAPTER EIGHT

1. J. Barton Payne, *The Theology of the Older Testament,* p. 285.

CHAPTER TWELVE

1. Merrill C. Tenney, "Luke," in *Wycliffe Bible Commentary,* ed. Charles F. Pfeiffer and Everett F. Harrison (Chicago: Moody, 1968), p. 1048.
2. Charles F. Pfeiffer and Howard Vos, *Wycliffe Historical Geography of Bible Lands* (Chicago: Moody, 1967), p. 109.
3. Charles C. Ryrie, *Balancing the Christian Life,* pp. 123-24.

CHAPTER THIRTEEN

1. E. J. Young, "The Book of Isaiah," in *The New International Critical Commentary,* 1:440-41.
2. Ibid.
3. For an extended treatment, see J. Dwight Pentecost, *Your Adversary, the Devil;* and Lewis Sperry Chafer, *Systematic Theology,* 2:47-50.

CHAPTER SIXTEEN

1. Merrill F. Unger, *Demons in the World Today,* p. 10.
2. Merrill F. Unger, *Biblical Demonology,* p. 36.
3. Ibid., p. 59.
4. Ibid.
5. Ibid., p. 60.
6. Ibid., pp. 60-61.
7. Ibid., p. 61.
8. Ibid.
9. Ibid., pp. 55-57; and Gerhard Kittel and G. Friedrich, eds., *Theological Dictionary of the New Testament,* 2:2.
10. Unger, *Biblical Demonology,* p. 58.
11. A. T. Robertson, *Word Pictures in the New Testament,* 1:70.
12. Charles R. Smith, "The New Testament Doctrine of Demons," *Grace Journal,* Spring 1969, 10:28.
13. W. F. Arndt and F. W. Gingrich, *A Greek-English Lexicon of the New Testament,* p. 168.
14. Smith, p. 27.
15. Ibid.
16. *Theological Dictionary of the New Testament,* 2:16-19.

CHAPTER SEVENTEEN

1. Merrill F. Unger, *Demons in the World Today,* pp. 13-14.
2. *Theological Dictionary of the New Testament,* 2:6-7.
3. Kenneth S. Wuest, *First Peter in the Greek New Testament,* pp. 99-100.

4. Merrill F. Unger, *Biblical Demonology*, pp. 43-44.
5. John C. Whitcomb, Jr., *The Early Earth*, pp. 115-34.
6. Unger, *Demons in the World Today*, p. 14.
7. Charles R. Smith, "The New Testament Doctrine of Demons," *Grace Journal* 10 (Spring 1969):32.
8. Unger, *Demons in the World Today*, p. 14.
9. Ibid.
10. Unger, *Biblical Demonology*, pp. 44-45.
11. Lewis Sperry Chafer, *Satan*, p. 63.
12. Unger, *Demons in the World Today*, pp. 15-16.
13. For a list of scholars pro and con, see Unger, *Biblical Demonology*, pp. 46-47.
14. Smith, p. 33.

CHAPTER EIGHTEEN

1. Merrill F. Unger, *Biblical Demonology*, p. 67.
2. Ibid., p. 64.
3. Ibid. For extrabiblical evidence from case studies on the power of demons to manifest themselves or to cause apparitions, see Kurt E. Koch, *Christian Counseling and Occultism*, pp. 29-40, 137-53.
4. Merrill F. Unger, *Demons in the World Today*, pp. 38-41.

CHAPTER NINETEEN

1. Merrill F. Unger, *Biblical Demonology*, p. 30.
2. Merrill F. Unger, *Demons in the World Today*, p. 150.
3. Ibid., p. 152. For God's defeat of the gods of Egypt, see Donald Grey Barnhouse, *The Invisible War* (Grand Rapids: Zondervan, 1965), pp. 205-12; and C. Theodore Schwartz, *The Program of Satan* (Chicago: Good News, 1947), pp. 147-91.
4. Unger treats several major non-Christian religions and connects them with the distracting influence of demons in *Demons in the World Today*, pp. 152-57.
5. Ibid., pp. 168-73.
6. A psychiatrist distinguishes between the demonic and disease in Kurt Koch, *Occult Bondage and Deliverance*, pp. 133-98.
7. Ibid., pp. 166-78.
8. Unger, *Biblical Demonology*, p. 69.

CHAPTER TWENTY

1. Merrill F. Unger, *Demons in the World Today*, p. 102.
2. Ibid., p. 113.
3. Merrill F. Unger, *Biblical Demonology*, p. 95.
4. Unger, *Demons in the World Today*, p. 102.
5. Kurt Koch, *Occult Bondage and Deliverance*, pp. 57-59.
6. Ibid., p. 58.
7. Unger, *Demons in the World Today*, pp. 102-8.
8. Koch, pp. 64-67; see also Kurt Koch, *The Strife of Tongues*.
9. Cited in Koch, *Occult Bondage and Deliverance*, pp. 136-53.
10. F. C. Coneybeare, "Christian Demonology," *Jewish Quarterly Review*, pp. 600-1.
11. T. K. Oesterreich, *Possession, Demoniacal and Other, Among Primitive Races in Antiquity, the Middle Ages, and Modern Times*, pp. 199-235; see also Edward Langton, *Supernatural: The Doctrine of Spirits, Angels, and Demons from the Middle Ages to the Present Time*.
12. John L. Nevius, *Demon Possession and Allied Themes*, 5th ed., pp. 9-94.
13. Unger, *Biblical Demonology*, pp. 82-89; and *Demons in the World Today*, pp. 102-13.

14. Koch, *Occult Bondage and Deliverance*, pp. 57-67.
15. Ibid., pp. 149-53.
16. Ibid., pp. 153-98.
17. Unger, *Biblical Demonology*, p. 100.
18. Unger, *Demons in the World Today*, pp. 116-17.
19. Koch, *Occult Bondage and Deliverance*, pp. 67-71.
20. Ibid., p. 69.
21. Ibid., pp. 70-71.
22. Hal Lindsey, *Satan Is Alive and Well on Planet Earth*, pp. 159-60.
23. Ibid., p. 160.
24. Unger, *Demons in the World Today*, p. 189.
25. Koch, *Occult Bondage and Deliverance*, p. 189.
25. Koch, *Occult Bondage and Deliverance*, p. 189.
26. *Theological Dictionary of the New Testament*, 2:18-19.

CHAPTER TWENTY-ONE

1. Kurt Koch, *Occult Bondage and Deliverance*, p. 16.
2. Merrill F. Unger, *Demons in the World Today*, p. 56.
3. For a more detailed treatment, see ibid., pp. 56-72; and Koch, pp. 18-26.
4. Unger, p. 57.
5. Ruth Montgomery, *A Gift of Prophecy*, p. 26.
6. Unger, p. 71.
7. Koch, p. 21.
8. Unger, p. 76.
9. Ibid., p. 79.
10. Koch, p. 20.
11. Merrill F. Unger, *Biblical Demonology*, p. 148.
12. For detailed analysis, see ibid., pp. 148-52.
13. Unger, *Demons in the World Today*, p. 38. For more detail and description of the phenomena, see Kurt Koch, *Between Christ and Satan*, pp. 38-50.
14. See James M. Gray, *Satan and the Saint;* Raphael Gasson, *The Challenging Counterfeit;* and Victor H. Ernest, *I Talked with Spirits.*
15. For a summary of the popularity of occultism, see Unger, *Demons in the World Today*, pp. 17-18. For an extended treatment, see John P. Newport, *Demons, Demons, Demons;* and Roger C. Palms, *The Christian and the Occult.*
16. Unger, *Demons in the World Today*, p. 10.
17. Kurt Koch, *Christian Counseling and Occultism*, pp. 232-33.
18. Koch, *Occult Bondage and Deliverance*, p. 19.
19. Ibid., pp. 12-13.
20. Ibid., p. 32.
21. Koch, *Occult Bondage and Deliverance*, pp. 38-41; see also Unger, *Demons in the World Today*, pp. 177-87.
22. Koch, *Occult Bondage and Deliverance*, pp. 35-36.
23. Ibid., p. 37.
24. Ibid., pp. 39-40.
25. Ibid., pp. 88-128; and Unger, *Demons in the World Today*, pp. 192-203.
26. Koch, *Occult Bondage and Deliverance*, pp. 90-92.

APPENDIX

1. See Merrill F. Unger, *Biblical Demonology*, pp. 45-52 for a complete discussion of the problem. Pages 46-47 give a list of scholars on each side.
2. Ibid., p. 48.
3. Ibid., pp. 48-49.
4. For a concise and complete treatment of 1 Pe 3:18-21 identifying the "spirits" and treating Gen 6 as well (identifying "the sons of God"), see Kenneth S. Wuest, *First Peter in the Greek New Testament*, pp. 92-109.

BIBLIOGRAPHY

REFERENCE WORKS

Arndt, William F., and Gingrich, F. Wilbur. *Greek-English Lexicon of the New Testament.* Chicago: U. Press, 1952.

Davidson, Gustave. *A Dictionary of Angels.* New York: Macmillan, 1967.

Hastings Dictionary of the Bible. Vols. 1, 4. New York: Scribner's Sons, 1902.

International Standard Bible Encyclopedia. Grand Rapids. Eerdmans, 1939.

Interpreter's Dictionary of the Bible. New York: Abingdon, 1962.

Jewish Encyclopedia. New York: Funk & Wagnall, 1903.

Kittel, Gerhard, and Friedrich, G., eds. *Theological Dictionary of the New Testament.* Vols. 1 and 2. Trans. G. W. Bromiley. Grand Rapids: Eerdmans, n.d.

1974 World Almanac. New York: Newspaper Enterprise Assoc., 1974.

Pfeiffer, Charles F., and Vos, Howard F. *The Wycliffe Historical Geography of Bible Lands.* Chicago: Moody, 1967.

Robertson, A. T. *Word Pictures in the New Testament.* Nashville: Broadman, 1930.

Scofield, C. I. *New Scofield Reference Bible.* New York: Oxford U. Press, 1967.

THEOLOGIES

Bauer, Paul. *Christianity or Superstition.* London: Marshall, Morgan, Scott, 1966.

Barth, Karl. *Church Dogmatics.* Vol. 3. Edinburgh: T. & T. Clark, 1960.

Berkhof, L. *Systematic Theology.* Grand Rapids: Eerdmans, 1939.

Berkouwer, G. C. *The Triumph of Grace in the Theology of Karl Barth.* Grand Rapids: Eerdmans, 1956.

Brunner, Emil. "The Christian Doctrine of Creation and Redemption." In *Dogmatics,* vol. 2. Trans. Olive Wyon. London: Lutterworth, 1952.

Chafer, Lewis Sperry. *Systematic Theology.* Vol. 2. Dallas: Seminary Press, 1947.

Davidson, A. B. *The Theology of the Old Testament.* Edinburgh: T. & T. Clark, 1904.

Hengstenberg, E. W. *Christology of the Old Testament.* Grand Rapids: Kregel, 1970.

Hodge, Charles. *Systematic Theology.* Vols. 1-2. Grand Rapids: Eerdmans, n.d.

Oehler, Gustave Friedrich. *Theology of the Old Testament.* Grand Rapids: Zondervan, n.d.

Payne, J. Barton. *The Theology of the Older Testament.* Grand Rapids: Zondervan, 1962.

Ryrie, Charles Caldwell. *Biblical Theology of the New Testament.* Chicago: Moody, 1959.

Strong, Augustus. *Systematic Theology.* New York: Griffeth & Roland, 1908.

BIBLICAL STUDIES

Alexander, William Menzies. *Demonic Possession in the New Testament.* Edinburgh: T. & T. Clark, 1902.

Archer, Gleason L., Jr. *A Survey of Old Testament Introduction.* Rev. ed. Chicago: Moody, 1974.

Chafer, Lewis Sperry. *Satan.* Chicago: Moody, 1942.

Chambers, Art. *Man and the Spiritual World.* Philadelphia: George W. Jacobs, 1900.

Corte, Nicolas. *Who Is the Devil?* New York: Hawthorn, 1958.

DeHaan, Richard W. *Satan, Satanism, and Witchcraft.* Grand Rapids: Zondervan, 1972.

Delitzsch, Franz. *Biblical Commentary on the Prophecies of Isaiah.* Grand Rapids: Eerdmans, n.d.

————. *Biblical Commentary on the Psalms.* Grand Rapids: Eerdmans, n.d.

Froom, L. E. *Spiritualism Today.* Washington, D. C.: Review & Herald, 1963.

Fleming, John. *The Fallen Angels and the Heroes of Mythology.* Dublin: Hodges, Foster, & Figgis, 1879.

Gaebelein, A. C. *The Angels of God.* Our Hope, 1924.

Godet, Frederick Louis. *Studies of Creation and Life.* London: James Clarke, 1900.

Gray, George B. *The International Critical Commentary.* Edinburgh: T. & T. Clark, 1912.

Gray, James M. *Satan and the Saint.* New York: Revell, 1909.

Gromacki, Robert G. *The Modern Tongues Movement.* Philadelphia: Presbyterian & Reformed, 1967.

Jennings, F. C. *Satan.* New York: Gaebelein, n.d.

Jewett, Edward H. *Diabology.* New York: Whittaker, 1889.

Joppie, A. *The Ministry of Angels.* Grand Rapids: Baker, 1953.

Langton, Edward. *Good and Evil Spirits.* New York: Macmillan, 1942.

————. *The Angel Teaching of the New Testament.* London: James Clarke, n.d.

Latham, H. *A Service of Angels.* Cambridge: Deighton, Bell, 1894.

Lindsey, Hal, and Carlson, C. C. *Satan Is Alive and Well on Planet Earth.* Grand Rapids: Zondervan, 1972.

Matson, William A. *The Adversary.* New York: Ketcham, 1891.

Mayor, J. B. "The General Epistle of Jude," *The Expositor's Greek New Testament.* Grand Rapids: Eerdmans, n.d.

Morgan, G. Campbell. *The Teaching of Christ.* Old Tappan, N.J.: Revell, 1913.

Newell, W. R. *The Book of Revelation.* Chicago: Moody, 1935.

Nordmo, J. M. *Demons Despoiled.* London: Lutterworth, 1950.

Pache, Rene. *The Future Life.* Trans. H. I. Needham. Chicago: Moody, 1962.

Parsons, William. *Satan's Devices.* Boston: Parsons, 1864.

Pentecost, J. Dwight. *Your Adversary the Devil.* Grand Rapids: Zondervan, 1969.

Ryrie, Charles Caldwell. *Balancing the Christian Life.* Chicago: Moody, 1969.

————. *Revelation.* Chicago: Moody, 1968.

Schwarze, C. Theodore. *The Program of Satan.* Chicago: Good News, 1947.

Scott, Walter. *Existence of Evil Spirits Proved.* London: Jackson & Walford, 1853.

Tenney, Merrill C. "Luke," in *Wycliffe Bible Commentary*. Ed. Charles F. Pfeiffer and Everett F. Harrison. Chicago: Moody, 1962.

Theilicke, Helmut. *Man in God's World*. Trans. and ed. John W. Doberstein. New York: Harper & Row, 1963.

Unger, Merrill F. *Biblical Demonology*. Wheaton, Ill.: Scripture Press, 1957.

————. *Demons in the World Today*. Wheaton, Ill.: Tyndale, 1971.

Walvoord, John F. *The Revelation of Jesus Christ*. Chicago: Moody, 1966.

Whitcomb, John C., Jr. *The Early Earth*. Winona Lake, Ind.: BMH, 1972.

Wuest, Kenneth S. *First Peter in the Greek New Testament*. Grand Rapids: Eerdmans, 1942.

Young, E. J. "The Book of Isaiah," in *New International Critical Commentary*. Grand Rapids: Eerdmans, 1965.

Occult Studies and Counseling

Baldwin, Stanley. *Games Satan Plays*. Wheaton, Ill.: Scripture Press, 1971.

————. *Wizards that Peep and Mutter*. Westwood, N. J.: Revell, 1967.

Bayly, Joseph. *What About Horoscopes?* Elgin, Ill.: David C. Cook, 1970.

Bounds, Edward M. *Satan: His Personality, Power and Overthrow*. New York: Revell, 1922.

Bubeck, Mark. *The Adversary*. Chicago: Moody, 1975.

Demon Experiences, A Compilation. Wheaton, Ill.: Tyndale, 1972.

Dolphin, Lambert T., Jr. *Astrology, Occultism and the Drug Culture*. Westchester, Ill.: Good News, 1970.

Ernest, Victor H. *I Talked with Spirits*. Wheaton, Ill.: Tyndale, 1970.

Gasson, Raphael. *The Challenging Counterfeit*. Plainfield, N.J.: Logos, 1966.

Gerstner, John H. *The Theology of the Major Sects*. Grand Rapids: Baker, 1960.

Godwin, John. *Occult America*. Garden City, N.Y.: Doubleday, 1972.

Gray, James M. *Spiritism and the Fallen Angels.* New York: Revell, 1920.

Hammond, Frank, and Hammond, Ida Mae. *Pigs in the Parlor.* Kirkwood, Mo.: Impact, 1973.

Kluckhohn, Clyde. *Navaho Witchcraft.* Boston: Beacon, 1944.

Koch, Kurt E. *Between Christ and Satan.* Grand Rapids: Kregel, 1968.

————. *Christian Counseling and Occultism.* Grand Rapids: Kregel, 1965.

————. *Demonology, Past and Present.* Grand Rapids: Kregel, 1973.

————. *Occult Bondage and Deliverance.* Grand Rapids: Kregel, 1970.

————. *The Strife of Tongues.* Grand Rapids: Kregel, 1969.

Lang, Andrew. *The Making of Religion.* London: Longmans, Green, 1898.

Langton, Edward. *Essentials of Demonology.* London: Epworth, 1949.

————. *Supernatural: The Doctrine of Spirits, Angels, and Demons from the Middle Ages to the Present Time.* London: Rider, 1934.

Larkin, C. *The Spirit World.* Philadelphia: Moyer & Lotter, 1923.

Leonard, Arthur Glyn. *The Lower Niger and Its Tribes.* London: Macmillan, 1906.

Lewis, C. S. *The Screwtape Letters.* New York: Macmillan, 1961.

Lyons, Arthur. *The Second Coming: Satanism in America.* New York: Dodd, Mead, 1970.

MacMillan, J. A. *Modern Demon Possession.* Wheaton, Ill.: Christian Pubns., n.d.

Meade, Russell. *Victory over Demonism Today.* Wheaton, Ill.: Christian Life, 1962.

Michelet, Jules. *Satanism and Witchcraft.* New York: Citadel, 1939.

Montgomery, John Warwick. *Principalities and Powers.* Minneapolis: Bethany Fellowship, 1973.

Montgomery, Ruth. *A Gift of Prophecy.* New York: Morrow, William, 1965.

Murrell, Conrad. *Practical Demonology.* Pineville, La.: Saber Pubns., n.d.

Nevius, John L. *Demon Possession and Allied Themes*. New York: Revell, n.d.

Newport, John P. *Demons, Demons, Demons*. Nashville: Broadman, 1972.

Oesterreich, T. K. *Possession, Demoniacal and Other, Among Primitive Races in Antiquity, the Middle Ages and Modern Times*. New York: Long & Smith, 1930.

Palms, Roger C. *The Christian and the Occult*. Valley Forge, Pa.: Judson, 1972.

Penn-Lewis, Jesse, and Roberts, Evan. *War on the Saints*. Abridged ed. Ed. J. C. Metcalfe. Fort Washington, Pa.: Christian Literature Crusade, n.d.

Peterson, Robert. *Are Demons for Real?* Chicago: Moody, 1972.

Phillips, McCandlish. *The Spirit World*. Wheaton: Scripture Press, n.d.

Pike, James A. *The Other Side*. New York: Dell, 1969.

Sloan, Mersene Elon. *Demonosophy Unmasked in Modern Theosophy*. St. Paul: The Way, 1922.

Timmons, Tim. *Chains of the Spirit—A Manual for Liberation*. Washington, D.C.: Canon, 1973.

Unger, Merrill F. *The Mystery of Bishop Pike*. Wheaton, Ill.: Tyndale, 1968.

Vogt, Evon Z., and Hyman, Roy. *Water Witching U.S.A.* Chicago: U. of Chicago Press, 1959.

Woods, Richard. *The Occult Revolution*. New York: Herder & Herder, 1971.

Wright, J. Stafford. *Christianity and the Occult*. Chicago: Moody, 1971.

———. *Man in the Process of Time*. Grand Rapids: Eerdmans, 1956.

Yoseloff, Thomas. *Materials Toward a History of Witchcraft*. New York: Yoseloff, 1957.

PERIODICALS

"Boom Times on the Psychic Frontier," *Time*, March 4, 1974.

Conybeare, F. C. "Christian Demonology," *Jewish Quarterly Review* 9 (1896-97).

"Occult: A Substitute Faith," *Time*, June 19, 1972, pp. 62-68.

"Occult Explosion." *McCalls,* March 1970, pp. 62-77.

Smith, Charles R. "The New Testament Doctrine of Demons," *Grace Journal* 10(Spring 1969).

"Witches," *Time,* October 31, 1969, p. 94.

Zuck, Roy B. "The Practice of Witchcraft in the Scriptures," *Bibliotheca Sacra* 128(Oct.-Dec. 1971).

Moody Press, a ministry of the Moody Bible Institute, is designed for education, evangelization and edification. If we may assist you in knowing more about Christ and the Christian life, please write us without obligation to: Moody Press, c/o MLM, Chicago, Illinois 60610.